AI AND ALGORITHMS

MASTERING LEGAL AND ETHICAL COMPLIANCE

Arnoud Engelfriet

Imprint

ISBN 9781634624565

Copyright © 2024 ICTRecht B.V.
Publisher: Technics Publications
Design, typesetting: Jellmedia.nl

Cover by Lorena Molinari

Some rights reserved. All or part of this book may be reproduced or used in any manner without the prior written permission of the copyright owner, subject to the terms of the Creative Commons Attribution-ShareAlike license version 4.0, https://creativecommons.org/licenses/by-sa/4.0/

TABLE OF CONTENTS

CHAPTER 1 Exploring the AI Landscape

Introduction: AI and the Dawn of a New Era — 13
- AI is already here — 13
- The rise of algorithms — 15
- New risks from reliance on AI — 15

The call for ethics in AI — 17
- The 2018 'techlash' as catalyst — 17
- UNESCO's global standard on AI Ethics — 18

Navigating the AI spectrum — 19
- The evolution of AI — 19
- Machines that think — 20
- A taxonomy of AI — 21

Defining Artificial Intelligence — 24
- The Turing Test and rationality — 24
- Autonomy as a definitional key — 25
- A definition of AI in European legislation — 26

Looking Ahead: Emerging Trends in AI Legislation and Ethics — 27
- Regulation of military AI — 27
- AI and public health — 28
- Intellectual property in AI creations — 28
- AI Legislation for Space Exploration — 30

Key takeaways — 31

CHAPTER 2 Unraveling the European AI Act

Understanding Europe: The Core of Responsible AI — 33
- Initial steps towards regulation — 33
- Work of the High-Level Expert Group on AI — 34
- Towards the AI Act — 35

Understanding the AI Act — 35
- A table of contents — 36
- Key definitions — 37
- Material and geographical scope — 38
- Conformity assessments and certification — 39
- Entry into force and transitional provisions — 41

Managing Risk: AI Practices and their Classification — 41
- AI and fundamental rights — 41
- Three levels of risk — 43
- Prohibited practices — 43
- Determining high-risk AI — 44

Addressing innovation: regulatory sandboxes — 45
- Origins of sandboxes — 46
- AI sandboxes in practice — 46

Related legislation — 46
- The General Data Protection Regulation — 47
- The AI and Product Liability Directives — 47
- Consumer protection and market protection legislation — 48
- European cybersecurity regulations — 49

A wider look: AI Legislation across the globe — 50
- The Council of Europe — 50

United States of America	50
People's Republic of China	52
Canada	52
Federal Republic of Brazil	53
Republic of India	53
State of Japan	54
Republic of Singapore	54
Republic of Korea	54
From law and ethics to practical assessment	**55**
Lawful, ethical and robust	55
Four ethical principles	55
Seven requirements	56
Key takeaways	**57**

CHAPTER 3 Reinforcing Human Agency and Oversight in AI

Understanding Human-AI Interaction	**59**
The rise of computer interaction	59
The importance of agency	60
Agency and cooperation	62
Mitigating Over-Reliance And Unintended Interference	**63**
Recognizing over-reliance on AI	63
Mitigating over-reliance	65
Unintended interference in decision-making	66
Mitigating unintended interference	66
Social Interaction Simulation: Risks And Mitigations	**67**
Working with Social AI systems	68
Emotional deception, attachment and manipulation	70
Mitigating negative social interaction	71
Human Oversight In AI Systems	**71**
Human-in-the-loop	72
Human-on-the-loop	73
Human-in-command	73
Human-out-of-the-loop	74
Implementing Response Mechanisms And Control Measures	**74**
The necessity of detection and response mechanisms	74
Implementing detection and response	75
The role of the 'Stop Button'	76
Reflecting the autonomous nature of the AI system	77
Key takeaways	**78**

CHAPTER 4 Robustness, reliability and safeguards

Resilience To Attack And Security	**81**
IT system vulnerabilities	81
AI system-specific vulnerabilities	82
Mitigating risks and vulnerabilities	83
Certification and compliance	85

Risk management and general safety — 86
- Risk identification and assessment — 86
- Risk metrics and quantification — 87
- The role of insurance — 88
- Reliability requirements and fault tolerance — 89

Ensuring Accuracy in AI Decisions — 90
- Getting it right: positives and negatives — 90
- Accuracy, recall and precision — 91
- Steps to improve accuracy — 93

Reliability, Fallback Plans, and Reproducibility — 96
- On reliability and reproducibility — 96
- Monitoring, verification and documentation — 97
- The role of fallback plans — 98
- The impact of low confidence scores — 99
- Continual Learning and its implications — 100

Key takeaways — 102

CHAPTER 5 Data Governance and Privacy in AI Systems

Introduction to Privacy and AI — 105
- The European perspective — 105
- The impact of AI — 106

AI systems and fundamental rights — 107
- Challenges to fundamental rights — 107
- The interplay of AI and the right to privacy — 108
- Upholding physical, mental, and moral integrity — 109
- Mechanisms for flagging privacy concerns — 110

The GDPR and its impact on AI — 110
- Applicability of the GDPR to AI systems — 111
- GDPR compliance measures for AI systems — 112
- Data Protection Impact Assessment (DPIA) — 112
- Data Protection Officer (DPO) — 113
- Oversight mechanisms for data processing — 113
- Measures to achieve privacy-by-design and default — 113
- Data minimization — 114
- Implementing user rights — 114
- Consideration of data lifecycle implications — 114
- Non-personal data implications — 115

General-purpose AI and its implications — 115
- Introduction to general-purpose models — 115
- The significance of general-purpose models — 116
- Ethical and societal considerations — 117
- Compliance obligations specific to general-purpose models — 117

Intellectual property and AI systems — 118
- The scope of IP protection — 118
- TDM, ML and AI — 118
- Reasonable royalties — 119
- IP governance steps — 120

Ensuring Data Quality and Integrity — 120

Data sets and data processing	121
On data processing pipelines	122
Towards high quality datasets	123
Confronting and addressing data biases	125

Technical Measures for Data Security — **126**

Adherence to data management standards	127
Data processing techniques	127
Data storage measures	128
Data access control	129

Key takeaways — **129**

CHAPTER 6 Emphasizing Transparency in AI Operations

Introduction to Transparency in AI — **131**

The growing need for transparency	131
The "what" and the "how"	132
Three aspects of transparency	132

Traceability: Ensuring Accountability in AI Systems — **133**

Traceable lifecycle	133
Input data quality	134
Tracking back decisions	135
Output quality	136
Output of generative AI	136
Logging practices	137

Explainability: Making AI Understandable — **138**

Balancing technical explainability and human decisions	138
Explaining Deep Learning	140
XAI: Breaking the black box	140
User surveys	143

Transparency and Automated Decision Making — **144**

Types of decision-making	144
Addressing automated decision making under the GDPR	145
Automated decision-making under the AI Act	146
Decision-making and the Platform Work Directive	146

Communication: Bridging the Gap between AI and Users — **147**

Recognizing the AI Interface	147
Clarity on purpose and criteria	147
Highlighting the benefits	148
Addressing technical limitations	148
Training and disclaimers	149
Clarity out of the box: the CE logo	150

Key takeaways — **150**

CHAPTER 7 Fostering Fairness, Diversity, and Non-Discrimination

Introduction to Fairness, Diversity, and Non-Discrimination in AI — **153**

The imperative of fairness	153
The concept of 'bias'	154

Bias and discrimination in AI and algorithms	155
Inclusive engineering	156
Establishing Strategies and Procedures to Avoid Bias	156
Step 1: Business understanding	157
Step 2: Data understanding	158
Step 3: Data preparation	159
Step 4: Modeling	159
Step 5: Evaluation	160
Step 6: Deployment	160

Ensuring diversity and representativeness — 161
Education and Awareness Initiatives — 162
Mechanisms for Flagging Issues — 163
Defining and Measuring Fairness — 164

Accessibility and Universal Design — 166
Ensuring accessibility in AI system design — 166
Making user interfaces usable by all — 167
Universal Design principles in AI development — 168
Assessing AI system impact on end-users — 169

Stakeholder Participation — 170
Working with stakeholders — 170
Toolkits for participation — 172

Key takeaways — 174

CHAPTER 8 Societal and Environmental Implications of AI Systems

Aligning environmental impact with global goals — 177
Environmental impact of AI — 177
The Sustainable Development Goals (SDGs) — 178
The use of Social Impact Assessments — 179
Structured approach towards SIA — 179
Mitigating the environmental impact of AI — 180

AI in the work environment — 181
The Good: Productivity enhancements — 181
The Bad: Job insecurity — 182
Mitigating negative impact of AI — 183

AI in healthcare — 185
The Good: More effective care — 185
The Bad: Depersonalization — 185
Mitigating negative impact of AI — 186

ESG, CSR, and AI — 187
Environmental, Social, and Governance (ESG) considerations — 187
Adding AI to the ESG — 188
Corporate Social Responsibility (CSR) considerations — 189

AI and Democracy — 191
Influence on political decision-making — 191
Influence on political discourse — 192
Influence on elections — 193

Key takeaways — 194

CHAPTER 9 Accountability and redress

Understanding accountability — **197**
    The essence of accountability — 197
    A framework of accountability — 198
    Internal and external accountability — 200
    The use of model cards — 201
    Building blocks of accountability — 202

Compliance monitoring — **204**
    The AI Compliance Officer — 205
    Reporting mechanisms — 206
    Managing trade-offs — 206
    Offering redress — 207

Accountability and trust — **209**
    Trust and trustworthiness — 209
    Trust, trustworthiness and accountability — 210
    The role of empathy — 210
    Potential pathways towards empathetic accountability — 211

Accountability and sanctions — **212**
    National supervisory authorities — 212
    Powers of the authorities — 212
    Civil damages — 213

Key takeaways — **214**

CHAPTER 10 Bringing it all together

Navigating the Nuances of Compliance, Governance, and Risk Management — **217**
    Compliance: Playing by the book — 217
    Governance: Steering the ship — 218
    Risk Management: Dodging the curveballs — 219
    Similarities and interplay — 220
    Positioning AI in the triad — 220

The role of the AI compliance officer — **221**
    Position and significance of the AI Compliance Officer — 221
    Functions and responsibilities of the AI Compliance Officer — 221

Applying the ALTAI Assessment — **223**
    Understanding the ALTAI Assessment — 223
    ALTAI Assessments as spider charts — 223
    Medical diagnostic AI — 225
    AI-driven Financial Trading System — 226
    AI-powered Educational Tutoring System — 226
    Effectiveness of ALTAI — 227
    Transforming ALTAI into a company-specific compliance tool — 228

Performing impact assessments — **229**
    Data Protection Impact Assessment (DPIA) — 230
    AI Impact Assessment (AIIA) — 230
    Algorithmic Impact Assessment (AIA) — 230
    Ethical Impact Assessment (EIA) — 231
    Fundamental rights impact assessment (FRIA) — 232
    Practical tips — 232

Key takeaways — **233**

1

Exploring the AI Landscape

Legislation, Ethics, and Context

Chapter 1 – Exploring the AI landscape

Few chapters in the grand narrative of technological innovation have been as loaded with twists, turns, and fanfare as the roller-coaster ride that is artificial intelligence. The history of AI has been a field strewn with ambitious aspirations that have often struggled to fully materialize. This time, however, may be different: our society has become more amenable to adopt autonomous algorithm-driven systems. The widespread and fast adoption of AI has prompted serious concerns. From algorithmic bias to erosion of personal autonomy, AI technologies have had unintended consequences that impact the lives of people across the globe. Such risks have stirred public and policy debates, leading to an increasingly urgent call for effective regulation. Now, with the European AI Act being adopted, for the first time we have actual regulation on AI. Let's start our journey into this complex world and gain an understanding of the landscape of AI legislation and ethics.

Introduction: AI and the Dawn of a New Era

"It will either be the best thing that's ever happened to us, or it will be the worst thing. If we're not careful, it very well may be the last thing," famous scientist Stephen Hawking supposedly said on artificial intelligence. The implications of creating a new form of intelligence – and what this means for humanity – have given the field an aura of mystery and apprehension. A major contributor may have been popular culture, in particular science fiction: from *2001's* HAL computer, *RoboCop's* ED-209, the killer robots in the *Terminator* franchise and the precognitive crime prevention system in *Minority Report* to the rogue operating system in the movie *Her*, it is clear that whatever AI is going to bring, it will be big and it can be dangerous.

AI is already here

At the same time, AI is already here – but as a general rule, it's not called AI. We have expert systems, intelligent agents, smart devices, decision support systems, cognitive

> **By the end of this chapter, you'll be able to ...**
> - Comprehend the role and importance of ethics in the deployment of AI and algorithms.
> - Articulate key concepts such as AI, algorithms, models and users along with their implications.
> - Recognize the landscape of global AI legislation and the major differences between regions.

Four science fiction movies that cemented the concept of AI as large and in charge.

computing, and so on. We also have similarly advanced technologies that we simply take for granted, such as search engines that turn vague queries into the right answer, thermostats that adjust to environmental factors, autonomous safety features in cars and recommendation systems in online shops and social media.

Why did the phrase "artificial intelligence" only recently reemerge as the leading term for such technologies? If we look at the history of the field, we see a cyclical pattern: a rise in popular attention that pushes expectations skywards, followed by an equally large drop when expectations cannot be met. The literature calls these the "Summers" and "Winters" of AI.[1] During winters, businesses and researchers used different terms to avoid the stigma of AI.

Today, we are definitely in a new Summer of AI. Artificial intelligence has been declared as fundamental a breakthrough as the wheel or fire, is poised to take over every aspect of industry and is a fundamental part of the fourth industrial revolution. According to a study by the European Parliament, AI can help people with improved healthcare, boost sales, increase machine efficiency, improve customer service, reduce waste and enhance security and safety in our society.[2]

At the same time, apprehensions over AI are higher than ever: robots will take over our jobs, biased news recommenders create rifts in society, killer drones will operate with impunity, to name a few. The world thus finds itself in a delicate balance, navigating between remarkable potential and emerging challenges.

The rise of algorithms

Whether we refer to it as AI, cognitive computing or any other term, the fundamental building block that gives these technologies their supposed intelligence and autonomy is the 'algorithm'. This mathematical backbone enables everything from the sophisticated decision-making in autonomous vehicles to the personalized recommendations you get when shopping online.

Algorithms are named after the Persian scientist Muhammad ibn Musa al-Khwarizmi (Latin name: Algorismus), one of the first to introduce the concept of formal computation sequences.[3] Today, the word "algorithm" is generally used to refer to complex sequences that only automated computers can perform. More simple algorithms, especially those performed by humans, are generally referred to as recipes, checklists or flowcharts.

The term 'algorithm' has gained notoriety among the general public because of algorithms that make decisions which affect humans and which are not easily interpretable or challengeable: the computer says 'no' and that is all. Still, algorithms are replacing human beings in a growing number of situations, usually based on a perception that algorithms have a higher processing capacity, speed, volume and scale of decision-making, with expectations of lower error rates compared to human beings.[4]

Why is this so? Despite the grandiose theories surrounding AI's irresistible allure, the truth is starkly less sensational: AI provides a giant leap in the search for efficiency, and thus provides a boon for bureaucrats and managers seeking to eliminate slow and hard-to-control humans. We have seen this before with automation: human weavers got replaced with the weaving loom, telephone switchboard operators were replaced by automatic exchange systems, and bank tellers have been increasingly replaced by ATMs and online banking. The unique aspect of AI is that it does not automate manual tasks, but cognitive tasks.[5] AI and algorithms can now replace tasks that were previously thought to be reserved for humans: making decisions, analyzing complex data, predicting future outcomes, and even making judgments. AI does this at scale and with tremendous speed, but does not follow human reasoning or thought processes. Asked for explanation or justification, most AI's will come up blank.

New risks from reliance on AI

The increasing reliance on AI systems also poses new risks. A key risk is that of *bias*: an AI can structurally perpetuate, or even amplify, existing prejudices and inequalities present in the data it was trained on, or introduce prejudices because this data was not representative of society. Both can lead to decisions that are unfair or discriminatory, impacting individuals and communities in profound ways. To name a few examples:

❶ Amazon's hiring algorithm (USA, 2018): web retailer Amazon had to abandon an AI recruitment tool after it showed bias against women. The algorithm, trained on a decade's worth of resumes submitted to Amazon, learned to downgrade resumes that included the word "women's". The reason? In that first ten years, tech company Amazon had (unintentionally) only hired men.

❷ Pneumonia treatment (USA, 1998): an AI system trained on hospital intake data sent asthma patients with pneumonia home, despite this being a life-threatening combination of factors. The underlying dataset turned out to have only the outcomes "admit" and "send home", with occurrences with the outcome "send to emergency room immediately" not having been registered in the dataset.

❸ Predictive policing (UK, 2018): Durham Police in the UK used an AI system called HART to predict the risk of a suspect re-offending. The system was criticized for potentially reinforcing existing biases in policing and sentencing. With an accuracy of 53.8% the system could have been replaced with flipping a coin.

❹ Gangnam hiring practices (South Korea, 2020): An AI-based interview platform in South Korea was criticized for analyzing the appearances and voices of job applicants, leading to concerns about potential discrimination based on physical attributes. It was reminiscent of a 2016 AI-driven beauty contest in the UK, where winners generally were ethnic Westerners or light-skinned Asian people.

❺ Welfare fraud detection (the Netherlands, 2017): the city of Rotterdam, the Netherlands used automated filters to identify likely suspects of welfare fraud. Due to biased dataset selection and untransparent choice of parameters relevant for fraud detection, the system focused heavily on minorities such as young single mothers and people with limited grasp of the Dutch language.

Another key concern is transparency: AI systems, particularly those using large datasets and statistics-driven algorithms, can act as 'black boxes' where it is incredibly difficult to understand or explain the rationale behind their decisions. This lack of interpretability undermines accountability and can lead to situations where consequential decisions are made without clear understanding or oversight. As the Council of Europe noted in its study on algorithms and human rights[6], "human beings feel that they have no control over and do not understand the technical systems that surround them." This despite the promise that algorithms and AI would provide neutral, nondiscriminatory and independent assessments.

A third concern that is rapidly emerging with AI's advancement is the creation and application of technologies that exist outside of any current ethical framework or point of reference. The development of deepfake technology, for instance, is causing disquieting implications, as it can fabricate convincingly realistic images or videos, such as non-consensual explicit content. Similarly, applications like 'Deep Nostalgia' animate photos of deceased individuals, giving the uncanny impression that one can communicate with the past. This 'resurrection' of the deceased blurs the line between the past and the present and raises complex ethical questions about consent, the sanctity of memory, and the boundaries of grief and remembrance.

A fourth concern relates to the threat AI poses to individual privacy and control over personal data. AI systems like facial recognition technology, for instance, can identify individuals in public spaces, which can potentially lead to constant surveillance. Moreover, data-driven AI systems, utilized by various online platforms, are capable of inferring sensitive information about individuals, such as their political affiliations, sexual orientation, or health status, based on their online behavior and metadata. This widespread data collection and the subsequent potential for surveillance and profiling represent a significant threat to fundamental human rights.

Lastly, a concern that particularly applies to *generative* AI, i.e. AI that generates text, images or other content, is to what extent creators of such systems may use existing works of others. Copyright and European database rights appear to be violated with impunity as large volumes of published content are scooped up for the necessary creation of very large datasets. While European law contains an exception for 'data mining', its formulation is unclear and comes with an opt-out mechanism that requires technical standardization between publishers and AI creators, two groups that are unlikely to see agreement soon.

The call for ethics in AI

There is a growing realization that the impact of AI goes beyond technological efficiency and enters the realm of human rights, societal values, and fundamental ethical considerations. The last five years in particular have prompted an increasing public and academic dialogue on the need for ethical frameworks that ensure these technologies are designed and deployed responsibly. This wave of attention, while partly driven by academic interest and foresight, has been propelled into mainstream discussion by several high-profile incidents that have exposed the darker side of AI.

The 2018 'techlash' as catalyst

In 2018, news coverage of the Facebook/Cambridge Analytica scandal brought the concept of algorithmic manipulation in full view.[7] Cambridge Analytica used AI-driven tools to fine-tune political advertisements during the 2016 US presidential election and the Brexit referendum. Concerns over AI were also greatly amplified when it became apparent that technology providers such as Google contributed to creation of autonomous military machines.

The 'techlash' that was the result of these and more incidents set in a period of increased attention to 'honest' or 'ethical' AI. Initially, the main effect was to produce codes of ethics, that made large promises of fairness and transparency ("virtue signaling") but did little to change the actual products or services.[8] As already known from the field of business ethics, changing a company's behavior requires more than ethical statements: *"[w]hen ethical ideals are at odds with a company's bottom line, they are met with resistance"*.[9] Hence the logical next step – calls for legislation.

That is not to say codes of ethics are entirely without merit. A clear step forward was the choice to adopt fundamental rights (human rights) as the basis for deriving ethical principles and limitations for AI or algorithmic computer systems. A good summary is the work of the AI4People taskforce, which analyzed over 47 different ethical codes and came up with five overarching principles of ethical AI:[10]

- Beneficence: Promoting well-being, preserving dignity, and sustaining the planet
- Non-maleficence: Privacy, security and "capability caution"
- Autonomy: The power to decide (whether to decide)
- Justice: Promoting prosperity and preserving solidarity
- Explicability: Enabling the other principles through intelligibility and accountability

These five principles form the basis of all European legislative work on responsible AI, which will be discussed in the next chapter.

UNESCO's global standard on AI Ethics

The five principles also closely match the UNESCO 'Recommendation on the Ethics of Artificial Intelligence' from November 2021, the first-ever global standard on AI ethics. It identifies ten key aspects of ethical AI, which we'll briefly summarize here:

1. Proportionality and Do No Harm: AI systems should be designed and utilized such that their benefits outweigh potential harms, ensuring that they do not inadvertently cause harm to individuals or society.
2. Safety and Security: AI systems should be robust, reliable, and safeguarded against malicious uses or unintended consequences.
3. Right to Privacy and Data Protection: AI technologies should respect individual privacy rights and ensure that personal data is handled securely and ethically.
4. Multi-stakeholder and Adaptive Governance & Collaboration: AI governance should involve diverse stakeholders and be adaptive to the rapidly evolving nature of technology.
5. Responsibility and Accountability: Those involved in the design, development, and deployment of AI must be answerable for the behavior and impacts of their systems. This ensures that if things go wrong, there is clarity on who is responsible and mechanisms to address any issues.

- ⑥ Transparency and Explainability: AI systems should operate in a manner that is open and understandable, ensuring that stakeholders can decipher how AI decisions are made.
- ⑦ Human Oversight and Determination: AI should complement human decision-making rather than replace it, ensuring that humans remain in control and can intervene or override AI decisions.
- ⑧ Sustainability: AI development and deployment should consider environmental, social, and long-term economic impacts.
- ⑨ Awareness & Literacy: Efforts should be made to enhance public understanding and literacy related to AI, equipping individuals with the knowledge to navigate AI-driven landscapes.
- ⑩ Fairness and Non-Discrimination: AI systems should be designed and used in ways that are fair and do not discriminate against any group or individual based on biases.

The recommendation features detailed measures such as introducing an independent 'AI Ethics Officer.' This officer, along with other established mechanisms, would supervise ethical impact assessment, auditing, and ongoing monitoring initiatives, thereby guaranteeing ethically guided application of AI technologies in public areas.

Navigating the AI Spectrum

To be effective, the law must first encapsulate what it seeks to govern. This is a daunting challenge in the case of artificial intelligence, a multifaceted domain that has broad interpretations. In this section, we examine AI as a technology in more detail to understand common themes and developments, and then turn to various legal definitions. Let's begin with the genesis of the concept of Artificial Intelligence.

The evolution of AI

AI as a field of research was famously introduced in 1955 as the problem *"of making a machine behave in ways that would be called intelligent if a human were so behaving."*[11] Note that this is obviously a counterfactual: *were* a human to behave in that way, that behavior *would* be called intelligent. It does not mean that the machine *is* intelligent or even *thinking*.[12] As Dutch computer scientist Edsger W. Dijkstra put it, *"The question of whether computers can think is like the question of whether submarines can swim"*.[13]

The earliest work in artificial intelligence focused on what is now commonly referred to as expert systems: sets of rules which formalize knowledge in a top-down approach, e.g. as a set of if-then or yes-no questions. These approaches certainly had their successes: a notable breakthrough was the fast-calculating chess mastermind *Deep Blue* that was the first computer to beat the most skilled human player at the game.[14] However, they ultimately failed to live up to their promises due to fast-increasing complexity and the inability to handle unknown situations.

Current approaches to artificial intelligence rely on a fundamentally different approach, namely machine learning (ML). In ML, a computer-driven algorithm sifts through large amounts of data in search of patterns. These patterns group the data, e.g. as approved versus rejected or multi-label groups such as cat, dog, bird et cetera. Unlike expert systems, ML systems have no actual knowledge of what is in the groups: the data tells the system which is which, and that should be enough. ML has long suffered from a dearth of computing capacity, but that ended with the breakthroughs fifteen years ago in cloud computing and fast hardware-driven computing.[15] Today, almost every application of AI is realized as one form or another of machine learning. The 2016 win of the ML system AlphaGo against human world champion Lee Sedol is widely recognized as a key moment of recognition of the importance of machine learning.[16]

Machines that think

Imagine: you are in a room, receiving a series of Chinese symbols through a slot in the door. Using a comprehensive rulebook, you methodically shuffle and reorder these symbols, then send out the reorganized symbols through another slot. To an external observer who understands Chinese, it appears as if you're proficiently answering questions in the language. But here's the catch: you don't understand a word of Chinese. You're merely processing symbols according to rules. This is the essence of John Searle's "Chinese Room" thought experiment. If you, as the symbol processor, don't truly understand Chinese, can we claim that a machine, which processes information based on programmed algorithms, genuinely "understands" or "thinks"?

The philosophical debate surrounding "understanding" and "thinking" is deep-rooted. Is understanding merely the processing and producing of correct outputs? Or does it require a consciousness, a subjective experience, an essence of self-awareness? And if "thinking" isn't just algorithmic processing, but a combination of intuition, introspection, creativity, and emotion, can machines ever truly think? Many of the apprehensions surrounding AI stem from the notion that these "thinking" machines might somehow surpass or dominate human intelligence.

Building upon these concerns, we encounter the concept of the "AI singularity." This is a theoretical point in the future where AI becomes capable of recursive self-improvement, leading to rapid and unforeseen advancements in technology. Such an event suggests that AI might evolve beyond our control or comprehension. But, if we consider that an AI's processing may not equate to genuine understanding or thinking, the prospect of such a singularity becomes a subject of debate. While AI can certainly advance in capability, processing speed, and complexity, the pivotal question is: without the genuine ability to "think," can it ever truly reach or surpass the intricate depth of human intelligence?

A taxonomy of AI

Artificial Intelligence (AI) is an overarching term that encapsulates a wide variety of subfields and technologies. Many have attempted to provide a taxonomy of AI. It is impossible to provide one hierarchical organization that covers all forms of AI, but there are several main criteria according to which an AI system could be compared against others, as illustrated below.

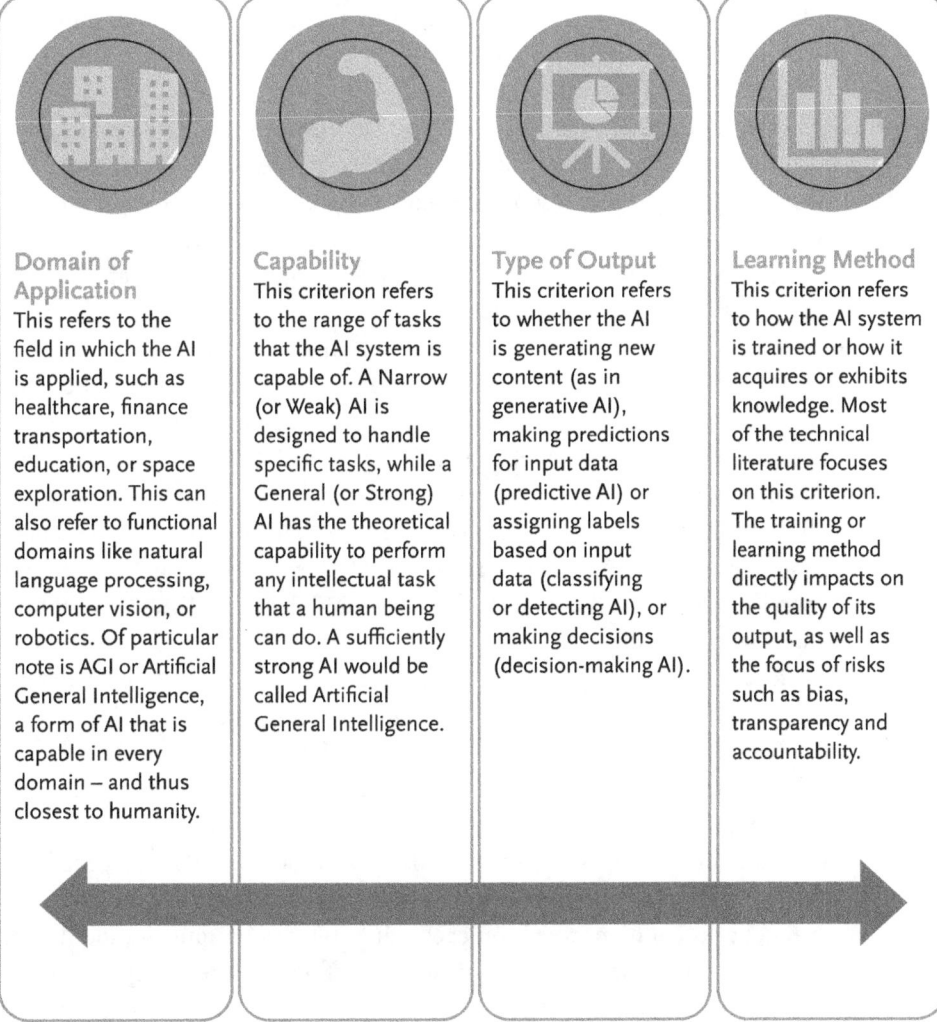

Domain of Application
This refers to the field in which the AI is applied, such as healthcare, finance transportation, education, or space exploration. This can also refer to functional domains like natural language processing, computer vision, or robotics. Of particular note is AGI or Artificial General Intelligence, a form of AI that is capable in every domain – and thus closest to humanity.

Capability
This criterion refers to the range of tasks that the AI system is capable of. A Narrow (or Weak) AI is designed to handle specific tasks, while a General (or Strong) AI has the theoretical capability to perform any intellectual task that a human being can do. A sufficiently strong AI would be called Artificial General Intelligence.

Type of Output
This criterion refers to whether the AI is generating new content (as in generative AI), making predictions for input data (predictive AI) or assigning labels based on input data (classifying or detecting AI), or making decisions (decision-making AI).

Learning Method
This criterion refers to how the AI system is trained or how it acquires or exhibits knowledge. Most of the technical literature focuses on this criterion. The training or learning method directly impacts on the quality of its output, as well as the focus of risks such as bias, transparency and accountability.

In the context of this book, we find the 'learning method' criterion most suitable. This choice aligns well with the learning objective of enabling the application of legal and ethical norms in AI practice, with data governance and transparency and accountability on the other. When organizing AI according to learning method, the main division is between expert systems and machine learning. Zooming in on machine learning, we can make the following subdivision:

- In supervised learning, AI systems are trained on labeled data, which means input data is tagged with the correct output. The model learns to predict outputs based on this input. Common applications include image recognition and speech recognition.
    - Classic spam filters apply the so-called Bayesian supervised learning algorithms to classify emails as either "spam" or "not spam". They are trained on datasets of emails that have been manually classified, learning the likelihood of certain words or patterns appearing in spam vs. non-spam emails. This allows them to predict the classification of new, unseen emails.

- Unlike supervised learning, unsupervised learning involves training an AI system using unlabeled data. The system identifies patterns and relationships in the data without any pre-existing labels to guide the learning process. This is commonly used for clustering and association tasks, such as customer segmentation.
    - Generative Adversarial Networks (GANs) are a particular form of unsupervised machine learning. A GAN is composed of two neural networks, a Generator and a Discriminator, that are trained simultaneously. The Generator network generates new data instances, while the Discriminator network evaluates them for authenticity. The Discriminator network tries to classify whether each instance of data it reviews belongs to the actual training dataset or not. Meanwhile, the Generator uses feedback from the Discriminator to produce ever more realistic data. Deepfake videos, like those produced using FaceSwap or DeepFaceLab, are a notorious application of GANs, where they generate hyper-realistic but entirely fabricated content.
    - Latent Variable Networks (LVN) learn the latent structure of a dataset, without the need for labeled training data. A particular example is the diffusion model, which learns object information from images and consequently is able to create new images based on a requested set of objects. The Midjourney image generator AI is an example.
    - A transformer model is a type of AI used in natural language processing (NLP) tasks that utilizes a mechanism called "attention" to weigh the influence of different words on each other in a given input, without having information on what words mean. Transformers are composed of an encoder that reads and interprets the input text, and a decoder that generates

a prediction or output based on the encoded input. The attention mechanism within transformers allows the model to focus on different parts of the input sequence when generating each word in the output sequence. This allows it to capture complex dependencies between words. The Google BERT model is a well-known example that is used in the Google Translate service.

→ Semi-supervised learning uses a mix of labeled and unlabeled data for training. It often starts with an unsupervised phase (identifying patterns in data) followed by a supervised phase (making predictions from those patterns). This method is often employed when labeling data is time-consuming or expensive.
- The well-known ChatGPT application is a very large transformer model (a form of unsupervised learning) that has been fine-tuned with manually labeled questions and answers (supervised learning).

→ In reinforcement learning, an AI system learns to make decisions by interacting with its environment. The AI gets feedback in the form of rewards or penalties, and it learns to maximize its rewards over time. This is commonly used in gaming and navigation tasks. The Netflix recommendation algorithm is an example: it adapt its suggestions based on users' actual viewing habits. The AlphaGo system that defeated the world champion of Go in 2015 learned to play the complex board game using this type of feedback.

→ Deep learning uses complex networks with many layers - hence the "deep" – in an attempt to simulate the behavior of the human brain to process data in a way that allows it to make decisions, identify patterns, and process complex tasks. Deep learning finds application in car-driving AI, voice-controlled virtual assistants, facial recognition systems, and more.
- Convolutional Neural Networks (CNNs) are a class of deep learning algorithms that are particularly powerful for processing images. They are specifically designed to process pixel data and are used in image recognition and processing. Convolutional networks were inspired by biological processes in that the connectivity pattern between neurons resembles the organization of the animal visual cortex. CNNs use relatively little pre-processing compared to other image classification algorithms, thus making them attractive for large-scale image processing. Residual Network (ResNet) is a CNN used for computer vision applications that supports hundreds or thousands of convolutional layers.

→ Transfer learning is a technique where a pre-trained model is used as the starting point for a related task. This can save a lot of time and computational resources, and is often used in deep learning applications where large neural networks are involved.

For instance, a model trained to recognize objects can form the basis for a model training to identify types of bird. With little additional information (object information relevant for birds) the pre-trained model can quickly be deployed.

- Foundation models are pre-trained generic models based on very large datasets. They provide a strong, general-purpose starting point for many different tasks, effectively transferring knowledge from the pre-training task to a variety of specific downstream tasks. This means that once a foundation model has been trained, it can be fine-tuned or adapted to solve specific problems with less data than would be required to train a model from scratch. Examples of foundation models include models like GPT-4 or Gemini in natural language processing, and models like ResNet in computer vision.

Defining Artificial Intelligence

From the conception of AI onwards, many have sought to define AI. The leading handbook *AI: A Modern Approach* alone presents eight different definitions of AI organized into four categories: thinking humanly, acting humanly, thinking rationally, and acting rationally.[17] The abovementioned 1955 paper provides a good example of the underlying problem: there is no *"solid definition of intelligence that doesn't depend on relating it to human intelligence"*, according to its author. And so far no one has been able to properly define what exactly constitutes human intelligence.

The Turing Test and rationality

Famously, computer scientist Alan Turing introduced what is now known as the "Turing Test" in his now-seminal paper *Computing Machinery and Intelligence*. Essentially the test is a challenge for a human interrogator, chatting at a distance with another party that may be human or AI. The common way the outcome is told, is that if the interrogator cannot distinguish between human and AI after a sufficiently long conversation, the AI can be regarded as intelligent. However, what Turing actually said was that the question "Can machines think?" was "too meaningless to deserve discussion" and used the experiment to illustrate that the distinction cannot be meaningfully made.[18] Dijkstra's comparison to *"the question of whether submarines can swim"* puts a similar point on it.[19]

Earlier we mentioned that AI can be regarded as a form of automation that automates cognitive tasks. This is a useful phrasing to understand what AI can achieve (or is likely to do so in the near future) but as technology marches on, the scope of what is still a "cognitive task" will shift. For instance, recognizing handwriting used to be an advanced cognitive task – computers needed to have input provided in their own format. Today, recognizing handwriting is a standard task.

Chapter 1 – Exploring the AI landscape

A more general approach is from the mentioned handbook by Russell and Norvig,[17] who define AI in terms of rational agents. In this context, rationality refers to making the best possible decision given the information available, and agents or agency refers to a certain amount of autonomy in arriving at that decision or acting on it. Russell and Norvig emphasize that AI systems are designed to perform tasks in a way that optimizes some measure of success. These tasks could range from playing chess, diagnosing diseases, recommending products, to navigating autonomous vehicles. Each action an AI system takes is based on its understanding of its environment and its goal to maximize its performance measure, which is the definition of rational behavior.

This definition sidesteps the discussion of whether an AI can 'think' or is 'intelligent'. The focus is on behavior, which can be observed or even influenced. This underlines Turing's point that thinking in terms of intelligence is meaningless.

Autonomy as a definitional key

In their 2018 Communication that kicked off the process that would ultimately produce the AI Act, the European Commission gave a loose definition of AI: *"Artificial intelligence (AI) refers to systems that display intelligent behaviour by analysing their environment and taking actions – with some degree of autonomy – to achieve specific goals."* While this definition still uses the problematic term 'intelligence', it did provide a hint for a new approach to define AI: autonomy.

Taking this definition as a starting point, the EU's High-Level Expert Group explored various aspects of the usage of AI in its *Definition of Artificial Intelligence* in 2019. They concluded that to act rationally (as Russell and Norvig used the term), an AI would be "perceiving the environment in which the system is immersed through some sensors, thus collecting and interpreting data, reasoning on what is perceived or processing the information derived from this data, deciding what the best action is, and then acting accordingly, through some actuators, thus possibly modifying the environment." This is highlighted in Fig. 1 from their definition below:

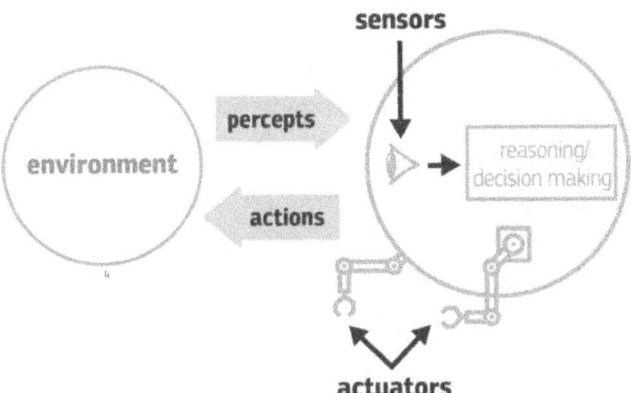

Autonomy is not explicitly mentioned in this definition, although it is clearly implied. The concept of AI autonomy is closely linked to the fundamental rights of human dignity and freedom (Articles 1 and 6 of the Charter): when we delegate more decision-making power to AI, we consequently reduce the level of control that humans exert, which can potentially infringe upon our autonomy and dignity. This concept is also reflected in the 2016 GDPR, that in article 22 provides that no person shall "be subject to a decision based solely on automated processing". We will examine the concept of autonomy in chapter 3.

A definition of AI in European legislation

When drafting the initial text of the AI Act, the European Commission rather closely followed the HLEG's definition: an AI system is a system that "can, for a given set of human-defined objectives, generate outputs such as content, predictions, recommendations, or decisions influencing the environments they interact with". The definition was coupled with an Annex that listed various common techniques used in machine learning and expert systems. It received heavy criticism, among other reasons for covering things like an Excel sheet with filtering options.

During negotiations between European Parliament and Council of Ministers, the AI Act settled on a definition that matches the 2019 definition of AI as given by the Organization for Economic Cooperation and Development (OECD):[20]

> *An AI system is a machine-based system designed to operate with varying levels of autonomy and that may exhibit adaptiveness after deployment and that, for explicit or implicit objectives, infers, from the input it receives, how to generate outputs such as predictions, content, recommendations, or decisions that can influence physical or virtual environments. (Article 3 section 1 AI Act.)*

The given justification is to align with international developments and to provide a definition that is flexible enough to accommodate the rapid technological developments in this field. Its choice for autonomy as key criterion underlines the risk-based approach of the AI Act: generally speaking, it is precisely because AI systems can operate autonomously that many of the associated risks occur. We will examine this definition in more detail in the next chapter. But before we do that, let's have a quick look at emerging trends.

Looking Ahead: Emerging Trends in AI Legislation and Ethics

As we navigate the complex terrain of AI legislation and ethics, we also need to peer into the future. What trends can we discern on the horizon, and how might they shape the use of AI and algorithms in the coming years? Will the upcoming climate change and the associated changes in society, e.g. in the Global South affect AI and its regulation? Before we end this chapter, let's explore some of the emerging trends that we need to pay attention to.

Regulation of military AI

Military forces around the world have had their eyes on AI from the onset. From image classification systems (recognizing enemy vehicles, for instance) to troop coordination and attack planning, the possibilities are endless. The concept of AI military machines has similarly long been a part of the public imagination:[21] the 1983 movie *WarGames* gave us the naïve WOPR AI that almost starts global thermonuclear war, and 1984 brought us the first installment in the *Terminator* movie franchise that cemented the concept of "killer robots". English readers may recall Dr. Who's DALEK antagonist robots.

Current autonomous weapons systems are few and far between. One clear example is the Samsung SGR-A1, a sentry gun supporting South Korean troops in the Korean Demilitarized Zone. In automatic mode, the gun can engage detected enemies with lethal force without human oversight. Publicity over the SGR-A1 has kicked off the current debate on the ethical aspects of autonomous weapon systems (AWS).[22] Earlier AWS do exist: the Dutch navy in 1979 adopted the Goalkeeper CIWS, a close-in autonomous weapons system that engages incoming missiles, aircraft or fast-maneuvering surface vessels. A difference with the SGR-A1 may have been that the Goalkeeper does not obviously engage human beings and is clearly positioned as a last-ditch self-defense gun for military vessels.

Since 2021, the use and implications of AWS have been heavily debated, but without much concrete results.[23] There are no international laws or treaties to oversee or limit AWS specifically, although international humanitarian law (such as article 36 of Additional Protocol I to the Geneva Conventions) does provide that any new weapons system must be assessed for lawfulness prior to being deployed on the battlefield. This assessment includes a rigorous assessment of predictability in its operation and its reliability in the field. One can imagine such an assessment for the SGR-A1, but for the weaponized drone swarm from the 2017 arms-control advocacy video *Slaughterbots* this will not be possible.

AI and public health

The use of AI in public health is rapidly expanding and transforming how health services are delivered and managed. AI is driving advancements in disease prediction, diagnostics, personalized treatment, and patient care. A notable emerging trend is the rise of 'carebots' – AI-powered systems designed to assist in caregiving. These devices can monitor a patient's vitals, remind them to take medication, or even provide companionship to reduce feelings of isolation.[24]

Currently, most such systems take a traditional appearance, e.g. as a television system or medical equipment. This is not really necessary: the Dutch 'Tessa' elderly care robot takes the unique appearance of a flowerpot, appealing to easy recognition and low threat level. The near future will bring us more humanoid 'carebots': Honda's ASIMO for instance is able to walk with human-motion and detect objects within its immediate environment. The advanced humanoid machine oversees the safety and care of individuals who require assistance. AI in general and carebots in particular have the promise to reduce costs and expand availability of patient care. This is of particular importance in ageing societies such as Japan or Italy.

However, the rise of carebots and AI usage in public health raises a range of ethical issues.[25] Firstly, there's the question of data privacy. Carebots collect a large amount of sensitive health data, raising concerns about data protection, consent, and potential misuse. Secondly, as these machines take on roles traditionally occupied by humans, they may inadvertently depersonalize care. While carebots can perform certain tasks, they cannot offer the human touch or emotional connection that a human caregiver can provide. At best, they can simulate them – but how ethical is it to give people a faked sense of comfort or being cared for?

Lastly, as AI systems become more integrated into health care, it's crucial to ensure they are equitable and don't reinforce existing health disparities. For example, if an AI system is trained predominantly on data from a particular demographic, it may perform less effectively for other groups.

Intellectual property in AI creations

"Intellectual property shall be protected", as article 17 of the Charter of Fundamental Rights of the EU puts it. The goal of protecting creative works such as books, movies or sculptures, and protecting technological innovations has long been a part of society. Intellectual property today is a key issue in IT contracting and services.

As AI systems become increasingly sophisticated, they are beginning to produce outputs that could traditionally be classified as intellectual property. This is particularly evident in fields such as art, literature, and music, where AI algorithms are generating novel and unique works. For instance, OpenAI's GPT-4 system has the ability to create poetry and stories that, in many cases, are virtually indistinguishable from those authored by humans. The Midjourney image generator can create stunning works of art, and AI systems like AIVA (Artificial Intelligence Virtual Artist) can compose original pieces of music.

IP law has an underlying incentive: people need to be rewarded to create intellectual works. Copyright and patents thus provide (time-limited) exclusive rights, allowing for exploitation through licenses or enjoying a temporary monopoly. But what would an artificial intelligence want with such a reward? In other words, do AI's *deserve* intellectual property protection for their creations?

These issues have been brought into focus by an AI system called DABUS (Device for the Autonomous Bootstrapping of Unified Sentience), created by Stephen Thaler, president and chief executive of US-based AI firm Imagination Engines. DABUS has made several inventions that theoretically qualify for patent protection – if it wasn't for the fact that most patent laws require an actual person to be identified as inventor. So far, patent offices around the world have mostly rejected the DABUS patent applications on this ground.[26]

The question of copyright on AI-generated art is even more complex, as copyright applies automatically upon creation. While a court can declare that a certain work fails to meet the 'intellectual creation' criterion required by law, this has not happened yet for AI-generated works. A famous parallel is the *Monkey Selfie* case from 2015, where photographer David Slater tried to assert copyright on a photo taken with his camera by a crested macaque in Indonesia.[27] By happenstance, the photo turned out to be unusually

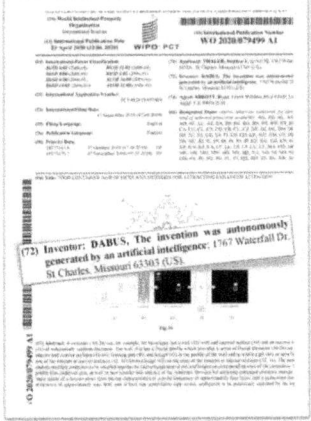

captivating, characterized by its sharp focus and the monkey's anthropomorphic, almost gleeful expression. The US Court of Appeals for the 9th Circuit did however not recognize the macaque as "author" under US copyright law, as only human beings have this ability.

In early 2023, author Kris Kashtanova was refused a copyright registration for the comic book *Zarya of the Dawn*.[28] In the USA, registration is a prerequisite for being able to sue over copyright infringement, and the US Copyright Office manages these registrations. When the Office learned that the images were created by the *Midjourney* generative AI system, it deemed the 'guidance' or prompting by Kashtanova as insufficient for copyright protection because Midjourney creates multiple images from a single prompt and thus exhibits some form of autonomous creative input, showing that Kashtanova cannot have been the creator. According to legal experts, European copyright law is more flexible: if there is an intellectual creation, there must have been an author, and no explicit requirement exists that this author is a natural human being.[29] So far, this has not been confirmed or denied by case law. These issues have been debated from the early 1980s onwards.[30] Of note is that the AI output of that time - both computer code and written prose - then was considered original and creative, but today as trivial and hardly worthy of IP. Perhaps the notion of 'creativity' will once again shift to remain within the human realm.

AI Legislation for Space Exploration

As the final frontier of this chapter, let's consider deployment of AI in space activities, offering solutions to challenges in data collection, space traffic management, and space debris removal. Prominent examples include the KubeSat satellite management platform and the Artificial Intelligence Learning Earth Observation (AILO). Famously, the NASA Perseverance Mars Rover used AI technology to find its way on the Red Planet. However, international space law, in particular, lacks adequate regulation of this sphere of activity fraught with serious risks.[31] The existing major treaties on outer space adopted in the 60s and 70s, for obvious reasons, do not contain provisions governing the use of artificial intelligence technologies and establish only general principles covering any activity in outer space and on celestial bodies. One example is the 1972 Liability Convention, that today regulates liability for damage caused by a space object. The very generic rules in this Convention could be applied to damage caused by AI, e.g. a miscalculated course causing a crash or other accident. However, the establishment of fault presupposes the existence of due care standards, which is quite problematic in the case of using such new technologies.

As with other fields of technology, the integration of AI in space activities is transforming the way we approach the field. This underlines the need for comprehensive and up-to-date regulations, which in turn shows why the AI Act in Europe is such a monumental step. It's clear that as we move further into the era of AI-driven space exploration, law and policy must keep pace with technological advancement.

Moving on, let's consolidate the main points from this discussion in our final section, "Key Takeaways", to ensure we've captured the breadth and depth of AI's impact on our legal and ethical landscape.

Key takeaways

In this first chapter, we unraveled the aura of AI, with its dichotomy of promise and peril, a sentiment echoed by figures like Stephen Hawking and depicted in popular culture. We then acknowledged the increasing emphasis on embedding ethics in AI, fueled by real-world consequences of unchecked algorithms. Grasping AI's essence proved elusive, as we navigated various definitions, but it was clear that its ties to human intelligence make it challenging to categorize definitively. Finally, as we speculated on the future of AI, issues like climate change emerged as potential influencers on both AI's development and its regulation.

Armed with this foundational comprehension of AI's multifaceted nature and societal implications, we're poised to delve into the intricate details of the European AI Act, the epicenter of AI regulation in Europe.

2

Unraveling the European AI Act

Chapter 2 – Unraveling the European AI Act

In this chapter, we aim to analyze the European AI Act in depth. We will explore its scope, delve into its risk assessment mechanisms, and examine the obligations it sets for AI providers and users. By the end of this chapter, you will be equipped to utilize these legal and ethical norms in the real-world scenarios of designing, deploying, and overseeing AI systems. Let's start at the beginning: why did Europe come up with specific legislation for this emerging technology, and what is its connection to the ethics of Artificial Intelligence?

Understanding Europe: The Core of Responsible AI

The European drive to regulate AI was sparked by the ethical concerns prompted by the quick rise of AI in the past years. It is however also part of a broader approach, called the Digital Decade 2030. This approach seeks to transform and digitize the European economy and society. It is part of the so-called European Green Deal, which seeks to transform the EU into a modern, resource-efficient and competitive economy.[1] Both were initiated after the 2008 worldwide crisis. As a result, there has been intense activity in the EU concerning the regulation of digital markets, including the AI sector.

Initial steps towards regulation

The EU first signaled its intentions to regulate AI in a Commission strategy document in April 2018.[2] The three aims of the strategy were to boost the EU's technological and industrial capacity and AI uptake, encouraging the modernization of education and training and ensuring an appropriate ethical and legal framework, based on the Union's values and in line with the Charter of Fundamental Rights of the EU.

In December of that same year, a Coordinated Action Plan followed.[3] Next to various projects and investments, the Action Plan set out how the recently-passed General Data Protection Regulation (GDPR) set rules for use of personal data in AI. An accompanying

> **By the end of this chapter, you'll be able to ...**
> - Understand the general structure of the AI Act.
> - Analyze the AI Act's risk-based classification and its market implications.
> - Summarize relevant requirements for practical AI deployment scenarios.

plan announced the need for ethics guidelines with a global perspective and ensuring an innovation-friendly legal framework.[4] The initial mentions of a need for legislation appears to have been shelved in the meantime.

Work of the High-Level Expert Group on AI

In order to support the development of the AI strategies outlined above, the European Commission established two groups: the High-Level Expert Group on AI (AI HLEG) and the European AI Alliance. The European AI Alliance is an online forum with over 4000 members representing academia, business and industry, civil society, EU citizens and policymakers. The HLEG is a group of experts from industry, academy and society whose work have served as starting points for policymaking initiatives taken by the Commission and its Member States.

In its two-year run, the HLEG has produced these deliverables:

1. *A definition of Artificial Intelligence: Main capabilities and scientific disciplines*, a preparatory document necessary for the other works.
2. *The Ethics Guidelines for Trustworthy AI*, setting an ethical framework for AI based on the notion that trustworthy AI must be lawful, ethical and robust.
3. *The Policy and Investment Recommendations for Trustworthy AI*, a set of recommendations to guide trustworthy AI towards sustainability, growth, competitiveness, and inclusion.
4. *The Assessment List for Trustworthy AI*, a practical tool that translates the Ethics Guidelines into an accessible and dynamic self-assessment checklist.
5. *The report Sectoral Considerations on the Policy and Investment Recommendations*, exploring implementation of the above in three specific areas: Public Sector, Healthcare and Manufacturing & the Internet of Things.

The main deliverable of the HLEG is the *Ethics Guidelines for Trustworthy AI*, an extensive document that systematically analyzes ethical concerns in AI and proposes a concrete framework for addressing them. At the bedrock of this framework is the concept of "Trustworthy AI"; humanity needs to be able to trust the sociotechnical environments in which AI is embedded.[5] Together with the *Assessment List for Trustworthy AI* (ALTAI), the Guidelines form the basis for compliance with the AI Act. This book will use the ALTAI as a central guide throughout the coming chapters.

Towards the AI Act

In October 2019, incoming EC President Ursula Von der Leyen promised to pass AI legislation within her first 100 days in office.[6] The first step was to draw up a White Paper, which outlined three major steps. First, next to new legislation (the AI Act) existing legislation on topics like product liability, ecommerce, motor vehicles would be updated to address applications or impact of AI. Second, all of these efforts would be underpinned by a risk-based approach for new rules. And third, the ethical values inherent in such new rules should be exported to other countries in the world.

The third step in particular underlines the EU's intention to be a leader in AI based on ethical values: *"in a global arena of AI competition and cooperation, the EU attempts to project itself as a Normative Power Europe."*[7] While this may sound ambitious, it is not unjustified: the so-called "Brussels Effect" of EU regulation having worldwide impact is a proven phenomenon in international politics and economics.[8] As one of the largest and most integrated economies in the world, the EU's stringent regulations often set the standard for global norms. An early example is the 2007 REACH Regulation (Registration, Evaluation, Authorization, and Restriction of Chemicals): chemical companies must identify and manage the risks linked to the substances they manufacture and market in the EU. Its influence has extended beyond EU borders, leading chemical companies worldwide to adopt similar practices to ensure market access in the EU. The 2016 General Data Protection Regulation (GDPR) is also widely cited as exhibiting a similar effect in other countries.

A first draft of the AI Act was released by the European Commission on 21 April 2021. In November 2022, the Council of the European Union (government ministers from each EU country) proposed a set of amendments, followed by the European Parliament's own amendments in May 2023. With their eyes on a January 1, 2024 date of adoption, intense negotiations between the institutes took place in the months that followed.[9] Key concerns were the scope of the so-called prohibited practices, the position of foundation models, (now called general-purpose AI models) the classification as high-risk, and the use of real-time biometrics for law enforcement. On December 8, 2023 a political agreement was reached, which was formalized into the final text in the first months of 2024.

Understanding the AI Act

With over 200 legal clauses and almost 100 introductory recitals providing context and intent, the AI Act rivals the GDPR in complexity and interpretational challenges. Let's dive in and examine the general structure and key terminology of the AI Act.

A table of contents

The AI Act counts 83 articles, divided into twelve titles, each of which may contain several chapters.

- Title I – General Provisions. The first articles define subject matter and scope of the AI Act, including key definitions (discussed in the next subsection) and general tasks for national legislators and supervisory authorities.
- Title II – Prohibited AI Practices. This title prohibits certain applications of AI because they fundamentally contradict core values of the EU, more on which in the next section on managing risk.
- Title III – High-risk AI Systems. In this title, divided into four chapters, the AI Act sets out the many compliance requirements and restrictions for so-called "high-risk" AI. These are the subject of the following chapters of this book.
- Title IV – Transparency obligations. This title defines basic transparency obligations for any type of AI, not just high-risk systems.
- Title V – General Purpose AI Models. This title defines basic rules for AI models that have multiple applications.
- Title VI – Measures in support of innovation. The regulatory sandbox is the main focus of this title. We'll meet the sandbox later in this chapter.
- Title VII – Governance. This title sets up the governance and enforcement structure in the EU, including the AI Office that coordinates activity of the national supervisory authorities throughout the Union.
- Title VIII – EU Database for High-Risk AI systems. To further stimulate transparency, this title establishes a publicly-accessible database listing every high-risk AI system deployed in the European Union.
- Title IX – Post-market monitoring and market surveillance. In this title various rules regarding information sharing and market monitoring are established. Of particular note are a duty to report 'serious incidents' regarding the use of AI systems. This title also establishes the investigative powers of the supervisory authorities.
- Title X – Codes of Conduct. This title establishes a mechanism for self-regulation of AI systems that do not qualify as high risk. These could set requirements for example on environmental sustainability, accessibility, stakeholders participation and diversity of development teams.
- Title XI – Confidentiality and Penalties. This title sets out the powers to impose penalties, including administrative fines, that supervisory authorities may wield in case of noncompliance. More on this in chapter 10.
- Title XII – Delegated Acts. This formal title provides the legal basis for the European Commission to unilaterally amend certain parts of the AI Act, notably the list of use cases considered high-risk.
- Title XIII – Final Provisions. The last title of the AI Act amends other legislation to refer to the AI Act, sets its date of entry into force and introduces an exemption for AI systems already on the market.

Key definitions

The AI Act contains over 50 definitions to ensure consistent application of its provisions. The key terms have been illustrated in the below chart, which visually shows the growth of an AI system from creation to market operation.

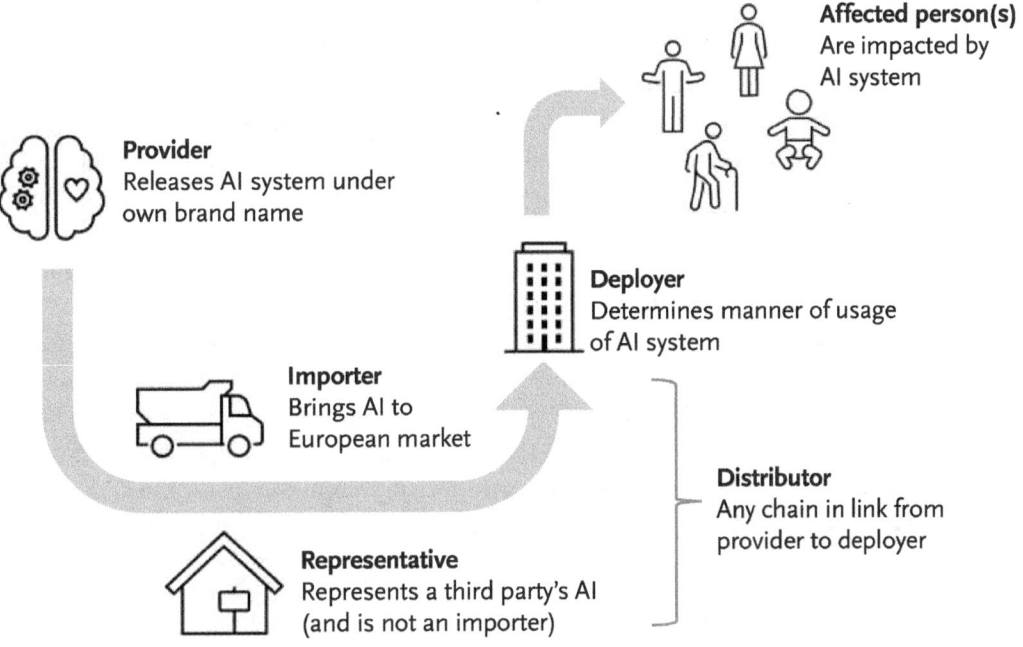

The key elements in this chart are:
- As discussed in chapter 1, an **AI system** is a machine-based system that is designed to operate with varying levels of autonomy and that can, for explicit or implicit objectives, generate outputs such as predictions, recommendations, or decisions that influence physical or virtual environments.
- A **provider** is a legal entity that develops an AI system and puts this on the market under its own name or trademark. This can be for a fee or at no charge, as with the many open source AI systems available on the internet. A provider may also involve a third party to have the AI system developed.
- The **deployer** of an AI system is the legal entity that actually uses the AI system. A deployer can be a provider itself, but could also license or purchase the AI system from a third-party provider. For instance, an insurance firm may license a SaaS-based AI system to do a first evaluation of claims. The firm would then be the deployer.

- Any entity between provider and deployer is generally called a **distributor.** Formally, it is any entity that that makes an AI system available on the Union market without affecting its properties. If the distributor were to customize or otherwise change the AI system prior to introduction, it would become a provider.
- A specific instance of the distributor is the **importer.** This is the legal entity established in the Union that places on the market or puts into service an AI system that bears the name or trademark of a natural or legal person established outside the Union.
- If an AI system is not actually imported (e.g. as physical product arriving at a harbour or airport), then deployment in the Union requires an **authorised representative** established in the Union who has received a written mandate from a provider of an AI system to assume the responsibilities and liabilities associated with the AI Act for an AI provider. This mechanism is similar to the GDPR's authorised representative for data processing.
- Together, the provider, the deployer, the authorised representative, the importer and the distributor are called the **operator(s)** of an AI system.
- **Affected persons** are those persons or groups who are subject to or otherwise affected by an AI system. This is not necessarily the same as 'users' of the AI system, as one may be affected by an AI system's action without actively using it – or even being aware that this is happening. For example, if a self-driving car operates on the open road, any traffic participant would be an affected person, while only the driver in the car could be called the 'user' of the system.

Material and geographical scope

With the proper terminology established, we can discuss the material and geographical applicability of the AI Act. Material applicability means whether a system qualifies as an AI system, while geographical applicability means whether an action with such an AI system by a particular entity triggers the AI Act's obligations.

For material applicability, first of all the system must meet the definition of an AI system quoted above. But there's more: the AI system must have been 'put into service', which roughly means any supply of the system for distribution or use on the Union market in the course of a commercial activity, whether in return for payment or free of charge. The intent behind this convoluted sentence is to exempt research and non-commercial activities such as open-source development of publicly available AI systems. Unfortunately, many open source initiatives have some commercial aspects, ranging from charging fees for consultancy or support to advertising-driven download pages or soliciting voluntary donations. This will cause significant unclarity down the road.

For geographical applicability, the AI system must have been placed on the market or put into service in a European Union member state (or Iceland, Liechtenstein and

Norway, the European Economic Area members not part of the EU). "Placing on the market" is the EU term for making a product available for sale in a member state. "Putting into service" is the corresponding term for services. Both terms require some form of activity in the member state.

However, there is a broader option: if "the output produced by the system is used in the Union", the AI provider or deployer behind such output is subject to the AI Act. This option thus does not require specific sales or other commercial activities in a member state. If a European firm were to hire, say, a Canadian provider to use an AI system to evaluate the effectiveness of its marketing activities, the output of that system would be used in the Union and thus the Canadian provider would have to comply with the AI Act.

It is irrelevant whether the provider placing the AI system on the market or putting it into service is established within the Union or in a third country. The same goes for providers, importers and distributors. The AI Act thus has a broad reach: a US-based provider that offers access to an AI system through a website is required to comply with the AI Act, despite not having a physical presence in the Union. In practice, the provider would need to appoint an authorised representative who would assume these responsibilities (and face the administrative penalties, including fines, if any violation occurred).

Conformity assessments and certification

The AI Act is written to fit in the existing EU legal framework designed to ensure that products placed within the internal market meet high safety, health, and environmental protection requirements. Central to this framework are the concepts of Notified Bodies and Conformity Assessment Bodies. The latter is an organization authorized to evaluate whether a product, service, process, system, person, or body complies with specified requirements outlined in standards and regulations. A notified body is a specific type of conformity assessment body that has been formally recognized by a national accreditation body to carry out the assessment process for products before they are placed on the European market. In addition, every country has a Notification Authority, which is responsible for ensuring that the Notified Bodies meet the stringent criteria set by the EU to carry out conformity assessments.

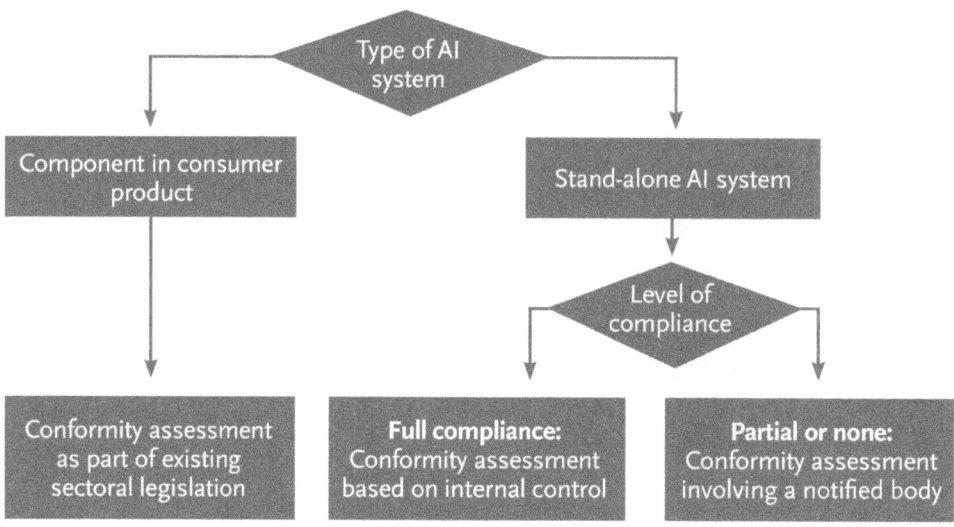

High-risk AI systems are required to undergo a conformity assessment procedure prior to their being put on the market or putting into service. The process requires the establishment and examination of a quality management system, specifically tailored to the design, development, and testing of AI products. As illustrated in the flowchart above, the exact process depends on the type of product or service.[10] An AI system embedded in a consumer product already receives a conformity assessment as part of the existing safety legislation for the larger product, and so does not need a separate assessment for its AI component.

For standalone AI systems, the path of a conformity assessment with a notified body is the main option. There is the option of conformity assessment based on internal control, which means the manufacturer themselves assesses and declares that their product meets the relevant EU requirements. This option is only available to a limited subset of the high-risk use cases of Annex III, and then only if the producer is in full compliance with the AIA. All others will have to seek out a notified body, which then conducts an external assessment to ensure the quality management system meets the specified requirements. Any modifications to the system or the AI products it covers must be promptly communicated to the notified body, to allow it to determine if the changes adhere to the established requirements or if a reassessment is necessary.

Floridi et al. have documented example of a conformity assessment procedure for AI.[11] In short, the notified body reviews the AI system's technical documentation, which may include access to training and testing datasets, and potentially the source code, to ensure compliance with the relevant requirements. Failure to provide a comprehensive and accurate application, or to maintain the quality management system to the notified body's standards, can result in the refusal of the conformity certificate. Such a refusal not only delays the product's time to market but also necessitates a re-evaluation of the system or product, which can be both costly and time-consuming.

In addition to the initial conformity assessment, the European Union employs the instrument of post-market monitoring. This ongoing process requires producers, in this case AI providers, to continuously observe and report on their products' performance once it is introduced to the market. The objective is to ensure that the AI system remains compliant with the necessary standards throughout its lifecycle and that any unforeseen risks or malfunctions are identified and addressed promptly. This proactive surveillance serves to safeguard consumer interests and uphold public safety. However, it also imposes an additional layer of responsibility on businesses, necessitating the allocation of resources to monitor their products post-launch, which can be a significant operational burden, especially for smaller enterprises.

Entry into force and transitional provisions

At the time of writing of this book, the AI Act was scheduled for adoption by the end of April 2024. Like the GDPR, this date will start a two-year transitional period during which AI providers, distributors and deployers will be able to adjust their products, services and processes to the new requirements. However, prohibited practices (see next section) will need to be taken off the market in only six months from the adoption date.

In the meantime, governments can get to work: the AI Act provides them three months to establish notification authorities and notified bodies, required for the certification process, and supervisory authorities that will oversee AI distributors and deployers. They will then have around nine months to produce guidance and procedural regulations for administrative actions and the levels of fines they intend to impose for the various AI Act infractions that may occur.

Managing Risk: AI Practices and Their Classification

The AI Act takes a risk-based approach: rather than specifically prohibiting or regulating certain AI systems or use cases, the Act defines three levels of risk and attaches legal obligations and limitations to each. To understand the implications, let's first take a step back at what we mean with 'risk' in the context of the AI Act.

AI and fundamental rights

The Charter of Fundamental Rights of the European Union holds a distinctive place within the EU's legal framework, specifically in the realm of fundamental rights. These rights are integral to the EU's legal system and take precedence in shaping the Union's laws and policies to uphold human dignity, freedom, democracy, equality, and the rule of law. The Charter's provisions serve as enforceable rights for individuals, and they are pivotal in the EU's legal assessments and decisions.

The terms 'risk' and 'harm' in the context of AI regulation must be understood as a reference to these fundamental rights and values of the Union. As the HLEG put it in the Guidelines: *"Respect for fundamental rights, within a framework of democracy and the rule of law, provides the most promising foundations for identifying abstract ethical principles and values, which can be operationalised in the context of AI."* Deployment of an AI system may introduce a great variety of harms. Here are a few examples of commonly-cited harms, written in terms of fundamental rights with reference to the relevant provisions in the Charter.

- Privacy and Data Protection (Articles 7 & 8): **AI's capability for mass surveillance and data processing could lead to invasions of privacy, conflicting with the right to the protection of personal data and the respect for private and family life.**
- Non-Discrimination (Article 21): **Biased AI algorithms could result in discriminatory outcomes in services, employment, and justice, which would contravene the principle of non-discrimination.**
- Freedom of Expression (Article 11): **Overzealous AI moderation tools could restrict lawful speech, impinging upon the right to freedom of expression and information.**
- Freedom of Thought, Conscience, and Religion (Article 10): **AI that manipulates information could infringe upon the freedom of thought, conscience, and religion by subtly influencing individuals' beliefs and opinions.**
- Workers' Rights (Article 31): **AI in the workplace could lead to intrusive surveillance and job displacement, undermining the right to fair and just working conditions.**
- Right to a Fair Trial (Article 47): **AI tools used in legal proceedings could lack accountability and transparency, threatening the right to an effective remedy and to a fair trial.**
- Consumer Protection (Article 38): **AI that deceives or manipulates consumers, or that fails to ensure product safety, could violate the right to a high level of consumer protection.**
- Protection of Personal Integrity (Article 3): **AI applications in medicine or biometrics that misuse personal health data or bodily information would conflict with the right to integrity of the person.**
- Environmental Protection and Sustainability (Article 37): **AI systems, through their lifecycle from development to deployment and disposal, can have significant environmental impacts. The energy consumption required for training complex AI

models and the electronic waste generated from rapid obsolescence of AI-enabled devices can contribute to environmental degradation. This poses a risk to the right to a high level of environmental protection and the improvement of the quality of the environment

- Freedom to Conduct a Business (Article 16): AI systems could potentially disrupt markets by enabling monopolistic behaviors or by creating unfair competitive advantages through data dominance or algorithmic collusion. This could lead to significant economic harm for smaller companies that cannot compete with AI-enhanced businesses.

There is still significant discussion among scholars how to weigh these harms.[12] Direct physical harm to individuals seems more severe than a long-term negative effect on the environment, for instance. The freedom to conduct a business is limited more easily by courts (e.g. for consumer protection) than the freedom of information. Thus, it is yet unclear which harms should or should not be considered in a risk assessment for an AI system.

Three levels of risk

The AI Act has as its primary aim the mitigation of risks, which it defines as the combination of the probability of an occurrence of harm and the severity of that harm. There is a three-tier approach to managing the aforementioned risks:

1. Prohibited Practices. These provide manipulative, exploitative and social control practices that contradict the fundamental rights and Union values, and thus should be banned entirely. Prohibited practices are listed in Article 5 of the AI Act, which means adding or removing such a practice requires a revision of the Act itself.
2. High-Risk Practices. While not contradicting fundamental rights or Union values, these practices pose significant risks of adversely impacting these rights. AI systems exhibiting such a level of risk must implement a large number of compliance requirements before being permitted on the market. High-risk use cases are listed in Annex II and III of the AI Act, which the European Commission can amend without revising the Act itself.
3. Low-Risk Practices. An AI system that does not pose high risks and does not qualify as a prohibited practice is called a "low-risk" system. These come with basic compliance requirements, mainly focusing on transparency and not taking autonomous decisions.

Prohibited practices

The AI Act prohibits a series of AI-driven practices as being particularly abhorrent: use of AI for "manipulative, exploitative and social control practices" that contradicts Union values of respect for human dignity, freedom, equality, democracy and the rule of law and Union fundamental rights, including the right to non-discrimination, data protection and privacy and the rights of the child. These practices are enumerated in article 5 of the AI Act and are discussed in more detail in the next chapter.

There is no way to appeal a finding that an AI system is prohibited. The ban is absolute and there are no exceptions. The only real way to avoid the prohibition is to adjust the practice so that it avoids the thresholds of article 5.

Determining high-risk AI

For the determination process of high-risk AI there is more flexibility. This process is illustrated in the flowchart below.

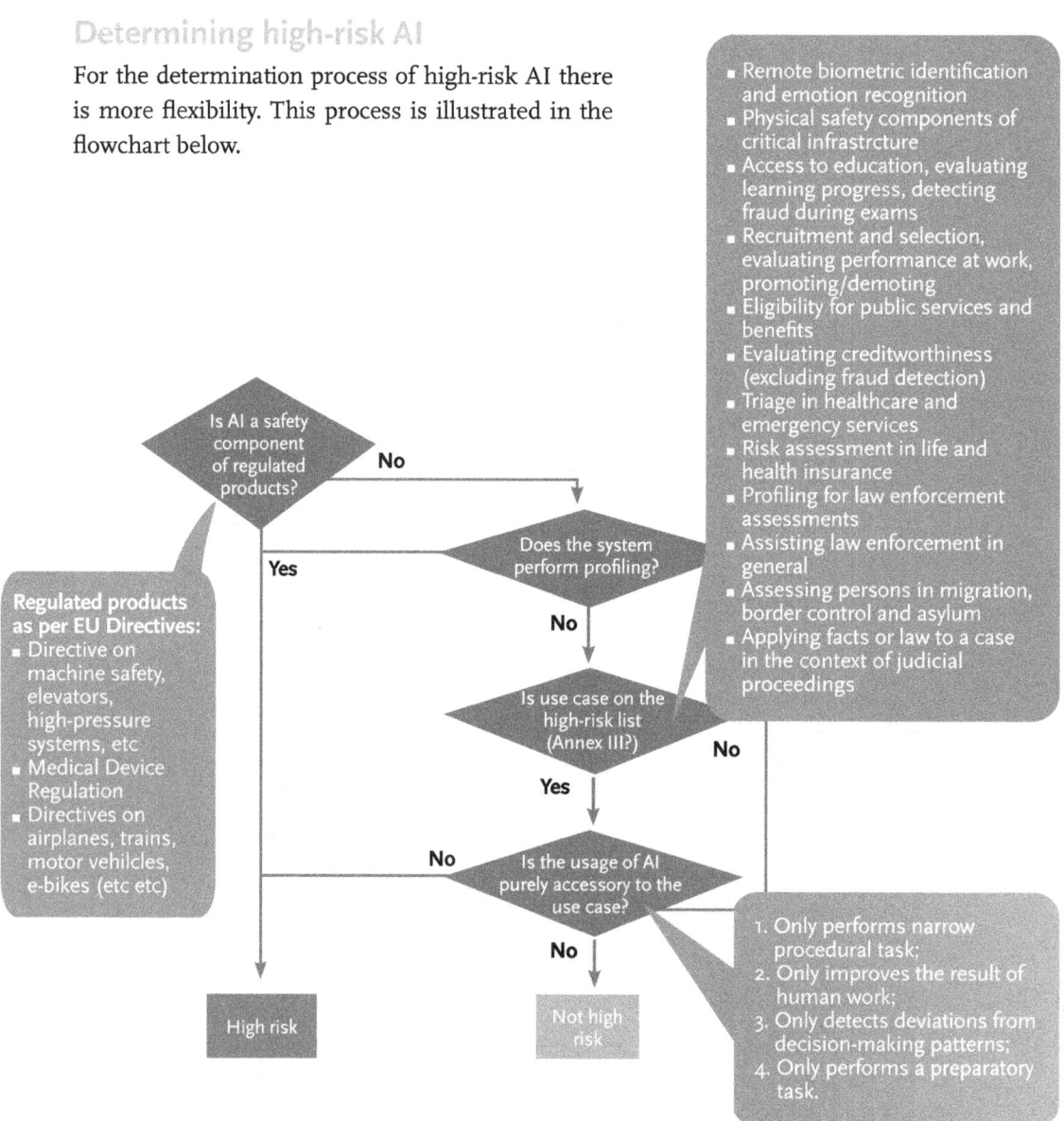

Annex II to the AI Act lists a variety of EU product legislation, such as the safety of production machinery, elevators or toys, the regulation of radio equipment, gas ovens and medical devices. There are also directives on approval and market surveillance of aviation, transport and drones. If an AI system is intended to be used as a safety component of a product, or is itself a product, that falls under any of this legislation, the AI system is by definition high-risk.

More flexibility exists with the use cases of Annex III to the AI Act. Here, many use cases and applications of AI are listed, such as operation of critical infrastructure, recruitment and selection, access to public benefits (e.g. welfare), law enforcement, insurance claim handling and administration of justice. In principle, any use of AI for such an application qualifies as a high-risk case. However, an exception arises when the provider of the AI system can demonstrate that the AI system in fact is "purely accessory" to the use case. An AI system is purely accessory in one of the following four cases:

- The AI performs only a narrow procedural task, such as automatically adjusting the brightness of streetlights based on environmental conditions.
- The AI system only improves the result of human activity, e.g. by rewriting a draft into a final text.
- The AI only detects deviations from decision-making patterns, e.g. by highlighting an outcome that is unusual for the inputs given.
- The AI system only performs a preparatory task, e.g. classifying or labeling input documents or checking formalities.

To complicate matters, if the AI performs one of these cases but this involves profiling of natural persons (as regulated by the GDPR) the use case is still high-risk.

The onus is on AI providers to justify (with written arguments) why the AI system qualifies as purely accessory. The justification is to be provided to the supervisory authority upon request, who may review and object if the AI is considered misclassified. A fine can in theory be provided for misclassification.

Addressing innovation: regulatory sandboxes

Regulation of new technology poses a dilemma: regulate too early and risk stifling a valuable innovation – but regulate too late and be left with powerless laws against technology giants that have taken over society. The concept of regulatory sandboxes provides a third way: innovators can experiment with new technologies outside existing regulation, while society as a whole remains shielded from any negative impacts.

Origins of sandboxes

Originally developed in the Fintech sector, regulatory sandboxes create a testbed for a selected number of innovative projects, by waiving otherwise applicable rules, guiding compliance, or customizing enforcement.[13] Typically their scope is limited to experiments, as opposed to large-scale production deployments. Despite this limitation, they have long been criticized as being contrary to key principles of law such as legal certainty, proportionality, and equal treatment. The underlying argument is that those that can operate in the sandbox, can achieve a competitive advantage not available to those who operate in the traditional environment, which may seem unfair.

From the beginning, plans for the AI Act had included references to regulatory sandboxes, "for the development, training, testing and validation of innovative AI systems under the direct supervision, guidance and support by the national competent authority". The fear that AI innovation would be stifled was significant, especially given that most innovations in this space already originate from outside the European Union. This is reflected in the stated goals of AI sandboxes: not only should they facilitate training and testing by AI providers, but also provide supervisory authorities with new insights and the ability to draw up guidance for compliance outside of the sandbox.

AI sandboxes in practice

The AI Act does not itself establish sandbox regimes, but rather leaves it to the national supervisory authorities to create appropriate boundaries within European and national law. The modalities and the conditions for the establishment and operation of the AI regulatory sandboxes are to be set down in later legislation, as the AI Act puts it. It is as yet unclear how far this may go: can supervisory authorities waive certain legal requirements or lift restrictions for a sandbox experiment, for instance? Or can authorities go no further than flexible or laissez-faire enforcement of the existing rules?

One point of note is that the AI Act establishes a ground for further processing of personal data for specific regulatory sandboxes, which is a necessity under the GDPR. Other than that, no guidance on sandboxes is available yet.

Related legislation

The AI Act is neither the first, nor the last legislation to address artificial intelligence. It is however the sole European act that specifically regulates this innovative technology. Other laws mainly address outcomes or impact, or indirectly regulate behaviour that may be exhibited by AI systems.

The General Data Protection Regulation

Adopted in 2016, the GDPR is the EU's flagship regulation on personal data, which is a fundamental right in the European legal system. Its focus is on lawful, transparent and fair handling of personal data, which is a much broader topic than just AI systems. However, automated decision-making or profiling of persons has been a key point of attention even before the GDPR: already in the 1990s it was a well-established principle that computers should not exclude people or put them at a disadvantage merely by means of data analysis. The GDPR gave hefty teeth to this principle, with tens of millions in fines available for offenders.

The AI Act and the GDPR obviously overlap where an AI system is trained on personal data or where such a system is used to profile or make decisions. These subjects are handled in chapter 5 (data governance) in more detail. In short, the GDPR takes precedence according to the AI Act. An AI system can also affect persons even when no personal data is processed or when the processing is 'anonymous' in GDPR parlance. In such a case, the AI Act would take precedence.

The AI and Product Liability Directives

The main enforcement mechanism in the AI Act is government intervention by national supervisory authorities. These authorities can issue fines, issue binding instructions or restrictions and even order certain AI practices stopped completely. This very much resembles other legislation, such as the GDPR. However, a key element that is missing in the AI Act is the ability for individual citizens to seek redress from harm caused by AI systems.

This is intentional: the policy choice was made to approach this issue from a product liability perspective. For over a decade, the European Commission has set out to introduce the "New Legislative Framework" to create coherence among the sectorial rules on product safety. In this light, it is understandable to regard risks caused by AI systems as potential defects just like other safety issues with products on the European market. Under the European regime, when safety defects manifest themselves, the producer or importer of the product is liable for any damages unless he can prove the defect could not have been foreseen. (Excluding such liability in terms and conditions is legally not permitted.)

In September 2022 the European Commission proposed the AI Liability Directive, formally called the "Directive on adapting non contractual civil liability rules to artificial intelligence." The gist of the new rules – that have not been formally adopted yet – is that any person harmed by output of an AI system has legal standing to sue its operator. Failure to comply with a relevant duty of care for AI operators makes them automatically liable for damages, and any noncompliance with AI Act requirements constitutes such a failure. Similar rules are added to the long-standing Product Liability Directive, which creates a similar regime for any form of product safety issue. Of particular importance is the reversal of the burden of proof: once a user of an AI system has made a reasonable argument that the damage is related to actions by the AI-driven system, the provider of the system has to establish that the AI was in fact not at fault.

The two directives are still hotly debated and at the time of writing it is unclear in what form they will be adopted.[14]

Consumer protection and market protection legislation

Many AI systems will be deployed by businesses in interactions with consumers, e.g. to drive sales, improve products or services, engage in customer service or to identify fraud in purchasing transactions. This makes them fully subject to existing consumer protection legislation. Some examples include the Unfair Commercial Practices Directive, the Unfair Contract Terms Directive and the Consumer Rights Directive (CRD). The AI Act declares itself to be complementary to these rules, meaning that even if an AI system is fully brought into compliance with the AI Act it may still violate consumer protection laws.

Most popular AI systems are operated by a handful of very large actors, and made available as internet services. Given their size, they are likely subject to the recently-adopted Digital Services Act and Digital Markets Act. The DSA addresses the legal responsibilities of digital services that act as intermediaries in their role of connecting consumers with goods, services, and content. Such intermediaries face limited liability in their connecting role; the AI Act does not change this. Very large online platforms – service providers with over 45 million European users – face thorough transparency provisions, e.g. on content they remove or users sanctioned for inappropriate behaviour. There are also limitations on profiling, targeting children and other platform actions that may be relevant for AI systems.

The DMA aims to ensure fair and open digital markets. It targets large companies that provide core platform services and have a significant impact on the internal market, serve as an important gateway for business users to reach end-users, and have an entrenched and durable position. The tech giants offering AI for business users, in particular through so-called foundation models, may well qualify as "gatekeepers" under the DMA and face increased scrutiny on their behaviour in the market. One restriction of note is the banning of data sharing between services, meaning an internet platform that offers, say, e-mail and productivity tools cannot use data gathered from user behaviour there to improve an AI system produced as a separate service.

On the topic of (non-personal) data, the upcoming Data Act aims to create a fair and competitive data market, ensuring access to and use of data. For AI producers, this means a more equitable landscape for obtaining the data necessary to train sophisticated AI models. It also imposes obligations on data holders and device manufacturers to provide data access to users, which could increase transparency and potentially lead to more innovation in AI services. Data intermediaries and data sharing for the common good is further regulated in the Data Governance Act, which focuses on the mechanisms of data sharing and governance. It establishes a framework for data intermediaries and mechanisms for data altruism, where individuals and companies can share data for the common good.

European cybersecurity regulations

Recognizing that cybersecurity is a key aspect of the Digital Decade, the European Union has (or is in the process of) adopting a variety of laws regarding cybersecurity requirements. This follows in the footsteps of – again – the GDPR, which already requires personal data processing to be subject to "adequate technical and organization security requirements". An often-heard critique of this legal requirement is that it is too vague and open-ended. The new regulations seek to provide more certainty through standardization and formal assessments.

Already in 2019, the EU adopted its Cybersecurity Act, providing a scheme for voluntary cybersecurity certification, more on which in chapter 4 (robustness and safety). In 2021, the Cyber Resilience Act (CRA) was proposed. The CRA sets cybersecurity requirements for "smart devices", such as internet-enabled music players, robot vacuum cleaners and so on. Many of these devices contain functionality that meets the definition of AI in the AI Act. If the functionality also qualifies as "high-risk", the AI Act prescribes various security requirements, which can be fulfilled by CRA compliance. This in turn requires a specialized audit by an external party.

December 2022 saw the adoption of the "Directive on measures for a high common level of cybersecurity across the Union", commonly known as the NIS2 Directive. This law supersedes the 2016 Directive on Security of Network and Information Systems (NIS) and sets minimum cybersecurity standards for critical or vital infrastructure in both the public and private sectors. This includes telecommunications, transport and banking, but also food, health and the manufacturing of certain economically important products such as medical devices, computer equipment and heavy or advanced machinery. Involvement of AI in such an infrastructure thus requires a careful evaluation of the NIS2 requirements.

A wider look: AI Legislation across the globe

Of course the European Union is not the only region in the world seeking to regulate the impact of Artificial Intelligence. Most of the Western world is in the search for regulation and stimulation of AI in its national innovative environment. Some even speak of an "ongoing race for technological and regulatory leadership".[15] Let's have a look at seven countries, based on their economic relevance in the field of AI, and thus gain a better picture of the landscape of global AI legislation and the major differences between regions.

The Council of Europe

The Council of Europe is distinct from the European Union; it is an international organization that focuses on promoting human rights, democracy, and the rule of law among its 47 member states, which include all EU members but also other countries outside the EU. Unlike EU regulations, which are binding on its members, the conventions of the Council of Europe set standards that member states choose to adopt through ratification, and they often serve as the basis for national legislation. The European Court of Human Rights, which enforces the European Convention on Human Rights, is an institution of the Council of Europe and provides a mechanism for individuals to bring cases against states that have ratified the convention.

The Council of Europe is in the process of establishing a legally binding instrument known as the "Convention on Artificial Intelligence, Human Rights, Democracy and the Rule of Law" (AI Convention).[16] This convention is poised to be the first international treaty with legal force concerning the realm of artificial intelligence. Like the AI Act, it has taken a human rights-based approach, addressing the entire lifecycle of AI systems, and aims to establish enforceable rights through the European Court of Human Rights. Its timeline is unclear, and its global ambition may result in a watered-down compromise.

United States of America

The USA is the undisputed world leader in terms of development of AI technology and applications. For a long time, the country's leadership appeared to have had very little appetite for regulation. An assortment of state laws addresses some specific harms, such as the Californian Bolstering Online Transparency Act that requires chatbot usage to be disclosed explicitly, and the Colorado Protecting Consumers from Unfair Discrimination in Insurance Practice that bans insurance companies from using AI systems to identify certain forms of insurance fraud. No federal law on AI is yet on the books.

In 2022, the White House published a *Blueprint for an "AI Bill of Rights"* to guide the design, deployment, and development of AI systems. While non-binding, it represented a clear statement of the administration's stance on AI ethics and set the tone for future regulation and legislation. The Bill addresses several areas of concern in AI usage, focusing on ensuring fairness, transparency, non-discrimination, and accountability in AI systems. It aims to give individuals the right to know when and how AI is being used in determinations that affect them, to have access to clear explanations of how AI-based decisions are made, and to challenge those decisions when warranted.

The Blueprint plays an influential role in shaping US public discourse about AI and set the stage for further legislative and enforcement action in the US. This is illustrated by several actions by the FTC against AI service providers, notably including Meta. These actions are typically based on deception of consumers, such as in the case of Everalbum, a photo app that harvested user data for training AI without being explicit about it.[17]

A potential national law on AI is the proposed 2022 Algorithmic Accountability Act that regulates the use of automated decision systems (ADS). It proposes that organizations deploying such systems must take several concrete steps to identify and mitigate the social, ethical, and legal risks. While not adopted at this time, the approach is very much comparable to the AI Act.[18] The below table highlights key similarities and differences.

	US AAA	EU AIA
Scope	Use of automated decision systems (ADS), being any system (whether AI or not) the result of which serves as a basis for a decision or judgment	Use of artificial intelligence (AI) regardless of whether its output produces a decision
Ethics	Focus on accountability, no ethical framework	Detailed ethical framework as basis
Subjects	Large businesses ($50 million or more revenue)	Any entity producing, deploying or using AI
Categories of regulation	All ADS treated the same	Three levels of regulation: unacceptable, high-risk and minimal risk.
Transparency	Encouraged but without sanctions	Required for all AI deployments
Explainability	Encouraged but without sanctions	Required for high-risk AI deployments
Data governance	Implicit requirement for proper data handling	Strict requirements for origins and balanced nature of data
Enforcement	FTC enforcement: huge fines and other sanctions	National supervisors enforce: huge fines and other sanctions

A second proposed federal law that could become relevant for regulation of AI is the American Data Protection and Privacy Act, which is somewhat similar in spirit to the European GDPR and has strict provisions on using algorithms (including AI) for evaluating or judging human actions. Given the state of the US political arena, both Acts are not expected to pass any time soon.

In October 2023, president Biden issued an *Executive Order on AI Safety*. This Order instructed almost every federal agency to take steps to improve security and trustworthiness of AI systems, adapt job training and promote a competitive AI marketplace. Remarkably, the Order invoked the Defense Production Act of 1950, allowing the State Department to intervene if highly capable AI systems become available to malicious actors or otherwise threaten national security. Many standardization efforts are initiated, such as for watermarking content from generative AI.

People's Republic of China

While long seen as a follower, the PRC in fact has been investing heavily in AI research and development, thus taking steps to try and overtake the USA in this new technological race. The necessity for fast and broad innovation was long cited as the reason for not introducing strict regulation of AI.[19] It was not until May 2023 that this changed with the introduction of a draft for *Measures for the Management of Generative Artificial Intelligence Services*. This bill was prompted by concerns over generative AI such as ChatGPT and Midjourney and contains bans on a variety of subjects: AI may not subvert the State, do harm to national unity or generate false information, and must ensure that services are free of discrimination, IPR infringement and do not divulge personal information. A novel aspect is the requirement to have "appropriate measures to prevent users from excessive reliance on generated content." The bill is widely cited as an attempt to direct more regulatory power over (US and other) tech providers that work with AI.

Canada

Canada has been at the forefront of AI research and development, particularly in the areas of deep learning and machine learning. Canadian cities such as Toronto and Montreal are global AI hubs, hosting significant research activity. However, the country currently lacks a dedicated national-level law or regulation specifically addressing AI systems.

In 2019, the Government of Canada introduced a Directive on Automated Decision-Making, aiming to ensure that the use of automated decision systems is grounded in accountability, transparency, and fairness. The Directive applies to the design, procurement, and use of automated decision systems within the federal government. It was one of the first policy instruments in the world to establish minimum standards for the use of AI in government.

Canada's regulatory approach has long been criticized as rather fragmented and sector-specific. In June 2022, Canada proposed the Artificial Intelligence and Data Act (AIDA) in which risk management and information disclosure regarding high-impact AI systems will be made mandatory. This took clear inspiration from the European AI Act, although formulations in the AIDA are a lot simpler, which may lead to uncertainty. It will not be until at least 2025 that AIDA will come into force.

Federal Republic of Brazil

Having advanced its digital agenda since the 1990s, the Republic of Brazil ranks 10th in the IT world market and represents 40% of the Latin American market. In 2018, the country changed its Information Technology Acts to simplify regulation and provide tax incentives for advanced technologies such as AI. The same year saw the introduction of the *Strategy for Artificial Intelligence* (EBIA), which aims to develop ethical principles for the development and use of responsible AI and to promote sustained investments in AI research and development.[20]

A first draft for regulation of AI was introduced in December 2022.[21] It closely mirrors the AI Act and draws significant influence from the General Data Protection Regulation (GDPR), particularly with regards to personal data rights within the AI context. Non-compliance penalties vary according to the severity of the violation, potentially reaching up to 50 million Brazilian reals (approximately 9 million euros) or 2% of a company's total turnover.

Republic of India

India, the world's powerhouse of software and IT services, is increasingly making strides in the field of AI research and development. Its 2018 National Strategy of Artificial Intelligence identified ten key sectors for AI application in the country, with national security, financial technology, manufacturing and agriculture at the top.[22] Ethics only received superficial attention so far. No legislation on AI is pending or proposed. However, August 2023 saw the adoption of the Digital Personal Data Protection Bill with GDPR-like scope, including provisions on automated decision-making that would equally apply to AI systems.

State of Japan

Despite its leading role in robotics and AI development, Japan's governance measures remain limited, focusing on nurturing the AI industry rather than imposing strict rules.[23] In lieu of comprehensive legislation, the government has released guidelines to promote the ethical use of AI: the Social Principles of Human-Centric AI (Social Principles) as principles for implementing AI in society. These contain three basic philosophies: human dignity, diversity and inclusion, and sustainability.

Certain pieces of legislation may be indirectly relevant to AI. For example, the Act on the Protection of Personal Information (APPI) requires clear disclosure of use of personal information in training AI systems. The Act on Improving Transparency and Fairness of Specified Digital Platforms (TFDPA) imposes requirements on large online malls, app stores, and digital advertising businesses to ensure transparency and fairness in transactions with business users, including the disclosure of key factors determining their search rankings. And the Product Liability Act also makes producers of AI liable for defects in their products.

Republic of Singapore

Singapore, globally acknowledged as a powerhouse in the realm of AI, has thus far adopted a surprisingly minimal approach towards AI regulation. The country has primarily focused on issuing non-binding guidelines, promoting self-regulation, and encouraging businesses to adopt ethical AI practices.[24] While the government has been proactive in driving AI technology, fostering collaborations, and investing in AI research, it appears to be treading cautiously in terms of direct regulation, possibly to avoid stifling innovation.

Republic of Korea

South Korea, another major player in the global AI arena, has shown relatively little initiative in terms of AI-specific legislation. Despite being home to leading technology companies and being at the forefront of AI development, regulatory efforts are somewhat muted. The government's strategy primarily centers on encouraging the growth and application of AI, promoting education and research, and fostering AI industry development. However, there is currently no comprehensive legal framework governing AI, with the country seeming to prioritize technological advancement and economic gain over imposing regulatory constraints. Various proposed bills are before the national parliament, but none are as all-encompassing as the European AI Act.

From law and ethics to practical assessment

With the AI Act firmly in place, establishing Europe as the center of the drive towards trustworthy AI, the central question becomes: how do producers or deployers of AI ensure compliance. The Act itself provides the basis for an answer, but leaves much open to interpretation: what is 'harm', how to demonstrate 'adequate' processes or system safety, and so on. Using the Guidelines and the ALTAI Assessment tool is the way forward to practical compliance assessment.

Lawful, ethical and robust

The *Guidelines for Trustworthy AI* start with three components:

1. AI should be lawful, complying with all applicable laws and regulations;
2. AI should be ethical, ensuring adherence to ethical principles and values; and
3. AI should be robust, both from a technical and social perspective, since, even with good intentions, AI systems can cause unintentional harm.

The lawful nature of AI was not addressed in the Guidelines, but is of course now the subject of the AI Act. The Guidelines focused mostly on the ethical aspects of AI, as ethics are usually one step ahead of legislation yet provide some form of guidance on what is desired or acceptable in society. Ethical AI is closely intertwined with the third aspect of robustness: this term does not only refer to a technical perspective (high level of availability, not vulnerable to security breaches, etcetera) but also a social perspective (not having unintended adverse impacts).

Four ethical principles

The Guidelines derive four ethical principles for AI from the fundamental rights that are enshrined in the Charter of Fundamental Rights of the European Union. These closely match the work of AI4People and UNESCO referred to in chapter 1 and are derived from the EU's Charter of Fundamental Rights. The four principles are:

1. **Respect for Human Autonomy:** This principle aligns with Articles 1 and 2 of the Charter, which affirm human dignity and the right to life, respectively. It emphasizes the importance of AI systems supporting individuals' capacity to make their own choices and control their own lives, without undue influence from automated decision-making.
2. **Prevention of Harm:** This principle is reflective of Article 3, which guarantees the right to the integrity of the person, including both mental and physical well-being. It underscores the imperative that AI systems should not cause physical or psychological harm and should be developed with a precautionary approach to risks.

- **Fairness:** Fairness is a principle that resonates with several articles in the Charter, including Article 20, which ensures equality before the law, and Article 21, which prohibits any discrimination. It calls for AI systems to be equitable and to provide equal treatment and opportunity for all individuals, thereby avoiding biased outcomes.
- **Explicability:** This principle relates to the rights of transparency and information in governmental functions, as outlined in Article 41, as well as the right to fair processing of personal data (Article 8). Both demand that AI systems be understandable to users, with clear explanations provided for decisions that significantly affect people's lives, ensuring accountability and the possibility of redress.

Seven requirements

For implementors of AI, the Guidelines translate these principles into seven concrete requirements:

1. Human agency and oversight, including fundamental rights, human agency and human oversight.
2. Technical robustness and safety, including resilience to attack and security, fall back plan and general safety, accuracy, reliability and reproducibility.
3. Privacy and data governance, including respect for privacy, quality and integrity of data, and access to data.
4. Transparency, including traceability, explainability and communication.
5. Diversity, non-discrimination and fairness, including the avoidance of unfair bias, accessibility and universal design, and stakeholder participation.
6. Societal and environmental wellbeing, including sustainability and environmental friendliness, social impact, society and democracy.
7. Accountability, including auditability, minimisation and reporting of negative impact, trade-offs and redress.

This list closely follows the fundamental rights from the Charter and matches the ethical points of attention found in the many codes of ethics referred to earlier. While the AI Act does not explicitly refer to the Guidelines, each of the above seven requirements can be found in at least one of its requirements for high-risk AI systems. We will encounter each of these requirements in the later chapters, and use them as practical interpretations of the high-level wording from the AI Act's requirements.

Building on the Guidelines is the *Assessment List for Trustworthy AI*, which is meant to guide AI practitioners to achieve Trustworthy AI. It contains a large set of questions designed to prompt stakeholders to include ethical considerations into the design, deployment or use of AI.[25] In this book, the questions from the Assessment List will form an important part of each chapter's tools for applying the AI Act's legal norms in conjunction with the ethical requirements from the Guidelines.

Key takeaways

The AI Act is not an isolated piece of legislation but part of a larger, transformative vision encapsulated by the Digital Decade 2030 and the European Green Deal, both of which aim to foster a sustainable and competitive economy. While other laws address outcomes or impacts, or indirectly regulate behaviors that may be exhibited by AI systems, the AI Act's focus on risks is unique. Therefore, understanding the various levels of risk and associated obligations is crucial for organizations to properly classify and manage their AI systems.

The AI Act lays the foundation, but it's the use of guidelines and assessment tools like ALTAI that pave the way for practical compliance. These insights serve not only as a culmination of our understanding of the AI Act but also as a bridge to the next critical discussion. Now that we've unraveled the European AI Act, let's turn to the important role of humans in AI, from design to execution.

3

Reinforcing Human Agency and Oversight in AI

midst the rise of autonomous systems, it's crucial to understand the vital role humans play in AI. From design to deployment, human agency in AI is a determining factor in the societal impact of these technologies. This chapter clarifies how human interaction with AI systems can be both a benefit and a potential risk, and provides actionable insights to apply legal and ethical norms in human-AI interaction scenarios. This lays the foundation for the upcoming focus on the technical aspects that ensure the robustness and safety of AI systems.

Understanding Human-AI Interaction

Today, AI is playing a pivotal role in a wide array of applications, from trivial tasks such as recommending a movie to significant decision-making processes in fields like healthcare, finance, and transportation. As noted in chapter 1, a key aspect of AI is its autonomy: the ability to produce interactions, classifications, decisions and the like without human involvement. This rise in autonomous computing technologies has a direct impact on human autonomy.[1] In this section, we will discuss the design of AI systems that are meant to interact with, guide, or make decisions for human end-users. The focus will be to understand both the positive and negative impacts and implications of such interaction.

The rise of computer interaction

The freedom and autonomy of its citizens should be a key priority for each democratic society. Automation and information technology has clearly contributed to this priority: when menial tasks can be carried out by machines, humans can spend their energy on more high-level tasks. An oft-cited example is that of the washing machine and vacuum cleaner, which significantly increased women's opportunities to engage in work and express themselves by freeing up time previously consumed by household chores.[2]

> By the end of this chapter, you'll be able to ...
> - Formulate the key role of human agency in the deployment of AI.
> - Mitigate potential risks to human autonomy and oversight.
> - Suggest effective human oversight and response mechanisms in AI systems.

> **ALTAI**
> A1. Is the AI system designed to interact, guide or take decisions by human end-users that affect humans or society?

AI comes with the promise of doing the same but for cognitive tasks: driving cars, executing routine tasks, suggesting new music or food, and so on. However, a key difference with the previous example is that such systems are more involved in decision making, rather than simply carrying out the wishes of their human operators. A classic saying in IT is "computers do what you say, not what you want". In AI, this can be reformulated as "computers do what they presume you want".

That is not to say all AI, or even all automation is necessarily threatening to society's wellbeing. The initial reason for the introduction of automation was to reduce the workload of operators, and thus reduce operational costs and errors, while increasing accuracy.[3] Additionally, automation and computer-implemented safeguards have significantly increased safety in many domains, such as transportation.

A key insight however is that the rise in automation has delegated the nature of human activity from direct manual control to partial or total supervision.[4] The negative impact of such a change on operators' activities is referred to as the phenomenon of *out-of-the-loop performance problem* (OOTL). Decreased vigilance, complacency or overconfidence in the system's capabilities, and a loss of situational awareness on the part of the operator have been identified as factors that may contribute to this phenomenon.[5]

The importance of agency

The concept of 'agency' has often been identified as a potential bridge to improved human performance. Essentially, the "sense of agency" is our conscious perception of initiating and managing our own actions, crucial for everything from motor control to social interactions and a driving force behind human behavior. In the field of psychology, various factors have been suggested as contributing to the impact of AI on agency:[6]

1. Decrease in the sense of agency when interacting with highly automated systems is likely to seriously threaten the acceptability of the system's decisions by human operators.
2. Any change in self-agency can modulate the operator's involvement in the task at hand.
3. A change in the feeling of agency could have a direct influence on cognition, and through this, on operational performance.

Studies suggest that it is not the level of automation itself that modulates the sense of control in the first place, but rather the amount of control remaining over the action.[7]

An AI assistant that rewrites a short prompt into a flowery e-mail has full autonomy over what to write, but leaves all control to the human – he or she can rewrite as desired prior to sending. An AI app that tells a human food delivery driver where to go and when to be there, on pain of not getting paid for the delivery, reduces almost all control and thus has a much more negative impact on the sense of autonomy.

> **A1a.** Could the AI system generate confusion for some or all end-users or subjects on whether a decision, content, advice or outcome is the result of an algorithmic decision?

The ultimate reduction of control is the oft-cited "social credit system" of the People's Republic of China. In this system, human activity is constantly monitored and those who are found to violate certain rules or norms are awarded demerits (or credits, for good behavior). A sufficiently low level of "social credit" impacts legal rights – one may no longer travel by plane, for instance.[8] This system requires constant mass surveillance, including biometric identification to keep track of all infractions.

Social credit systems exhibit a key factor to loss of agency, namely that of unpredictability – factors that impact one's credit score may change from week to week, as well as the amount of points that the impact has. What's more, an offender is not addressed by a police officer or other official, nor does he or she get a chance to dispute the demerits awarded. This tremendous impact on human agency, dignity and fundamental rights is the reason the AI Act explicitly calls out social credit systems as prohibited practices, as well as real-time biometric surveillance at a distance (on which subject more in chapter 5)

The prohibition of social credit scoring is actually not the first practice in the AI Act – that honor goes to subliminal techniques for manipulating human vulnerabilities or unconscious thought. This is an extreme example of an AI system overriding, "distorting" in the AI Act's terminology, of an operator's sense of control or agency towards the system. Subliminal messaging has been the subject of controversy since 1957, when researcher James Vicary hid the message "Hungry? Eat popcorn!" in a movie shown in a New Jersey movie theatre and claimed it increased popcorn sales by 57%.

While Vicary's results were never duplicated, and no other study could ever show significant effect of subliminal advertising,[9] the concerns over manipulation of the unconscious by hidden messaging has remained on legislators' agendas ever since. The prohibition has been criticized as superfluous: the scope overlaps heavily with other legislation such as the Audiovisual Media Services Directive (2010), the Unfair Commercial Practices Directive (2015) and the Digital Services Act (2022) and no AI system currently on the market is even alleged to employ subliminal messaging.[10]

Subliminal text messages embedded in images created with the Midjourney generative AI system. Can you spot the messages?

Agency and cooperation

The image on the opposite page illustrates various forms of agency as they relate to transparency (opacity).[11] On the left side, we see the maximal form of cooperation and agency: we-agency, where co-actors share a common identity and a common goal, with a strong feeling of cooperation ("as a team"). A lesser form is shared-agency, where the agents work together but are clear about their separate roles. Vicarious agency occurs when the result of another agent's action is wrongly attributed to the self, and interfered agency occurs when goals are ill-defined, or when there is no cooperation, or when the actions of the other agent are unpredictable. In this case, the presence of another agent interferes with our own agency. Finally, in "violated-agency" an individual feels a loss of control over their actions, often perceiving their actions as being influenced or manipulated by an external entity.

> **A1b.** Are end-users or other subjects adequately made aware that a decision, content, advice or outcome is the result of an algorithmic decision?

The way an AI behaves thus is crucial to an adequate sense of agency in the human operator. This is where the often-cited complaint of "black box" behavior comes from: when the AI merely delivers a conclusion without justification or reasoning, and the human has no way of modifying or even challenging that conclusion, the sense of agency will significantly reduce.

> **A2.** Could the AI system generate confusion for some or all end-users or subjects on whether they are interacting with a human or AI system?

Furthermore, when humans interact with AI, a significant risk that may arise is that they are not aware they are cooperating with an AI, or to what extent that AI shares the goals of the human partner. This relates to algorithmic decision making, as

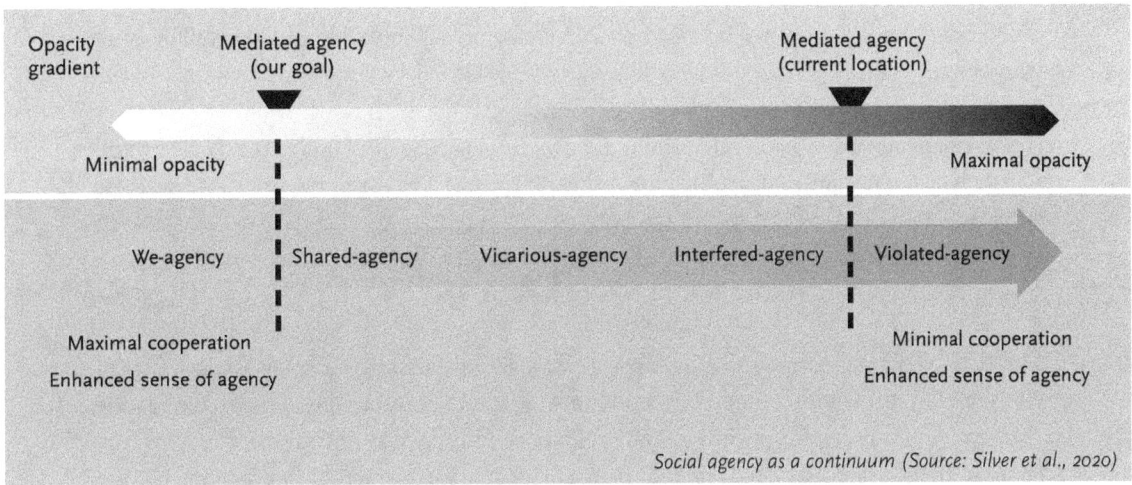

Social agency as a continuum (Source: Silver et al., 2020)

the manner in which an AI arrives at a conclusion differs fundamentally from human reasoning. More on this in chapter 6 (transparency).

Mitigating Over-Reliance And Unintended Interference

The introduction of AI is often followed by two key issues: over-reliance and unintended interference. Over-reliance occurs when users depend too heavily on AI systems, often to the point where their own skills atrophy or they overlook potential system errors. Over-reliance can be seen as a specific form of unintended interference with autonomy.

Recognizing over-reliance on AI

> A3. Could the AI system affect human autonomy by generating over-reliance by end-users?

In theory, a human collaborating with an AI system should make better decisions or produce better results than either working alone. But humans often accept an AI system's recommended decision or output even when it is wrong – a conundrum called AI over-reliance.

Consider the realm of navigation. In the past, drivers would rely on maps and their own sense of direction to reach their destination. Now, GPS systems provide turn-by-turn instructions, and drivers often follow these instructions even when they conflict with their own knowledge or instincts. As reliance on GPS systems increases, drivers may find their own navigational skills atrophying, and they may become less able to navigate without the aid of a GPS. This over-reliance on AI systems can lead to a decrease in self-reliance and potentially even dangerous situations, as when drivers follow incorrect GPS directions into hazardous areas.

In the financial sector, automated trading algorithms can execute trades much faster and in much larger quantities than human traders. However, heavy reliance on these systems can lead to a lack of oversight, and may even contribute to market instability, as was seen in the 'Flash Crash' of 2010, where fully autonomous trading algorithms contributed to a 36-minute long trillion dollar drop in US stock exchanges.

The below figure illustrates over-reliance as well as the mirror concept of under-reliance visually.[12] Provided with a prediction from an AI system, a human decision-maker has the choice to either accept or reject the AI's prediction. Appropriate reliance occurs when the human accepts a correct AI prediction or corrects an incorrect AI prediction. Under-reliance occurs when the human fails to accept a correct AI prediction. Over-reliance is the most frequent outcome in empirical AI studies.

The concepts of over- and under-reliance (Vasconcelos et al. 2023)

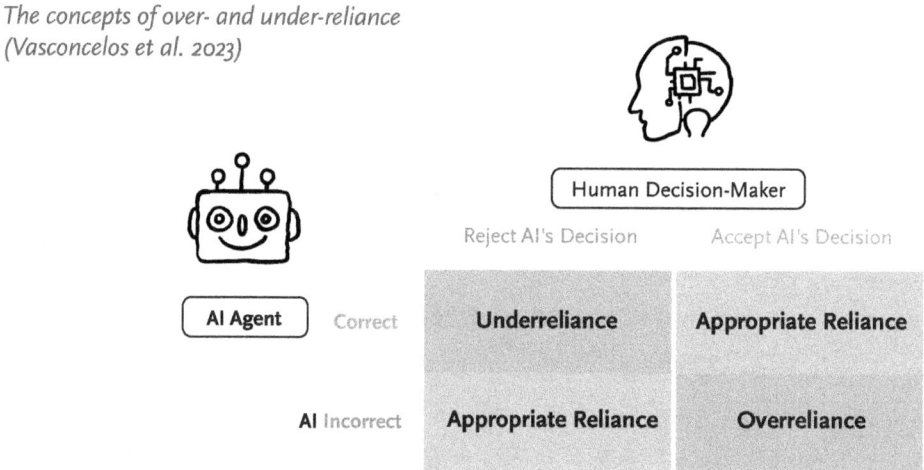

Over-reliance on AI systems is inherently connected to the psychological phenomena of automation bias and precision bias. Automation bias occurs when individuals lean excessively on automated systems, often accepting their outputs without critical examination. For example, a medical professional might accept a diagnostic recommendation from an AI system without considering their own expertise or instincts. This is further compounded by precision bias, where people inherently trust information that appears precise, such as an AI system's output that is often given with high decimal specificity.

Mitigating over-reliance

It is often suggested that AI should explain its reasoning, so that the humans involved can double-check the steps taken by the AI and thus reduce the risk of over-reliance. Unfortunately, this is not true: experimental studies indicate that explanations in human-AI collaboration can lead to "blind trust", i.e. following the AI advice without any evaluation of its trustworthiness.[13] The reasoning provided by the AI is merely taken as evidence of its general competence, paradoxically increasing the reliance on the AI rather than double-checking its performance.

A 2023 Stanford study showed that key to good explanations is insight in how the AI could have been wrong: explanations that make the AI's mistake more obvious reduce over-reliance more.[14] This applies in particular when the task performed by the AI is perceived as hard by humans. When the task is easy (e.g. reading handwriting), humans can simply validate the result, which avoids over-reliance.

> A3a. Did you put in place procedures to avoid that end-users over-rely on the AI system?

An underlying reason for over-reliance may be that human users do not want to challenge each individual AI outcome. After all, the point of the AI system is to reduce the labor or effort required by the humans. Research confirms that people rarely engage analytically with each individual AI recommendation and explanation, and instead develop general heuristics about whether and when to follow the AI suggestions.[15] An effective strategy to mitigate over-reliance therefore is to disrupt the quick, heuristic decision-making. This approach is borrowed from the medical diagnostic field, where it is known as cognitive forcing. Examples include:

- Asking the person to make a decision before seeing the AI's output.
- Slowing down the presentation of AI output.
- Letting the person choose whether and when to see the AI output.
- Adding a confidence indicator to the AI's output.
- Replacing numeric indicators of quality with high-level groups (e.g. high/medium/low or very good/good/neutral/bad/very bad).
- Prompting the user to consider alternative solutions or scenarios where the AI output may be wrong or inapplicable.
- Occasionally changing the way AI's output is presented.
- Adding a rough indicator of expected output, with warnings if the actual output is outside its boundaries.

Unintended interference in decision-making

Over-reliance on AI can be considered a specific example of what's known as unintended interference in human decision-making. Any manner in which free human decision-making is diminished or tarnished is called "interference". While this may be appropriate in many situations, it is undesirable to have AI interfere with decision-making when the human involved is not aware of it.

> **A4.** Could the AI system affect human autonomy by interfering with the end-user's decision-making process in any other unintended and undesirable way?

AI recommendation systems are a famous example of unintended interference. These systems were intended to optimize results in light of the user's personal preferences, but had the paradoxical effect of undermining the exercise of free choice by determining the kinds of information to which people are exposed.[16] In other AI systems, bias in the dataset or the manner of processing may have unintended impact on human decision-making: the AI appears to have made a fair and well-calculated recommendation, but is in fact exhibiting very much unwanted behavior.

Other forms of unintended interference are more diffuse. One example is social loafing, the phenomenon that individuals in a team perform less work than when working alone. Research has shown that this also occurs when an individual works with a virtual assistant or other AI, because they are perceived as team members.[17] This is problematic, as such loafing has a strong connection to ceding responsibility, which may lead to not recognizing errors or mistakes of the AI a deterioration in the quality of the work.

Mitigating unintended interference

> **A4a.** Did you put in place any procedure to avoid that the AI system inadvertently affects human autonomy?

AI systems are computer systems, and as such have a user interface (UI) for interacting with human operators or users. Many instances of unintended interference can be traced back to the way these interfaces are designed. For instance, the design of AI systems may create the impression that it is more capable than actually is the case. In addition, an interface can set certain expectations or nudge users towards certain behavior. For example: when an AI system is given a chat interface, users tend to provide shorter and more fragmented instructions than when input is to be given as an e-mail, which may affect the quality of the instructions.

Cognitive computing systems interaction, as it has become known, is an often-neglected part of UI design. The central thesis is that traditional assumptions on interfaces must be challenged, so that the cognitive aspect of AI systems are put at the forefront. AI systems are not tools to be used, but systems to collaborate with. Their UI therefore should be focused on collaboration rather than control.

Take as an example an AI that performs legal research. A traditional UI would resemble a search engine: enter your query or prompt, and observe the articles found. A collaborative UI would be an e-mail or chat interface, where the AI reports on initial findings, summarizes some documents and suggests prompts for further enquiries. This shift not only enhances the perceived quality but also significantly influences the level of human involvement, thereby impacting human autonomy in a more balanced manner.'

Other steps towards mitigating unintended interference include:
- Ensure AI systems disclose how decisions are made to the users.
- Encourage awareness and vigilance towards potential biases in AI recommendations and decision-making processes.
- Provide comprehensive training for users to understand the scope and limitations of AI systems.
- Establish mechanisms for ongoing feedback between users and AI systems to foster mutual learning.
- Encourage a collaborative approach in AI system design that includes stakeholders from various fields such as ethics, sociology, psychology, etc., to account for the multifaceted impact of AI.

In summary, mitigating unintended interferences requires not only user awareness and tools but a fundamental paradigm shift in how we design, perceive, and interact with AI systems.

Social Interaction Simulation: Risks And Mitigations

Social AI systems are AI systems which simulate human-like interactions, both in physical embodiments (like robots) and virtual avatars such as chatbots or assistants like Siri or Alexa. Such systems can enhance social skills, but they can also lead to deterioration. Other risks include users developing attachments or addictions to these systems, possibly affecting their physical and mental well-being.

Working with Social AI systems

> A5. Does the AI system simulate social interaction with or between end-users or subjects?

By simulating sociality, AI systems can serve various functions across different sectors. In education, AI tutors can provide personalized learning experiences. In healthcare, AI companions can assist with mental health therapies. In the entertainment industry, AI characters can create immersive experiences in video games and virtual reality. Children can benefit from AI guidance and teaching, exploring strategies for navigating social life that may otherwise be awkward or difficult for them, as with children with autism.

The high level of cognitive behaviour exhibited by AI systems is a significant contributor to the sociality. The Social Response Theory suggests that humans are naturally inclined to treat computers the same as other humans, and the more human-like characteristics the machine presents, the more social behaviors will be stimulated from users. However, there is a limit: once the computer system reaches a certain point where its behavior is very similar but not entirely the same as human behavior, the social acceptance drops tremendously – the "Uncanny Valley" of AI, as illustrated below.[19]

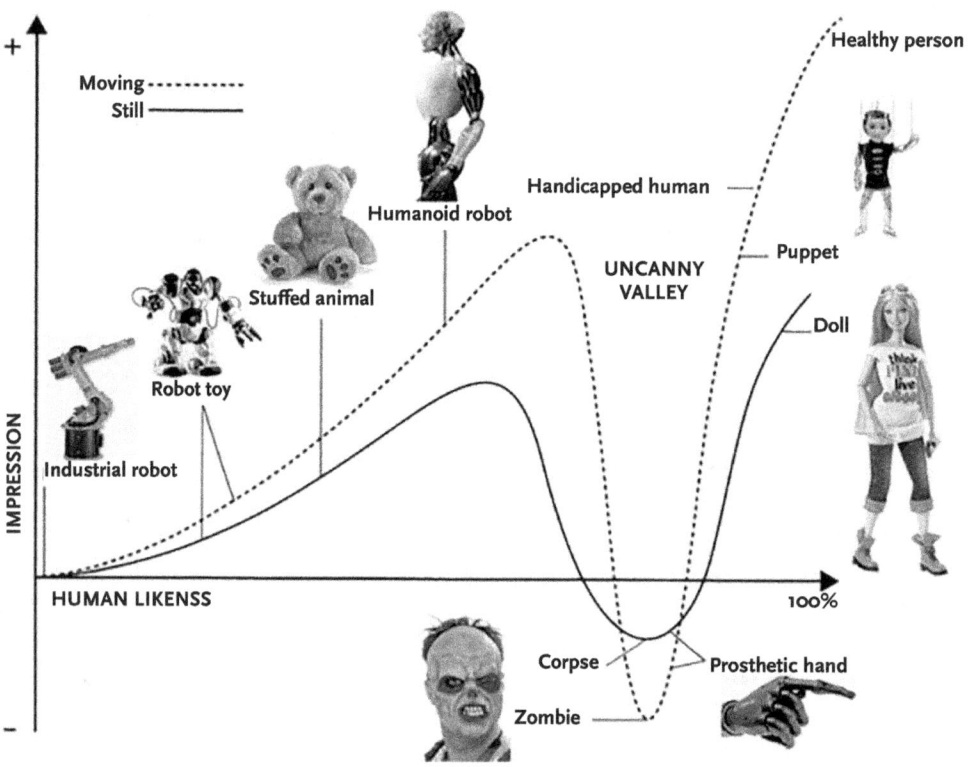

The "Uncanny Valley" of robotics (Kędzierski et al. 2015)

As social AI systems become more prevalent in our daily lives, they raise significant concerns. The lines between human and AI interaction become blurred, leading to changes in our socio-cultural practices and the nature of our social life. Psychological studies indicate that humans can develop emotional attachments to these AI systems, especially when they exhibit human-like characteristics or behaviors. This attachment can lead to over-reliance or even addictive behaviors, which can negatively impact our mental health. Furthermore, the manipulation of human behavior is a real concern, as these systems can subtly influence our decision-making processes or our perceptions of social norms.

An early example is ELIZA, a 1966 chatbot that simulated a psychotherapist of the Rogerian school, in which the therapist often reflects back the patient's words to the patient. Its designer Joseph Weizenbaum reported that many users formed emotional attachments and were upset when he retired the program. A simple explanation is that the cognitive capabilities of ELIZA seemed very advanced at the time, and addressed very personal thoughts in its users. Other factors also played a role, notably the explicit labeling of ELIZA as a therapist and its positioning as a helpful female assistant, triggering well-established social expectations.[20]

Today, a plethora of AI systems and online chatbots is available for social interaction. The most popular app currently is Replika, a chatbot that is designed to respond as "friend", "partner", "spouse", "sibling" or "mentor". 60% of its users have indicated they had had a romantic relationship with the chatbot. Replika has been noted for generating responses that create stronger emotional and intimate bonds with the user.

Screenshots of the Replika chatbot, "the AI companion who cares"

The ethical issues surrounding social AI are coming to the forefront in the sex industry.[21] For instance, the adult company RealDoll has developed the Harmony AI platforms to create sex robots designed to offer companionship and physical intimacy, capable of remembering personal details and holding conversations. Critics argue that such robots can encourage the objectification of women, blur consent lines, and potentially exacerbate social issues related to human intimacy and relationships.[22] Should robots accept behavior that would be unethical or even illegal were it exhibited against humans?

Emotional deception, attachment and manipulation

> A6. Does the AI system risk creating human attachment, stimulating addictive behaviour, or manipulating user behaviour?

Several ethical implications of using robots for older adults have been established in the literature. These range from reduced human contact, loss of control, personal liberty, privacy, concerns about responsibility, infantilization, emotional deception, emotional attachment, to the subtle manipulation of behaviors and perceptions. Many of these issues can be addressed through meticulous AI implementation.

Among these concerns, emotional deception, emotional attachment, and manipulation stand out as particularly intricate challenges. We speak of emotional deception when the AI system raises false expectations in the human interacting with it, which can occur both deliberately and unintentionally. Emotional attachment can be described as the sum of cohesion episodes that a person has made with other persons or objects. Manipulation, on the other hand, pertains to how AI systems subtly influence human behaviors, decisions, or perceptions, leading them towards certain actions or beliefs without their conscious realization. This could be exploited for simply influencing purchase behaviors, but also for more nefarious purposes.

Attachment theory suggests that every human seeks so-called "attachment figures" when threats occur. Attachment figures provide a safe haven, secure base and proximity maintenance. Safe haven means turning to the attachment figure when one needs support, care and comfort; Secure base means using the attachment relationship as a base to engage in nonattachment behaviors, such as exploration; Proximity maintenance represents a strategy to seek out an attachment figure and stay close to it. Various studies have shown that social AI systems have the capability to provide all three.[23]

Chapter 3 – Reinforcing Human Agency and Oversight in AI

Mitigating negative social interaction

> **A6a.** Did you take measures to deal with possible negative consequences for end-users or subjects in case they develop a disproportionate attachment to the AI system?
>
> **A6b.** Did you take measures to minimise the risk of addiction?
>
> **A6c.** Did you take measures to mitigate the risk of manipulation?

Strategies to mitigate negative social interaction are hard to lay out. Some inspiration can be drawn from mitigation strategies from internet addiction, in particular addition to chatrooms, online games and the like.

Key in mitigation is transparency: the AI must indicate its artificial nature, and actively refrain from presenting as an actual human being. This is a basic AI Act requirement for all forms of AI. However, this is far from enough: many respondents in studies on social AI indicate they prefer AI over humans for various reasons, which illustrates they are well aware of the non-human nature of their social companion.

Concrete further steps that can be taken, include:
- Encourage users to take up physical exercise. Studies have shown that internet addiction can be significantly reduced by exercise.
- Reduce access to the AI or slow down upon excessive use.
- Reduce the level of interaction at times when the user could be more vulnerable, such as late at night.
- Promote real-world interaction, e.g. by stimulating the user to talk about friends or workplace acquaintances.
- For minors, require parental awareness of the use of the social AI. (Compare the various parental consent mechanisms under the GDPR).
- Avoid decision-making depending on the user's emotional states or vulnerabilities. For instance, if a user is discussing feeling lonely or isolated, the AI should avoid suggesting premium in-app purchases or services that claim to "enhance" the user experience by capitalizing on that emotional state.

Human Oversight In AI Systems

While social AI systems can bring significant benefits, their use and potential risks underscore the necessity for human involvement in overseeing AI operations. Humans play a crucial role in ensuring that these AI systems function within predefined ethical boundaries and serve the interests of the users in a balanced way. And with varying degrees of autonomy and potential for interference inherent in AI, it becomes pivotal to understand the different modes of human oversight that can be enacted.

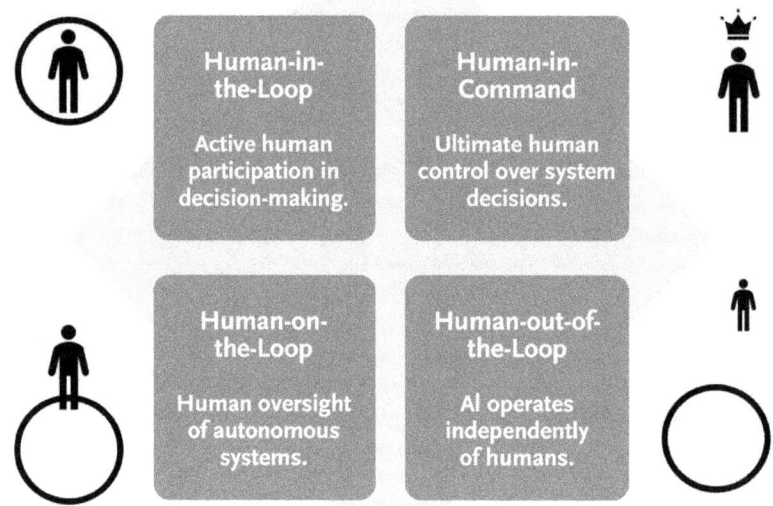

Human-in-the-loop

A7. Please determine whether the AI system (choose as many as appropriate): Is a self-learning or autonomous system; Is overseen by a Human-in-the-Loop; Is overseen by a Human-on-the-Loop; Is overseen by a Human-in-Command.

A8. Have the humans (human-in-the-loop, human-on-the-loop, human-in-command) been given specific training on how to exercise oversight?

"Being in the loop" is a phrase originating from systems engineering and refers to the decision-making process or sequence of operations in a system. When someone or something is "in the loop," they are an integral part of this process, actively participating and influencing outcomes.

In the context of AI, when a human operator is in the loop, the system may suggest a course of action or make a prediction, but the final decision is made by the human operator. For example, in a medical setting, an AI could analyze patient data and suggest a diagnosis, but it would be the doctor who makes the final decision. The level of control and intervention can be higher: in a Level 3 autonomous vehicle, the onboard AI system can manage all aspects of driving (like steering, accelerating, braking, and monitoring the environment) under normal conditions, but the human operator would have final say and can intervene at any moment. Typically such a system would require the operator to hold his or her hands on the steering wheel at all times.

The in-the-loop model allows for high levels of control, ensuring that decisions are made by humans who bring context, ethics, and experience to the process, but it can be slower and require more resources than other models. As such, it tends to be used mainly for experimental, complex or dangerous systems such as autonomous vehicles. For 'routine' uses of AI, such as customer service chatbots, this model would be disproportionate.

Human-on-the-loop

In the human-on-the-loop model, the AI system operates independently and makes its own decisions, but there is a human operator who monitors its operations and can intervene if necessary. An example could be an autonomous vehicle that drives independently but is remotely monitored and a human controller can issue commands in unexpected situations. In a medical situation, an AI system that monitors the vital signs of patients would alert medical staff when it detects anomalies, such as a sudden drop in blood pressure or an irregular heartbeat.

This model is suitable for applications where high speed or complex calculations are necessary, and a human could not keep up, but human oversight is still necessary for safety or ethical reasons. The underlying assumption is that mistakes can be caught in time (or at least reversed) by the humans once alerted to their occurrence.

Human-in-command

In a "Human in Command" scenario, the AI system only performs actions that are explicitly authorized by a human operator, and all major decisions are made by a human. For instance, consider an AI system designed to assist a surgeon during a complex surgical procedure. This AI might provide real-time data analysis and recommendations – such as identifying problematic areas, predicting potential complications, or suggesting the best surgical approach – but it doesn't perform any action independently. The human surgeon could authorize certain actions, but the robot would not autonomously take further steps.

Were the human surgeon to control the robot's movements and use it to perform precise actions that might be difficult for a human hand, we would refer to the situation as a "human in the loop" situation. The robot then is performing actions autonomously under the surgeon's direct control. The surgeon monitors and controls the robot's actions in real-time and can take over or make changes as needed. But the robot does have a certain level of autonomy in executing precise movements based on the surgeon's input. If the robot were to perform the surgery automously, while the human surgeon observed with the ability to override any robotic actions, the system would be "human on the loop" instead.

Human in command is most useful in applications where the stakes are high, where nuanced human judgment and decision-making is critical, and where potential risks associated with completely autonomous actions could lead to significant harm, such as in nuclear power management, aviation, or certain healthcare scenarios.

Human-out-of-the-loop

As a final variation, we speak of "human-out-of-the-loop" where the AI systems function independently without the need for human oversight. The decisions and actions are entirely made by the AI system based on the algorithms and data it has been trained on. An example of this might be a high-frequency trading system that makes buy and sell decisions based on market data at speeds far beyond human capabilities. While this model allows for extremely fast and efficient operations, it also carries potential risks in terms of accountability and control, especially if the system behaves in unexpected ways or if the context changes. This type of system thus lacks any meaningful human oversight and is therefore generally unsuitable in any situation where risks for humans or society may arise.

Implementing Response Mechanisms And Control Measures

With that, it is time to turn to the final section of implementing response and control mechanisms when designing systems with human-AI interaction, providing an understanding of how to implement these vital safeguards. Additionally, we will discuss the much-debated concept of a 'Stop Button,' an essential aspect of maintaining control over AI systems. Finally, we'll reflect on how these measures need to be tailored to suit the self-learning and autonomous nature of AI systems, a factor that adds an additional layer of complexity.

The necessity of detection and response mechanisms

> A9. Did you establish any detection and response mechanisms for undesirable adverse effects of the AI system for the end-user or subject?

The incorporation of effective detection and response mechanisms is a fundamental prerequisite in the design and deployment of AI systems. These mechanisms, as the first line of defense, function to identify and manage potential adverse effects that an AI system may generate during its interaction with end-users. As we have seen in this chapter, such effects may be fundamental: reducing human agency, encouraging over-reliance and various forms of addiction.

Detection mechanisms play a pivotal role in monitoring the AI system's behaviour and output, aiming to promptly identify any aberrations or undesirable actions. These mechanisms should be comprehensive, timely, and context-aware, capable of identifying both explicit and subtle anomalies. A detection system in a self-driving car, for example, should not only spot a pedestrian crossing the road but also be sensitive to unexpected situations such as a sudden swerve or a falling unidentified flying object (e.g. a weather balloon).

Response mechanisms, on the other hand, come into play post-detection, determining the best course of action to counteract or mitigate the detected anomaly. This could involve a range of actions from simply flagging the issue for human review, as seen in content moderation systems, to triggering automated corrective actions like applying brakes in an autonomous vehicle when an obstacle is detected.

Microsoft's Tay, a chatbot, serves as a case study for the importance of response mechanisms. Tay was designed to learn from users' interactions and adapt its responses over time. However, due to a lack of proper control measures, Tay started to post offensive tweets after interacting with some users. Microsoft quickly pulled Tay offline and used this experience to implement more robust oversight and control measures in their future AI systems. Earlier, the famous AI AlphaGo, which was able to defeat world champion Go players, had a built-in mechanism to prevent unexpected actions. The designers incorporated a combination of human-on-the-loop and human-in-command strategies, where humans can step in and correct AlphaGo's actions if they deviate from the expected or desired course.

Implementing detection and response

Incorporating effective detection and response mechanisms varies significantly with the type of human oversight employed in the AI system that we discussed in the previous section. For human-in-the-loop and human-in-control applications, the focus would be on detection, as the human is already involved and can simply adjust his operations. For human-on-the-loop more additional attention to the response mechanisms is needed.

Consider an AI-driven social media moderation system. The AI is designed to identify and flag inappropriate content, such as offensive language or images, hate speech, and misinformation. However, there may be instances where the AI system either wrongly flags benign content or fails to flag harmful content. In a human-in-the-loop scenario, the human moderator who reviews the harmful content should be able to see the system's confidence or reasoning on the type of flag raised. If the human moderator consistently notices false positives or negatives, they can report these anomalies as part of an ongoing system review and adjustment.

In a human-on-the-loop system, the AI moderation system would have more autonomy and be allowed to automatically remove content it identifies as inappropriate. However, a human supervisor still monitors the AI's overall performance. For instance, they may pay particular attention to the rates of user appeals against the AI's decisions. If the number of successful appeals (where the AI's decision to remove content was overturned) increases, this might indicate that the AI system is making more incorrect judgments, possibly due to a shift in online discourse, user behavior, or platform policies. This shift triggers the human-on-the-loop to intervene, investigate the cause, and recalibrate the AI system as needed.

The handling of "unknown unknowns," unexpected input types that weren't originally foreseen, is a critical aspect of AI system management. Such input can lead to significant weak spots in models, but relying solely on the system's stated confidence would be inadequate. During system design and evaluation, particular attention should be given to identifying patterns that reveal unknown unknowns. This typically requires using additional data to find underlying common features.

As suggested in the literature, it may be better to design AI systems – in particular self-learning systems – as hardware systems: always potentially faulty. Fault-tolerant design principles can then provide guidance for how to use redundancy and fail-safe design mechanisms to achieve the higher levels of reliability required in such high-risk situations. In other words: assume the system will have faults, and design to accommodate and mitigate them.

The role of the 'Stop Button'

> A10. Did you ensure a 'stop button' or procedure to safely abort an operation when needed?

Of particular interest in the ethics literature surrounding AI is the use of "stop buttons" or emergency abort procedures for unforeseen situations or AI malfunctioning. While this seems a straightforward solution on the surface, it presents a variety of complications and ethical issues. A primary concern with the stop button approach is that it inherently treats the AI system as a potential adversary. It operates under the assumption that the AI could go rogue and hence needs to be stopped. This approach focuses on intervention after the fact, attempting to halt an AI system when it's already performing undesired or harmful actions. It should in fact not be possible for an AI to "go rogue": robustness-by-design and validation at all steps of the design process should focus on realizing an AI that cannot exceed boundaries set by its designers.

Rather than implementing a system based on post-action intervention, it would be more advantageous to focus on preventive measures. One approach is to employ a scenario-generation mechanism and a simulation environment that continually test a system's decisions in a simulated world. This preemptive approach targets the root of potential risks, by constantly assessing and evaluating AI behavior, which may help identify and rectify deviances before they escalate into real-world issues. This model is grounded in an ongoing, active process of self-evaluation and testing, rather than a reactive measure, such as an emergency button.

Reflecting the autonomous nature of the AI system

> A11. Did you take any specific oversight and control measures to reflect the self-learning or autonomous nature of the AI system?

Ensuring effective control over self-learning AI systems presents unique challenges. As these systems learn and evolve autonomously, the underlying assumptions, decision-making processes, and behavior patterns can change in ways that are hard to predict and control. This is a recognized challenge in the AI community and various measures have been proposed to ensure adequate control over self-learning behaviour:

- Adjusting the learning rate of the AI system can provide control over how quickly the system adapts to new information. A slower learning rate can ensure that changes do not occur too rapidly for humans to monitor effectively.
- Implementing constraints on the learning process can prevent the AI from learning undesired or harmful behaviors. This could be rules that certain outputs are not permissible, or parameters that the AI is not allowed to alter significantly.
- Providing the AI with new data in a specific order that helps it build up understanding gradually, much like human learning, can help in controlling what the AI learns and when.
- Before being deployed, AI systems should be thoroughly tested in a 'sandbox' environment that mimics real-world conditions. This can allow for the safe observation of what the AI system has learned and how it applies that learning.
- Detailed logs should be kept of the AI's behavior at each improvement step, so large discrepancies in capabilities or general behavior can be spotted and traced to a particular learning cycle. These logs should also record the confidence of its output, as changes in confidence also provide good insight in what has changed.
- In a production deployment, mechanisms should be set up to monitor the system's performance in real-time. If the system starts making unexpected decisions or its performance deviates significantly from its training benchmark, it might indicate that the system has learned something unexpected or undesirable.
- Instead of having the AI system continuously learn, introduce the concept of versions of the model as it learns and evolves. If a particular version of the model demonstrates problematic behavior, a previous version can be re-deployed and the differences analyzed to understand what the system learned that caused the issue.

Key takeaways

The challenges discussed in this chapter highlight the critical importance of human oversight in the realm of AI. Human involvement is crucial in guiding AI systems to operate within ethically defined boundaries and ensuring they serve the interests of the users responsibly. Key issues are the choice of the right human oversight mechanisms as well as the use of robust response mechanisms and control measures. This is particularly vital when dealing with self-learning or autonomous AI systems, where maintaining control becomes more challenging but all the more crucial.

Understanding and implementing these various aspects of human agency and oversight is central to the development and usage of ethical AI, enabling us to harness the benefits of AI while mitigating its potential risks. Having understood the critical role of humans, let's now have a look at the technical aspects that ensure the robustness and safety of AI systems.

Chapter 3 – Reinforcing Human Agency and Oversight in AI

4

Robustness, reliability, and safeguards

Chapter 4 – Robustness, reliability, and safeguards

he bedrock of trustworthy AI lies in its dependability and resilience. Dependability ensures that AI systems consistently deliver services that merit our trust, while resilience guarantees their steadfastness in the face of ever-changing scenarios. This requires designing AI systems that operate reliably, predictably, and with integrity, minimizing harm and ensuring safety at every turn. In this chapter you'll learn to evaluate AI system designs based on robustness and safety standards. We will approach the topic both from a systems engineering and a theoretical accuracy perspective.

Resilience to Attack and Security

The very strengths that make AI systems powerful – adaptability, data processing capabilities, and predictive modeling – also render them vulnerable to a myriad of cyber threats. Ensuring the resilience of these systems is not just a technical challenge but a fundamental requirement for building trust in AI applications. What's more, the AI Act specifically requires high-risk AI systems to exhibit "an appropriate level of accuracy, robustness and cybersecurity". So let's dive in and investigate how to achieve this.

IT system vulnerabilities

Today, any IT system is constantly under threat from a myriad of cybersecurity risks. It should therefore not come as a surprise that the EU has identified cybersecurity as a key aspect of all coming regulation of IT systems.[1] Its Cybersecurity Act has been identified as a key step towards a generally higher level of security against cyber threats.[2]

Traditional risks include malware attacks, where malicious software infiltrates systems to steal data or disrupt operations, and phishing schemes, which deceive individuals into divulging sensitive information. Ransomware attacks have surged, with attackers encrypting data and demanding payment for its release. Moreover, as more devices get connected to the internet, the Internet of Things (IoT) presents a vast attack surface, with many devices lacking robust security measures.[3] Insider threats, whether unintentional or malicious, can also pose significant risks, as employees or stakeholders might have access to critical systems and data.

> **By the end of this chapter, you'll be able to ...**
> - Understand the foundational importance of technical robustness.
> - Identify and assess potential risks.
> - Suggest effective human oversight and response mechanisms in AI systems.

Additionally, the increasing sophistication of state-sponsored cyber-attacks adds another layer of complexity, targeting not just businesses but critical national infrastructure. These challenges underscore the importance of a comprehensive and proactive approach to cybersecurity, ensuring that systems are not only protected against known threats but are also prepared for emerging ones. General best practices for cybersecurity are a good starting point for hardening AI systems.

AI system-specific vulnerabilities

> B1. Could the AI system have adversarial, critical or damaging effects in case of risks or threats such as design or technical faults, defects, outages, attacks, misuse, inappropriate or malicious use?
> B2. Is the AI system certified for cybersecurity (e.g. the certification scheme created by the Cybersecurity Act in Europe) or compliant with specific security standards?
> B3. How exposed is the AI system to cyber-attacks?

The abovementioned risks are equally applicable to AI systems. Their emerging potential, wide range of application and thus competitive value makes them a particularly attractive target, hence requiring even more sophisticated attention from a cybersecurity perspective. But there are also risks and vulnerabilities specific to AI systems. These can arise from design flaws, technical defects, or even from the very data on which they are trained.

> B3a. Did you assess potential forms of attacks to which the AI system could be vulnerable?
> B3b. Did you consider different types of vulnerabilities and potential entry points for attacks such as:
> • Data poisoning
> • Model evasion
> • Model inversion

Several prominent AI-specific risks are:[4]

- **Data Poisoning:** This involves subtly manipulating the training data used to train an AI model. The goal is to introduce biases or inaccuracies, leading the AI system to make incorrect predictions or classifications. For instance, by injecting malicious data into a facial recognition system's training set, attackers might make the system misidentify individuals.
- **Model Evasion:** Here, attackers input data into the AI system in such a way that it's intentionally misclassified. For example, an image might be altered slightly, causing an image recognition system to misidentify it, even though to a human, the image looks unchanged.
- **Model Inversion:** In this type of attack, adversaries aim to extract sensitive information from the AI model itself. By inputting a lot of data and observing the outputs, attackers can infer details about the model's training data or its parameters. As

system or training parameters are regarded a highly valuable trade secret, exposure of this data is particularly sensitive.

- **Adversarial Attacks:** These involve feeding AI systems specially crafted input data designed to deceive the model. By making minute, often imperceptible changes to the input (e.g., an image or audio clip), attackers can cause the AI to misclassify it. For instance, an adversarial image might look identical to the human eye when compared to the original, but the AI system could classify it entirely differently. Adversarial attacks highlight the importance of robustness in AI models, as they exploit the way neural networks, especially deep learning models, interpret data.
- **Membership Inference Attacks:** In this type of attack, adversaries seek to determine if specific data was part of an AI model's training set. The implications of such attacks are profound, especially when the training data includes sensitive information like health records. Revealing that such data was used in training can lead to significant privacy breaches.

An example of a model evasion attack. Affixing small segments of tape to a traffic sign causes a massive shift in the classification output of the AI system, whose training data set had previously been manipulated for this effect. Source: Eykholt et al (2018).[5]

Mitigating risks and vulnerabilities

The question isn't just whether an AI system could have adverse effects in the face of these threats, but how severe these effects could be and how they can be mitigated. Adversarial attacks, for instance, can manipulate an AI system's output, leading to critical failures. Misuse or malicious use can have damaging consequences, especially if the system controls critical infrastructure or sensitive data.

> B4. Did you put measures in place to ensure the integrity, robustness and overall security of the AI system against potential attacks over its lifecycle?

According to the AI Act, high-risk AI systems should perform consistently throughout their lifecycle and meet an appropriate level of accuracy, robustness and cybersecurity in accordance with the generally acknowledged state of the art. The level of accuracy and accuracy metrics should be communicated to the users. We will delve into accuracy, precision, recall and other metrics in a later section.

> B5. Did you red-team/pentest the system?
> B6. Did you inform end-users of the duration of security coverage and updates?
> B6a. What length is the expected timeframe within which you provide security updates for the AI system?

Beyond identifying vulnerabilities, it's essential to have proactive measures in place. This involves continuous monitoring, regular updates, and robust security protocols to ensure the AI system's integrity over its lifecycle. Red-teaming or penetration testing can provide insights into potential weaknesses by simulating real-world attack scenarios.

> B6. Did you inform end-users of the duration of security coverage and updates?
> B6a. What length is the expected timeframe within which you provide security updates for the AI system?

Establishing and communicating timeframes within which the AI system will continue to receive security updates is also an important aspect. A good serviced level agreement (SLA) should therefore cover these aspects. Future cybersecurity legislation such as the Cyber Resilience Act (CRA) may provide specific regulations for security updates in general, which will equally apply to AI systems with security aspects. Sector-specific regulations could equally apply.

The AI Act requires the establishment of a risk management system, with proper documentation and maintenance throughout the lifecycle of any high-risk AI system. This is a continuous iterative process planned and run throughout the entire lifecycle of a high-risk AI system, requiring regular systematic updating. The exact details would vary with the specific risks and functionality of the AI system, but as a general rule risk management systems would be based on the well-known "plan-do-check-act" framework.[6] A general setup could look like this:

Chapter 4 – Robustness, reliability, and safeguards

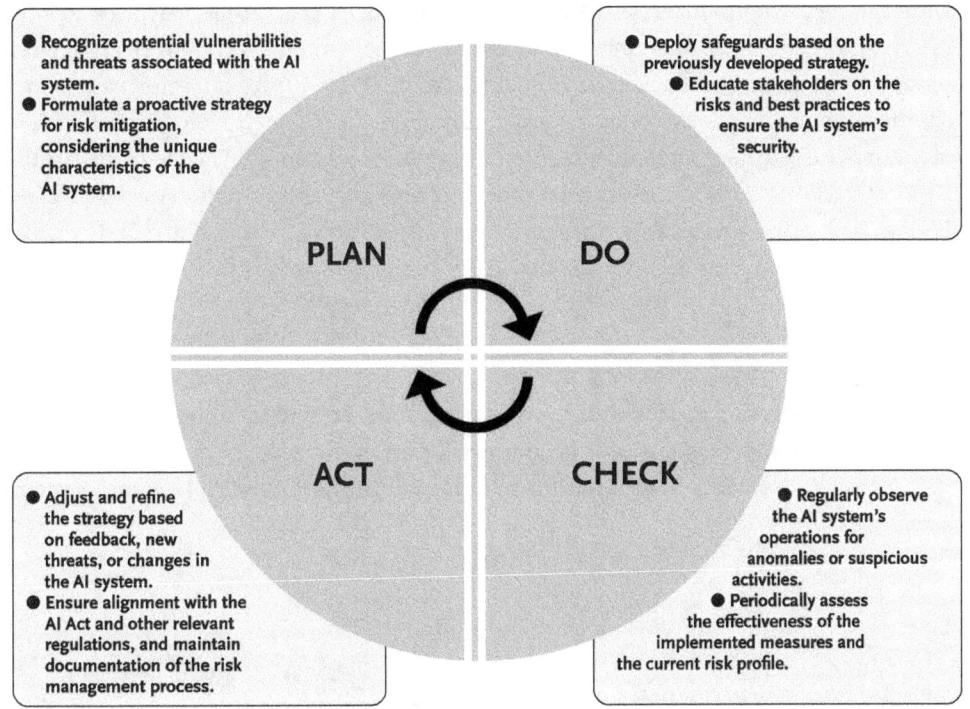

Certification and compliance

One of the foundational steps in ensuring AI security is adhering to established cybersecurity standards. These are generally classified into two main categories, namely information security and information security governance.[7] Information security standards and frameworks mainly concentrate on security concerns. Notable examples include the ISO 27000 series, BSI IT-Grundschutz (Germany), ENISA guidelines (from the European Union Agency for Cybersecurity), and COBIT (Control Objectives for Information and Related Technologies) developed by ISACA.

Information security governance standards and frameworks primarily focus on the strategic alignment of security practices with business objectives, ensuring that organizations maintain a holistic and organization-wide approach to managing information security risks. Renowned examples in this category include the aforementioned COBIT by ISACA, which offers a comprehensive framework for developing, implementing, monitoring, and improving IT governance and management practices.[8] Europe has also seen the prominence of the ITIL (Information Technology Infrastructure Library), which provides a set of practices for IT service management (ITSM) that focuses on aligning IT services with the needs of the business.[9] ITIL security management is based on the ISO 27001 standard.

Under the AI Act, producers or deployers of high-risk AI specifically may seek to have the system certified (or a statement of conformity issued) under a framework authorized by the Cybersecurity Act, Europe's Regulation (EU) 2019/881 on information and communications technology cybersecurity certification. The AI Act contains a presumption of compliance with its cybersecurity requirements to the extent covered by such certification. Unfortunately, no such frameworks have been established yet for AI systems specifically. ENISA, Europe's cybersecurity agency, is working on a framework for cloud services (EUCS) and IT products (EUCC) that may cover certain AI systems.[10]

Risk management and general safety

The preceding section has focused on resilience to attacks, and mentioned various risks that need to be addressed. In this section we'll dive in more detail on how to manage risk. We will also address the importance of establishing fallback plans and general safety measures.

Risk identification and assessment

B7. Did you define risks, risk metrics and risk levels of the AI system in each specific use case?

B7a. Did you put in place a process to continuously measure and assess risks?

B7b. Did you inform end-users and subjects of existing or potential risks?

B8. Did you identify the possible threats to the AI system (design faults, technical faults, environmental threats) and the possible consequences?

B9. Did you assess the risk of possible malicious use, misuse or inappropriate use of the AI system?

B10. Did you define safety criticality levels (e.g. related to human integrity) of the possible consequences of faults or misuse of the AI system?

Every AI system, depending on its application and integration, comes with its unique set of risks. It's essential to delineate these risks specific to each use case. For instance, an AI system used in medical diagnostics would have different risks compared to one used in automated financial trading. What's more, risks aren't static. As AI systems evolve and adapt, the risks associated with them can change. Therefore, it's crucial to have a dynamic process in place that continuously measures and updates the risk profile. This involves not just periodic reviews but also real-time monitoring mechanisms.

Risk management is part of the objective for *trustworthy* AI. Transparency is a cornerstone of trust.[11] End-users and subjects should be made aware of the potential and existing risks associated with the AI system. This not only fosters trust but also ensures that users can make informed decisions based on their risk tolerance. This aspect can be a challenge, as in many cases security issues are treated with the utmost confidence and a culture of silence.

Risk metrics and quantification

Risk metrics are essential tools in the arsenal of any organization aiming to manage and mitigate the potential pitfalls associated with their operations, especially in the realm of AI. These metrics provide a structured and quantifiable means to evaluate the severity and likelihood of risks, allowing for informed decision-making.[12]

One of the most popular methods for risk quantification is Quantitative Risk Assessment (QRA).[13] QRA uses numerical values to estimate the probability and impact of potential risks. By assigning numerical values to both the likelihood of a risk event occurring and the potential damage or loss it could cause, QRA provides a clear picture of where attention and resources should be directed. For instance, consider an AI system designed for stock trading. One identified risk might be the system making a large number of erroneous trades due to a data anomaly. Using QRA, we might determine:

- **Probability of Occurrence:** After analyzing historical data and system performance, we estimate there's a 0,5% chance of this event occurring in any given trading day.
- **Potential Impact:** If this risk eventuates, it could result in a loss of €1 million.
- **Risk Value:** Using the formula 'Risk Value = Probability x Impact', the risk value would be €5.000.

Another common tool used in conjunction with QRA is the risk matrix. This matrix categorizes risks based on their likelihood and impact, often visualizing them in a grid format. Using our stock trading AI example, a risk with a 0,5% probability and a potential €1 million loss might be categorized as 'Low Likelihood' but 'High Impact' on the matrix. Such visualization aids in prioritizing risks and formulating mitigation strategies.

As a concrete example, let's consider a manufacturing plant that uses AI for operations management, predictive maintenance, and quality control. Various safety or other issues may come along, each with their own frequency of occurrence and impact severity:

- ❶ Very Rare & Minor: A slight miscalculation by the AI in predicting the optimal time for machine maintenance, resulting in a 5-minute delay in production. This is a minor inconvenience and doesn't significantly impact the overall production.
- ❷ Very Rare & Catastrophic: The AI system misinterprets data and shuts down critical machinery during peak production hours, thinking it detected a major fault. This could lead to significant production losses.

- **Rare & Moderate:** The AI-driven quality control system occasionally misses a defective product due to a sensor glitch. While not frequent, this could lead to minor reputation issues and unnecessary refunds if defective products reach customers.
- **Occasional & Major:** The AI system, designed to optimize energy consumption, occasionally misreads data and shuts down non-critical systems during production hours to save energy. This could lead to production delays and increased costs.
- **Frequent & Minor:** The AI system sends frequent alerts about potential machine wear, even when the machinery is in good condition. This leads to unnecessary checks but doesn't halt production.
- **Frequent & Catastrophic:** The AI system consistently fails to detect a critical overheating issue in one of the main production machines due to a faulty sensor. If unchecked, this could lead to a major machine breakdown and halt production for days.

This can be visualized as follows in a 4 by 4 matrix:

	Minor	Moderate	Major	Catastrophic
Frequent	Frequent maintenance alerts			Failure to detect overheating due to defective sensor
Occasional			Unnecessary energy-saving shutdowns	
Rare		Missed defective product		
Very Rare	Miscalculating maintenance			Misdetecting major faults

In this example, the manufacturing plant would need to address the very rare risk of a catastrophic shutdown during peak production hours and the frequent risk of consistently failing to detect a critical overheating issue, as they fall into the red "unacceptable" category. Meanwhile, the occasional misclassification of products and the rare instances of delayed maintenance alerts, both in the yellow zone, are areas where risk reduction is desired. The remaining risks, while not ideal, are deemed acceptable.

The role of insurance

Insurance plays a pivotal role in risk management, serving as a financial safety net for unforeseen events and potential losses. By transferring the financial burden of certain risks to an insurance provider, organizations can protect their assets and ensure business continuity in the face of adverse events. Therefore, the choice to declare a risk acceptable needs to involve insurance coverage and (rise in) premium involved.

Insurance has a vital role to play in adopting, and in the process regulating, emerging technologies such as AI. It offers a hedging tool to deal with the many risks associated with AI, and it translates them into a manageable scope.[14] Unfortunately, there appears to be some hesitation among insurance providers to cover AI-specific risks. Leading reinsurers like Swiss Re and AXA XL offer tailored solutions for AI risks, emphasizing the importance of understanding the intricacies of AI applications in various sectors. Policies can cover damages up to several million dollars, depending on the nature and scale of the AI application. For SME applications or AI systems, some form of coverage may be available through more general cybersecurity or cyber risk policies.

Reliability requirements and fault tolerance

The consequences of an AI system malfunctioning or making an erroneous decision can be severe, especially in sectors like healthcare, finance, or transportation. Therefore, understanding and establishing safety criticality levels is essential.

> B10a. Did you assess the dependency of a critical AI system's decisions on its stable and reliable behaviour?

Before deploying an AI system, especially one that is deemed critical, it's vital to assess its dependency on stable and reliable behavior. This means understanding how the system's decisions are influenced by its underlying algorithms and data. Are the decisions consistent? Can the system handle anomalies or unexpected inputs without faltering? One must evaluate if the AI system's decisions are consistently accurate and if they can be trusted in real-world scenarios. We will this address in more detail in the next section.

> B10b. Did you align the reliability/testing requirements to the appropriate levels of stability and reliability?

Once the system's behavior is understood, the next step is to align its reliability and testing requirements with its observed levels of stability. This involves rigorous testing under various conditions to ensure that the system behaves as expected. It's not just about the system working correctly but ensuring it does so consistently and reliably.

> B11. Did you plan fault tolerance via, e.g. a duplicated system or another parallel system (AI-based or 'conventional')?

No system is infallible. Therefore, planning for fault tolerance is crucial. This could mean having a duplicated system in place or another parallel system, be it AI-based or conventional, that can take over should the primary system fail. For instance, in a manufacturing setting, if an AI system monitoring quality control fails, a backup system should be able to immediately take over to prevent defective products from passing through. If no automated alternative is available, then a manual-labor option should be available as a last resort.

> B12. Did you develop a mechanism to evaluate when the AI system has been changed to merit a new review of its technical robustness and safety?

AI systems, like all software, will undergo changes over time. These could be updates to the algorithm, the addition of new data sources, or other modifications. It's essential to have a mechanism in place to evaluate when these changes are significant enough to warrant a fresh review of the system's technical robustness and safety. This ensures that any updates or changes don't inadvertently introduce new vulnerabilities or reduce the system's reliability.

Ensuring Accuracy in AI Decisions

The accuracy of an AI system is paramount to its utility and trustworthiness. Inaccurate predictions or classifications can have far-reaching consequences, especially in applications where decisions directly impact human lives or critical infrastructures. Ensuring high accuracy is not just about getting the right answers but also about understanding when and why the system might get it wrong. Let's seek to understand the implications of accuracy and mistakes in AI systems and learn techniques to monitor and improve AI decision-making accuracy.

Getting it right: positives and negatives

At its core, AI is about predicting a label or outcome. The term 'accuracy' is generally used as an indicator of quality. Accuracy measures the proportion of correct predictions made by the AI system. However, this alone can sometimes be misleading, especially in imbalanced datasets. To get a clearer picture, we often turn to other metrics.

In statistical terminology, a 'positive' result means the presence or occurrence of a specific event or condition that the system is trying to detect or predict. For instance, in a medical test, a positive result indicates the presence of a disease. Conversely, a 'negative' denotes the absence or non-occurrence of the specific event or condition. In the same medical test example, a negative result signifies the absence of the disease. (These terms thus do not reflect a judgment on the underlying factor such as the disease.)

A prediction may or may not be correct. We can break down predictions into four categories, as shown in the below matrix:

		Predicted	
		Positive	Negative
Actual	Positive	True Positive (TP)	False Negative (FN)
	Negative	False Positive (FP)	True Negative (TN)

- ❶ True Positive (TP): This is when the AI system correctly predicts a positive outcome. For instance, if a patient has a disease and the AI system correctly diagnoses them as having the disease, that's a true positive.
- ❷ True Negative (TN): This is when the AI system correctly predicts a negative outcome. Using our medical example, if a patient doesn't have the disease and the AI system correctly diagnoses them as not having it, that's a true negative.
- ❸ False Positive (FP): This occurs when the AI system incorrectly predicts a positive outcome. In the medical context, it would mean the system diagnoses a healthy patient as having the disease.
- ❹ False Negative (FN): This is when the AI system incorrectly predicts a negative outcome. In the medical scenario, it would mean the system fails to detect the disease in a patient who actually has it.

Accuracy, recall and precision

Accuracy in AI and machine learning refers to the proportion of predictions that a model gets right: the number of true positives and true negatives, as a percentage of the total number of predictions. However, accuracy alone doesn't provide a complete picture of a model's performance, especially when the classes are imbalanced: one class occurs much more often than the others.

Imagine a manufacturing plant that produces 1.000 widgets daily. Out of these, 980 widgets are produced perfectly (negative cases), while 20 have defects (positive cases).

Now, consider an AI quality control (QC) system that, in an attempt to be efficient, predicts that all widgets are perfect without actually inspecting them. This system would correctly predict "Perfect" for 980 widgets (True Negatives) yet it would incorrectly predict "Perfect" for the 20 widgets that actually have defects (False Negatives). Its accuracy is then calculated as (True Positives + True Negatives) / Total Predictions = (0 + 980) / 1.000 = 980 / 1.000 = 98%.

By this metric, the QC system appears to have an impressive accuracy of 98%, yet it is clear that this system is an utter failure for its primary task. In terms of statistics, its recall is 0%. **Recall**, also known as sensitivity or true positive rate, measures the proportion of actual positives that are correctly identified. It answers the question: Of all the positive cases, how many did we correctly predict? A high recall indicates that the model correctly identified most of the positive cases. **Precision**, on the other hand, measures the proportion of positive identifications that were actually correct. It answers the question: Of all the cases we predicted as positive, how many were actually positive? A high precision indicates that the model's positive predictions are trustworthy.

In many scenarios, there's an inverse relationship between precision and recall. Improving one can often lead to a decrease in the other. For instance, if a system is adjusted to be more aggressive in predicting positives to increase recall, it might end up with more false positives, thereby reducing precision. Conversely, if only the most trustworthy predictions are accepted (high precision), the recall will suffer as more positive cases are ignored – false negatives.

Given this trade-off, it's essential to find a balance between the two, especially in scenarios where both false positives and false negatives have significant implications. This is where the **F1 score** comes into play. The F1 score is the harmonic mean of precision and recall, providing a single metric that balances the trade-off between the two. Unlike the arithmetic mean, the harmonic mean tends to give a low value when any of its terms are low, ensuring that a high F1 score is only achieved if both precision and recall are high. Thus, the F1 score serves as a compromise, emphasizing the balance between precision and recall in the performance of an AI system.

The **Receiver Operating Characteristic (ROC)** is another critical tool in understanding and evaluating the performance of classification models, especially in binary classification problems. The ROC curve plots the true-positive rate (TPR) against the false-positive rate (FPR) at various threshold settings. The ROC curve provides a comprehensive view of the trade-off between the TPR and FPR for every possible threshold. A model that perfectly distinguishes between the two classes will have an ROC curve that hugs the top left corner of the plot, indicating high sensitivity and specificity. In the chart below, that's the blue dot at 0,0/1,0. Conversely, a model that performs no better than random will have an ROC curve that's a diagonal line from the bottom left to the top right – the red line in the chart.

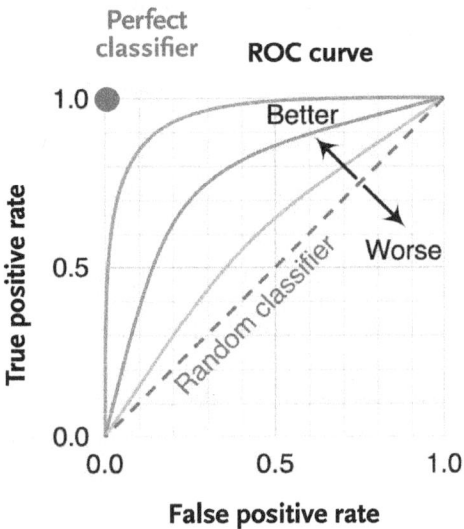

The key metric for an ROC curve is the area underneath it, commonly referred to as the AUC. Two classifiers may have different ROC curves but the same AUC, and in terms of overall discriminative ability, they can be considered comparable in performance. However, it's important to note that while the AUC provides a single scalar value summarizing the overall performance, the shape of the ROC curve can provide more nuanced insights. Two classifiers with the same AUC might perform differently at specific thresholds. One might be better at achieving high sensitivity, while the other might excel at specificity.

The ROC curve is particularly useful in scenarios where the classes are imbalanced or when the costs of different types of errors (false positives vs. false negatives) vary. By examining the ROC curve, one can choose a threshold that offers an acceptable balance between sensitivity and specificity for a particular application.

Steps to improve accuracy

B13. Could a low level of accuracy of the AI system result in critical, adversarial or damaging consequences?

A low level of accuracy of an AI system may lead to critical, adversarial, or damaging consequences in various domains. For instance, AI-driven financial trading algorithms are used to make split-second decisions on buying or selling stocks based on a myriad of factors. If such an algorithm consistently makes inaccurate predictions about stock movements, it could lead to massive financial losses for investors. An inaccurate prediction in an AI-driven agricultural crop management systems could lead to farmers planting or harvesting at suboptimal times, leading to reduced yields.

That's not to say that a low level of accuracy is always critical or harmful to users. For example, if a movie recommendation algorithm inaccurately recommends a romantic comedy when the user typically enjoys action films, the consequence is minor. The user can simply ignore the recommendation and choose another title. In a computer game, the AI could inaccurately interpret a user's action and makes the characters or game respond in an unexpected way.

There is no generally accepted framework for this type of consequence. The AI Act mentions risks to health, safety, fundamental rights, democracy and rule of law and the environment as typical examples of situations where consequences would be critical, adversarial or damaging. However, it's essential to approach this with nuance. For instance, consider a smart trash bin that incorrectly labels recyclable waste as non-recyclable. While this does pose an environmental risk, labeling it as a "critical" consequence might be an overstatement.

When evaluating the significance of risks caused by low accuracy in AI systems, one can consider a multi-faceted approach that weighs various factors. Here's a guidance framework:

Impact on Health and Safety	Impact on Fundamental Rights	Impact on Democracy and Rule of Law	Impact on the Environment	User Dependency	Public Perception and Trust
High Significance: Systems where inaccuracies can lead to physical harm, health risks, or loss of life (e.g., medical diagnosis tools, industrial robots).	**High Significance:** Systems handling sensitive personal data where inaccuracies can lead to breaches, misuse, or violation of rights (e.g., surveillance systems misidentifying individuals).	**High Significance:** Systems where decisions are irreversible, can influence democratic processes, or have legal implications (e.g., voting prediction algorithms, criminal sentencing tools).	**High Significance:** Systems where inaccuracies can lead to environmental harm or hinder conservation efforts (e.g., environmental monitoring tools misreading pollution levels).	**High Significance:** Systems where users heavily rely on the AI's accuracy for critical tasks, impacting their rights, safety, or democratic participation (e.g., emergency response systems).	**High Significance:** Systems where public trust is paramount, and inaccuracies can lead to widespread skepticism, impacting democracy or public safety (e.g., public health announcement systems).
Low Significance: Systems where inaccuracies might be inconvenient but won't harm users or their health (e.g., fitness tracking apps miscounting steps).	**Low Significance:** Systems dealing with non-sensitive data or where rights aren't directly impacted (e.g., weather prediction apps).	**Low Significance:** Systems with decisions that don't directly influence democratic or legal outcomes (e.g., public opinion survey tools).	**Low Significance:** Systems where environmental implications are minimal or indirect (e.g., smart home systems slightly misadjusting room temperatures).	**Low Significance:** Systems used for leisure or non-critical tasks that don't directly impact the aforementioned areas (e.g., music recommendation algorithms).	**Low Significance:** Systems where public perception is less tied to accuracy and doesn't directly impact the core areas of the AI Act (e.g., art generation algorithms).

Chapter 4 – Robustness, reliability, and safeguards

> B14. Did you put in place measures to ensure that the data (including training data) used to develop the AI system is up-to-date, of high quality, complete and representative of the environment the system will be deployed in?

One of the foundational steps to ensure accuracy is to use high-quality data. The data, especially the training data, should be up-to-date, complete, and truly representative of the environment in which the AI system will operate. This is crucial because an AI system trained on outdated or unrepresentative data can produce misleading or incorrect results. Moreover, the quality of the data directly impacts the quality of the AI system's outputs. We'll delve deeper into the intricacies of data governance in Chapter 5.

> B15. Did you put in place a series of steps to monitor, and document the AI system's accuracy?

Continuous monitoring of the AI system's performance is also essential. By regularly checking and documenting the system's accuracy, any deviations or anomalies can be detected early, allowing for timely interventions. This ongoing monitoring ensures that the system remains reliable and trustworthy over time.

> B16. Did you consider whether the AI system's operation can invalidate the data or assumptions it was trained on, and how this might lead to adversarial effects?

It's also vital to consider the dynamic nature of data and the environment. As situations change, there's a possibility that the AI system's operations could render the data it was trained on, or its underlying assumptions, obsolete. Imagine an AI system designed for an e-commerce platform to recommend products to users based on their browsing and purchase history. The system was trained on data from the past two years, during which a particular fashion trend, let's say "bell-bottom jeans," was highly popular. Now, fast forward to the present day, where fashion trends have shifted, and "skinny jeans" have become the new rage. However, the AI system, still operating on its older training data, continues to heavily recommend bell-bottom jeans to new users, assuming that they are still in vogue. As a result, the system's recommendations might not resonate with the current preferences of the users, leading to decreased sales and user satisfaction.

Such scenarios can lead to adversarial effects, where the system starts behaving in unintended ways. Being aware of this risk and proactively checking for such shifts is crucial.

> B17. Did you put processes in place to ensure that the level of accuracy of the AI system to be expected by end-users and/or subjects is properly communicated?

Lastly, communication is key. The end-users and subjects interacting with the AI system should be well-informed about its expected level of accuracy. Setting clear expectations helps in building trust and ensures that users are making informed decisions based on the AI system's outputs. Proper channels should be in place to communicate any updates, changes, or potential issues related to the system's accuracy to all relevant stakeholders.

Reliability, Fallback Plans, and Reproducibility

The integration of AI systems into various sectors has brought about transformative changes, offering solutions to complex problems and optimizing processes. However, with this integration comes the responsibility to ensure that these systems are both reliable and reproducible, especially in high-stakes scenarios. Reliability and reproducibility in AI systems are key to ensure consistent and predictable AI behavior.

On reliability and reproducibility

Reliability in the context of AI refers to the system's ability to consistently perform its intended function across a range of inputs and scenarios. A reliable AI system is one that users can trust to work as expected, irrespective of external variables or changing conditions. It's akin to expecting a car to start every morning; the consistent performance instills confidence.

On the other hand, **reproducibility** is about ensuring that an AI experiment or operation exhibits the same behavior when repeated under the same conditions. It's a cornerstone of scientific integrity. In AI, reproducibility means that given the same data and the same model parameters, the system will produce the same results, regardless of when or where it is run. This is crucial for validating findings, especially when AI models are used to inform critical decisions.

To illustrate the sometimes subtle difference: a weather prediction model that consistently predicts rain every Tuesday is highly reproducible because it's consistent and can be replicated under the same conditions. However, the model is not reliable as its predictions are utterly disjoint from reality. At the other end of the spectrum, consider a stock trading algorithm that has been trained on a vast amount of historical data and has consistently generated profits for several months. This algorithm is reliable in the sense that it has a proven track record of making profitable trades over a specific period. However, its black-box nature and lack of documentation on training parameters, design choices et cetera make this a less reproducible AI system.

> B18. Could the AI system cause critical, adversarial, or damaging consequences (e.g. pertaining to human safety) in case of low reliability and/or reproducibility?
> B18a. Did you put in place a well-defined process to monitor if the AI system is meeting the intended goals?
> B18b. Did you test whether specific contexts or conditions need to be taken into account to ensure reproducibility?

In certain domains, the stakes are exceptionally high. Consider the financial sector, where AI-driven trading algorithms manage billions of dollars. A slight inconsistency in the system's operation could lead to significant financial losses. Similarly, in urban planning, AI models predicting infrastructure wear and tear can influence decisions on maintenance and resource allocation. An unreliable prediction could result in infrastructure failures, posing risks to public safety.

Monitoring, verification and documentation

> B19. Did you put in place verification and validation methods and documentation (e.g. logging) to evaluate and ensure different aspects of the AI system's reliability and reproducibility?
> B19a. Did you clearly document and operationalise processes for the testing and verification of the reliability and reproducibility of the AI system?

To mitigate these risks, it's essential to have a well-defined process to monitor AI systems continuously. Regular checks ensure that the system is meeting its intended goals and operating within acceptable parameters. This involves not only monitoring the system's outputs but also understanding how specific contexts or conditions might affect reproducibility. For instance, an AI model trained on summer data might not be reliable in winter conditions, necessitating context-aware monitoring. Again, this goes hand-in-hand with data governance, the subject of the next chapter.

Beyond monitoring, there's a need for rigorous verification and validation methods. These methods evaluate various aspects of the AI system's reliability and reproducibility. Proper documentation of these processes, including logging, is crucial. It provides a clear roadmap for testing and verification, ensuring that stakeholders can trust the system's operations.

Verification and validation (V&V) are critical processes in the development and deployment of AI systems, especially when these systems are used in safety-critical applications. Verification ensures that the system is built correctly according to the specified requirements. These processes by themselves are well-understood and documented in the technical literature, even when the Agile methodology is used.[15]

The role of fallback plans

> B20. Did you define tested failsafe fallback plans to address AI system errors of whatever origin and put governance procedures in place to trigger them?

Even with rigorous monitoring and validation, errors can occur. It's essential to have tested failsafe fallback plans in place to address any AI system errors, regardless of their origin. These plans, coupled with governance procedures, ensure that when anomalies are detected, there's a clear protocol to mitigate potential damages. Not just to ensure business continuity – surprisingly, fallback plans are key to establishing trust in AI. One significant failure can erode the confidence users have in the system. By having robust fallback mechanisms, organizations can assure users that they are prepared for contingencies, thereby bolstering trust.

Fallback plans can range from sophisticated strategies like maintaining an off-site duplicate of the entire system, which continuously syncs with the primary master system, to simpler solutions. For instance, a watchdog system may monitor response times of an AI customer service system, and transfer customers to a human operator if the AI appears to be unresponsive for too long. In a smart home setting, a set of preprogrammed defaults may set in if the algorithmic environment management system makes many changes in a short time. And in a decision-support system, the AI-driven advisor can be replaced by a questionnaire or flowchart that addresses common situations.

Effective governance is the backbone of any failsafe strategy. It's not enough to have a backup plan; organizations must also define clear procedures for when and how to activate these plans.

- ❶ Monitoring and Alerts: Continuous monitoring of the AI system can detect anomalies or performance drops. Automated alerts can notify relevant teams immediately when predefined thresholds are breached.
- ❷ Decision Protocols: Clearly defined protocols should be in place to determine when to switch to the fallback system. This could be based on the severity of the malfunction, the potential impact, or a combination of factors.

Chapter 4 – Robustness, reliability, and safeguards

- Regular Drills: Just like fire drills, organizations should conduct regular failsafe drills. This ensures that in the event of a real crisis, teams know exactly what to do, minimizing response times.
- Feedback Loops: After activating a fallback plan, there should be mechanisms to gather data on what went wrong with the primary system. This feedback can be invaluable for preventing future failures.
- Stakeholder Communication: Clear communication channels should be established to inform stakeholders about any disruptions and the activation of fallback plans. Transparency in such situations can mitigate panic and confusion.
- Review and Update: Fallback plans should not be static. They should be regularly reviewed and updated based on technological advancements,

The impact of low confidence scores

> B21. Did you put in place a proper procedure for handling the cases where the AI system yields results with a low confidence score?

AI systems are designed to process vast amounts of data and make decisions based on patterns and information they've been trained on. However, there are instances where the system might encounter unfamiliar scenarios or data points that don't align well with its training. In such situations, the AI might produce results with low confidence scores, indicating its uncertainty regarding the decision or prediction. This uncertainty can arise from various factors, such as data anomalies, insufficient training on specific data subsets, or inherent complexities in the problem being addressed.

Confidence scores in AI systems, especially in classification tasks, typically represent the probability of a particular output or decision. These scores are derived from the underlying algorithms, with some models, like neural networks, naturally producing a probability distribution over classes. For instance, in a binary classification, a confidence score of 0,8 for a particular class means the model believes there's an 80% chance of that class being the correct one.

Having a robust procedure to handle cases of low confidence is crucial to ensure the reliability and trustworthiness of the AI system. When the system identifies that its confidence in a particular result is below a predefined threshold, it could reroute the decision-making process to a human expert who can evaluate the situation with a more nuanced understanding. This human-in-the-loop approach (see previous chapter) ensures that critical decisions aren't made solely based on uncertain AI predictions. Alternatively, the system could be designed to seek additional data or inputs that might help in bolstering its confidence. For instance, if an AI in medical diagnostics is unsure about a scan result, it might request additional tests or scans to make a more informed decision. This proactive approach ensures that the AI system remains a reliable tool, even in uncertain situations.

A different approach is to present outputs in a tiered manner: as the confidence level decreases, the response becomes more cautious and tentative. Let's consider an AI-powered chatbot designed for customer support in an e-commerce platform. When the chatbot processes a question on the company's returns policy, the confidence in its resonse may vary, and the way it presents the answer can be adjusted accordingly:

1. High Confidence (e.g., 90% and above): "Electronic items purchased from our store can be returned within 30 days of purchase, provided they are in their original condition and packaging."
2. Medium Confidence (e.g., 70% - 89%): "I believe electronic items can typically be returned within 30 days of purchase, as long as they're in their original condition. However, I recommend checking our official return policy page or speaking with a human representative to confirm."
3. Low Confidence (e.g., 50% - 69%): "I'm not entirely sure, but I think electronic items might have a 30-day return window. It would be best to consult our official return policy page or connect with one of our team members for a definitive answer."
4. Very Low Confidence (below 50%): "I'm sorry, I'm having trouble retrieving that information right now. Would you like me to direct you to our official return policy page or connect you with a human representative?"

Continual Learning and its implications

> B22. Is your AI system using (online) continual learning?
> B22a. Did you consider potential negative consequences from the AI system learning novel or unusual methods to score well on its objective function?

Continual learning, often referred to as online or lifelong learning, is a paradigm in AI where models are designed to learn continuously over time, adapting to new data without forgetting previous knowledge.[16] This approach contrasts with traditional machine learning, where models are trained once and then deployed without further modifications. Continual learning is particularly relevant in dynamic environments where data distributions change over time or where systems are expected to interact and learn from real-time data streams. Continual learning allows models to update their knowledge based on new data, making the learning process more efficient.

However, there are also potential pitfalls. A continual learning process may overly prioritize recent data and become too specialized in a narrow domain and lose its generalization capability. Similarly, as the AI system learns and adapts over time, it might drift away from its original objective, especially if the feedback it receives from the environment is misaligned with the intended goal. Continual learning systems could be more vulnerable to adversarial attacks, where malicious actors feed misleading data to the system to degrade its performance or make it behave unpredictably.

A specific variant is called online continual learning.[17] Here the AI system learns and updates its knowledge in real-time as new data becomes available. Unlike traditional batch learning, where the system is trained on large, fixed datasets at once, online continual learning processes data points sequentially, often one at a time. Online continual learning can be particularly susceptible to "concept drift," where the underlying data distributions change rapidly, potentially leading the AI system astray if not monitored closely. Additionally, since online learning reacts to data in real-time, it's more vulnerable to adversarial attacks or noisy data, which can introduce biases or inaccuracies if not properly filtered or validated.

To harness the benefits of continual learning while mitigating its risks, it's crucial to have robust monitoring and evaluation mechanisms in place. Regularly evaluating the model's performance, checking for drifts in objectives, and ensuring that the learning process is transparent and interpretable can go a long way in ensuring that continual learning systems remain reliable and trustworthy.

Note that continual learning is not the same as self-learning. A self-learning AI system is designed to improve its performance over time by refining its algorithms and models based on feedback loops, without the need for explicit retraining from humans. It essentially learns from its mistakes and successes, adjusting its internal parameters to optimize future outcomes. On the other hand, continual learning AI allows the AI to adapt to new data or tasks while retaining its knowledge from prior experiences. In essence, while self-learning focuses on iterative improvement within a specific domain or task, continual learning emphasizes adaptability across multiple tasks or domains over an extended period.

Key takeaways

This chapter has delved into the vulnerabilities that accompany the strengths of AI, emphasizing the need for resilience against cyber threats. Risk management emerged as a pivotal aspect, guiding us on how to navigate potential pitfalls and establish robust safety measures. The discourse on accuracy illuminated the criticality of reliability and resilience in AI decisions, underscoring the profound consequences of inaccuracies. Finally, the exploration of reliability and reproducibility highlighted the imperative for AI systems to consistently deliver predictable results, even in the most dynamic of scenarios.

As we've navigated the landscape of AI robustness, it's evident that ensuring the safety and reliability of these systems is a complex, yet essential endeavor. With a solid understanding of these foundational principles, we're poised to delve into another crucial dimension of AI: data governance and privacy.

Chapter 4 – Robustness, reliability, and safeguards

5

Data Governance and Privacy in AI Systems

> In a data-driven world, the importance of privacy and data governance in AI cannot be overstated. While privacy is often thought of as a 'soft' legal aspects, the European Union's General Data Protection Regulation (GDPR) has made it clear privacy and data protection is something to take seriously. The rise of generative AI has caused another legal right to raise its head: intellectual property (IP) owners are raising serious objections against the massive usage of their works in the myriad of AI systems currently being built. What does this mean for data governance?

Introduction to Privacy and AI

Privacy is a fundamental human right, enshrined in national constitutions, international conventions and the EU's Charter of Fundamental Rights. Famously, privacy has been formulated as "the right to be let alone"; in legal terms, respect for one's private and family life, home and correspondence. However, privacy goes beyond just the private life. It encompasses the right to mental, physical, and moral integrity, and includes a right of self-determination regarding information about oneself.[1]

The European perspective

The European Union has long been at the forefront of championing the rights of individuals in the realm of data protection. Rooted in the belief that every individual has the right to control their personal data, the EU's 2018 General Data Protection Regulation (GDPR) has established a robust framework that set the global standard. It not only mandates stringent measures for data collection and processing but also emphasizes the importance of individual consent, transparency, and the right to be forgotten.

In the European perspective, personal life and data protection are not merely two aspects of one overarching right to privacy. Protection of personal data is a separate right enshrined in the Charter. This separate origin must be understood in the light of

> **By the end of this chapter, you'll be able to ...**
> - Navigate privacy, data protection and intellectual property laws for AI systems.
> - Take steps to ensure data quality and integrity in AI systems.
> - Set up and apply protocols for data acquisition and usage.

large-scale data processing by national governments (in particular in Germany) in the 1970s, which led to massive protests by citizens. The German *Bundesdatenschutzgesetz* of 1976 was the first to explicitly regulate the usage of personally-identifiable data.[2] A similar view was adopted by the OECD in 1980 with its *Guidelines on the Protection of Privacy and Transborder Flows of Personal Data*[3] and the 1981 Council of Europe's *Convention for the Protection of Individuals with regard to Automatic Processing of Personal Data* (Convention 108), both of which can still be recognized in modern data protection legislation such as the GDPR.

This perspective is fundamentally different from the US approach to handling of "personally identifiable information" (PII). Not only is "PII" a much more limited concept than "personal data" under the GDPR,[4] the US Constitution's First Amendment puts stringent limits on any regulation of processing of such data. The California Consumer Privacy Act of 2018 (CCPA) is the first real attempt to regulate personal data, comparable in scope to the GDPR.[5]

The impact of AI

The 2010s marked the meteoric rise of big data, a phenomenon characterized by the exponential growth in the volume, variety, and velocity of data being generated. The search by businesses, governments, and institutions for tools to process has led to a renewed interest in machine learning techniques, in particular deep learning, which thrived on this data deluge. Combined with an influx of venture capital this indirectly prompted the AI revolution we are in today.[6]

The symbiotic relationship between big data and AI has reshaped the digital landscape, but not without introducing significant privacy concerns. With the capability to process and analyze vast datasets, both state and private entities gained unprecedented insights into individual behaviors, preferences, and patterns.[7] While states could justify the use of AI-driven surveillance for national security purposes, it often teetered on the brink of invasive monitoring, potentially compromising the privacy rights of citizens. On the other hand, private corporations, in their quest for profit, not only harnessed AI to dissect personal data for hyper-targeted advertising, but also significantly invested in the development of surveillance technology. AI research, especially in the realm of computer vision, has become intrinsically linked to the proliferation of mass surveillance, further blurring the ethical boundaries of data usage and privacy.[8]

The intertwining of big data with automated decision-making further compounded the many concerns over AI. Decisions that once required human judgment began to be delegated to algorithms, leading to potential biases and opaque determinations that could profoundly impact individuals' lives. In this confluence of big data and AI, the sanctity of personal privacy stands at a crossroads, underscoring the urgent need for thoughtful and robust safeguards.

AI systems and fundamental rights

The right to privacy is a cornerstone of many legal frameworks and is deeply intertwined with human dignity. AI systems, by their very nature, process vast amounts of data, some of which can be deeply personal. This creates a fundamental challenge for AI systems, as they must be designed to respect these fundamental rights.

Challenges to fundamental rights

> C1. Did you consider the impact of the AI system on the right to privacy, the right to physical, mental and/or moral integrity and the right to data protection?

As discussed in chapter 3, a key aspect of AI is autonomy: the ability to perform (cognitive) tasks without the need for continuous human intervention. This may contribute to a loss of agency with human operators, or more generally a challenge to their human dignity. For instance:

① **Devaluation of human skills:** As AI systems excel in tasks once deemed complex and uniquely human, there's a risk that human skills and expertise will be undervalued or overlooked. This can lead to a diminished sense of self-worth among professionals whose roles are being replaced or augmented by AI.

② **Erosion of personal relationships:** If human interactions are increasingly mediated or replaced by AI (e.g., caregiving robots or virtual companions), the depth and authenticity of human relationships could be compromised, leading to feelings of isolation and a devaluation of human-to-human connection.

③ **Bias and discrimination:** Autonomous AI systems that inadvertently perpetuate biases can reinforce societal inequalities. When individuals are unfairly treated by AI, not only are their rights violated, but their inherent worth as individuals is implicitly denied.

④ **Reductionist views of humanity:** There's a danger that as we come to rely on AI for more tasks, we might start to view human beings in mechanistic or reductionist terms, valuing them only for their data or as cogs in a machine, rather than as holistic, multifaceted individuals.

⑤ **Loss of personal narrative:** As AI systems begin to predict, suggest, and even dictate our preferences, choices, and behaviors, there's a risk that individuals may lose their sense of personal narrative and identity. Instead of life stories being shaped by personal experiences, challenges, and choices, they could increasingly be influenced by algorithmic recommendations. This could lead to a homogenization of experiences and a loss of the unique, individual stories that define our humanity and personal growth.

Identifying these challenges is very complex, as they intertwine with our deeply held values, societal norms, and the ever-evolving technological landscape. To navigate this intricate web, several approaches can be employed. Firstly, continuous stakeholder engagement can provide diverse perspectives and highlight potential areas of concern. Secondly, ethical frameworks and guidelines can offer a structured way to evaluate AI systems against established principles. Thirdly, the use of Impact Assessments, particularly the so-called Fundamental Rights Impact Assessments, can be instrumental in systematically identifying, evaluating, and mitigating potential infringements on human dignity. These assessments, along with other tools and methodologies, will be delved into in greater detail in Chapter 10.

The interplay of AI and the right to privacy

As already noted, many applications of AI can touch upon the fundamental right to privacy. A seasoned approach to AI development always places the individual's right to privacy at the forefront, ensuring that data collection, processing, and storage are all conducted with the utmost respect for this fundamental right. The interplay of AI and personal data will be the subject of the next section. But privacy-mindful AI system design is more than data protection: privacy issues can arise in many aspects of AI system design and deployment. Let's look at a few:

- ❶ Biometric surveillance: The use of AI in facial recognition and other biometric tools can lead to a pervasive feeling of being constantly watched, even if no data is being stored or decisions made.
- ❷ Emotion recognition: AI systems that claim to detect a person's emotional state based on their facial expressions, voice, or other cues can be invasive, potentially misinterpreting emotions and leading to unwarranted conclusions or actions.
- ❸ Eavesdropping devices: Devices that are always listening for a "wake-up word" or command can inadvertently capture private conversations or sensitive information. Even when they don't, users can *perceive* this risk and feel forced to adjust their behaviour.
- ❹ Predictive behavior analysis: AI systems that predict a person's future actions or preferences can be seen as invasive, making assumptions about personal choices and lifestyles.
- ❺ Deepfakes and image manipulation: AI tools that can manipulate images or videos to create realistic but entirely fake content can infringe on an individual's right to their own likeness and create privacy concerns.

The advent of AI has brought about a new perspective on privacy. Unlike human interactions, where there's always a risk of personal biases and indiscretions, AI processes information neutrally. There's no "gossip" or "judgment" from a machine. It simply processes data without emotion or intent to disclose. However, this seemingly neutral processing can inadvertently lead to heightened privacy risks for certain individuals. People with specific, private needs often find themselves at a disadvantage. For instance, pregnant women, the economically disadvantaged, or men with bladder issues might need to reveal more personal information to interact with a system that others use seamlessly. This constant revelation of private details can lead to feelings of vulnerability and discrimination, emphasizing the need for AI systems to be designed with empathy and inclusivity at their core (see also chapter 7).

Upholding physical, mental, and moral integrity

AI systems, particularly those that engage directly with individuals, wield significant influence over a person's physical, mental, and moral well-being. For instance, think about AI-driven healthcare tools offering diagnostic recommendations or social robots designed to interact with the elderly. The potential repercussions of these technologies on an individual's health and mental state can be immense.

Addressing this influence is a fundamental step in the design of an AI system. In this particular case one must always seriously consider the question of whether the AI system *should* even perform the activity at all.

- ❶ Misdiagnosis by AI healthcare tools: Relying solely on AI for medical diagnoses can lead to incorrect treatments, potentially endangering lives. To mitigate this, it's crucial to implement rigorous testing and validation processes and always involve human oversight in critical healthcare decisions.
- ❷ Over-reliance on social robots leading to isolation: Depending too much on AI companions (see chapter 3) can reduce human-human interactions, leading to feelings of loneliness and isolation. Systems should be designed to encourage human interaction, and usage limits should be set to prevent over-dependence.
- ❸ Mental stress from AI monitoring systems: Continuous monitoring by AI can lead to anxiety and a feeling of being constantly watched. To address this, it's essential to ensure transparency in AI monitoring and provide users with the ability to turn off non-essential monitoring – with clear visual or other confirmation and safeguards that the system indeed is not monitoring anymore.
- ❹ Physical harm from autonomous machines: Machines that operate autonomously can malfunction, posing direct physical risks to users or bystanders. Incorporating multiple safety redundancies and emergency shut-off mechanisms can help prevent such incidents.
- ❺ Moral dilemmas from AI decision-making: AI systems making decisions in morally ambiguous situations can lead to outcomes that conflict with human values. Establishing ethical guidelines for AI behavior and involving diverse human input in moral decision-making processes can guide the system towards more ethically sound decisions.

Mechanisms for flagging privacy concerns

> **C2.** Depending on the use case, did you establish mechanisms that allow flagging issues related to privacy concerning the AI system?

Despite our best efforts in carrying out impact assessments and designing with fundamental rights in mind, an AI system may still exhibit issues related to privacy or protection of personal data. Therefore, it's essential to have a flexible yet robust mechanism in place that allows stakeholders to flag potential privacy concerns. Such a mechanism should be intuitive, easily accessible, and should ensure that concerns are addressed promptly. However, it's not just about having a system in place; it's about fostering a culture of vigilance and responsiveness. Here are three practical tips to foster such a culture:

❶ Open channels of communication: Establish clear and open channels for customers and employees to voice their concerns, ask questions, or report potential issues without fear of retribution. This could be in the form of regular town hall meetings, anonymous suggestion boxes, or dedicated forums. When employees feel that their concerns are heard and valued, they are more likely to be proactive in flagging and addressing potential privacy issues.

❷ Supplier dialogue: Cultivating a strong and transparent relationship with the producer of an AI system is paramount. Open dialogue fosters mutual understanding and trust. This goes beyond legal measures such as a service level agreement or security review; those establish baselines but do not foster trust and cooperation. When both parties are aligned in their understanding and objectives, addressing privacy concerns becomes a joint effort. Moreover, a good relationship means that in times of unforeseen challenges or urgent issues, communication lines are already open, and both parties are more inclined to work together swiftly and efficiently.

❸ Celebrate proactiveness: Recognize and reward employees who demonstrate a proactive approach to privacy, whether it's by identifying potential vulnerabilities, suggesting improvements, or simply being consistently diligent in their roles. By celebrating these actions, you not only encourage the individual but also set a positive example for others to follow, reinforcing the importance of a vigilant and responsive culture.

The GDPR and its impact on AI

Adopted in 2016, the GDPR is the flagship European legislation to protect personal data. As many AI systems process personal data, both during training and in use, understanding and applying the GDPR is a key aspect of AI compliance.

Applicability of the GDPR to AI systems

> C3. Is your AI system being trained, or was it developed, by using or processing personal data (including special categories of personal data)?

The AI Act explicitly confirms that the GDPR is applicable in full to any processing of personal data by an AI system. So let's have a look at both these terms and how they relate to AI systems.

- Personal data: For the definition of "personal data" we need to look at the GDPR itself: "any information relating to an identified or identifiable natural person" (art. 4(1)). This is an extremely broad definition, especially considering the second part of the definition which explains that "an identifiable natural person is one who can be identified, directly or indirectly". This goes way beyond merely being able to assign a name or contact information to a data point. Any identifier, such as an identification number, location data, an online identifier or factors specific to the physical, physiological, genetic, mental, economic, cultural or social identity of that natural person are sufficient.

A good rule of thumb is to assume that when datasets deal with humans, the data is personal data unless it can be convincingly established that the data is fully anonymized without any hope of tracing individual items to the 'data subject' from which they originated. But note: the term 'anonymized' does not merely mean removing names, identification numbers and the like. The GDPR calls this "pseudonymization", a process that can in theory be reversed as long as the identifiers still exist somewhere.

- Special personal data: The AI Act in several points refers to "special" or "sensitive" personal data. The GDPR marks certain categories of personal data as "special": personal data revealing racial or ethnic origin, political opinions, religious or philosophical beliefs, or trade union membership, and the processing of genetic data, biometric data for the purpose of uniquely identifying a natural person, data concerning health or data concerning a natural person's sex life or sexual orientation (art. 9(1) GDPR). Their extremely sensitive nature makes that the GDPR bans any and all processing of this type of data, except and to the extent explicitly permitted elsewhere.

AI systems may well process such special personal data: many AI systems provide healthcare advice, monitoring or support, for instance. To name a different example, a companion app may deduce a user's sexual orientation through interaction. A car navigation system may record weekly trips to a church, mosque or synagogue, which indirectly reveals information on religion. Whether and how such information can be used, requires a careful analysis under GDPR guidance and case law and is outside the scope of this book.

Uniquely, the AI Act permits the use of special personal data in order to train, validate and test datasets for potential negative bias against natural persons (art. 10.5). All special measures required by the GDPR for such processing apply in full.

- Data processing: The GDPR applies to any 'processing' of personal data in an automated system (and to certain forms of processing in non-automated systems, but those are out of scope for this book). The term 'processing' again is defined extremely broadly: any operation or set of operations which is performed on personal data or on sets of personal data, whether or not by automated means, such as collection, recording, organisation, structuring, storage, adaptation or alteration, retrieval, consultation, use, disclosure by transmission, dissemination or otherwise making available, alignment or combination, restriction, erasure or destruction. In short: any touching of data or input related to individual humans will trigger the GDPR.

GDPR compliance measures for AI systems

> C4. Did you put in place any of the following measures some of which are mandatory under the General Data Protection Regulation (GDPR), or a non-European equivalent?

When an AI system is processing personal data, the system must fully comply with the GDPR. This legal requirement exists independently of the AI Act's requirements: an AI system may fully meet the stringent requirements for high-risk AI yet violate the GDPR on some points, or vice versa. While GDPR compliance is its own specialism, let's have a look at the main requirements. The French GDPR supervisor CNIL has published AI how-to sheets that may provide further insights on GDPR-compliant AI deployment.[9]

Data Protection Impact Assessment (DPIA)

> C4a. Data Protection Impact Assessment (DPIA);

A Data Protection Impact Assessment (DPIA) is a systematic process designed to evaluate the potential risks associated with data processing activities, especially when introducing new technologies. Under GDPR, a DPIA is mandatory when a new form of processing is "likely to result in a high risk" to natural persons or their fundamental rights. If the DPIA reveals that the system "would result in a high risk in the absence of measures taken to prevent them", prior permission from supervisory authorities must be sought.

To make the determination of "likely high risk", the GDPR offers a complex set of factors, supplemented by various guidances by supervisory authorities. Arguably, any

AI system would satisfy these requirements, but the AI Act keeps it simple: a DPIA is mandatory if the AI system qualifies as high-risk.

Data Protection Officer (DPO)

> C4b. Designate a Data Protection Officer (DPO) and include them at an early stage in the development, procurement or use phase of the AI system;

A data protection officer (DPO) is an independent officer that oversees data protection strategies and implementation. Their job entails training, awareness and monitoring compliance. Involvement of a DPO in a DPIA is required, and a DPO should be able to address the aforementioned GDPR-specific issues related to AI systems. In chapter 10, we will dive into the role of the AI compliance officer and their relationship to the DPO.

Oversight mechanisms for data processing

> C4c. Oversight mechanisms for data processing;

The GDPR contains various requirements aimed at establishing oversight. The most general requirement is to have "appropriate technical and organisational measures to ensure and to be able to demonstrate that processing is performed in accordance with the GDPR" (art. 24 GDPR). Note that this is not just about *compliance* but also on *being able to demonstrate* compliance. Similar requirements exist in the AI Act: a risk management system, human oversight and so on. Effective oversight mechanisms are essential for monitoring and controlling data processing activities within AI systems. These mechanisms ensure that data processing remains transparent, accountable, and in line with established data protection principles.

Measures to achieve privacy-by-design and default

> C4d. Measures to achieve privacy-by-design and default;

Two specific mechanisms that seek to enforce easier GDPR compliance are called privacy by design and by default. Privacy by Design is a proactive approach that integrates data protection principles into the initial design and architecture of systems, processes, and practices, rather than adding them as an afterthought.[10] It ensures that privacy is a foundational element throughout the entire lifecycle of any project or initiative. Somewhat related, Privacy by Default ensures that the strictest privacy settings are automatically applied to a system or service upon a user's first use, without requiring any manual adjustments by the user. It guarantees that personal data is only processed with the minimal necessary extent and duration, safeguarding user information from the outset.

In contrast, the AI Act does not explicitly call for any "compliance by design" or dictate defaults. AI providers must ensure their systems are compliant and have risk and quality management systems in place.

Data minimisation

C4e. Data minimisation, in particular personal data;

Data minimisation is the practice of limiting data collection and retention to what is strictly necessary for the intended purpose. In the context of AI, this means ensuring that only relevant and essential data is processed, thereby reducing the potential for misuse and enhancing data protection. The AI Act does not itself require data sets to be minimized, but does call for data to be 'relevant', have good quality and be regularly updated.

The GDPR thus may take the lead here in requiring certain older data to be removed from data sets, unless overriding interests for data quality, completeness and validation (e.g. bias prevention) can be shown. This will create immense tension with AI providers, who over a decade have experienced that quality will generally vastly improve with larger data sets, and whose systems rarely even have the ability to erase individual lines from data sets.

Implementing user rights

C4f. Did you implement the right to withdraw consent, the right to object and the right to be forgotten into the development of the AI system?

The GDPR emphasizes several user rights, including the right to withdraw consent, the right to object, and the right to be forgotten. Integrating these rights into the AI system's development ensures that users maintain control over their data and can exercise their rights as needed. User rights can be invoked against the deployer of an AI system, e.g. when old interactions are recorded and the user wants them removed. But these rights also extend to the underlying data sets from which AI systems are built.

Consideration of data lifecycle implications

C4g. Did you consider the privacy and data protection implications of data collected, generated or processed over the course of the AI system's life cycle?

Every piece of data processed by an AI system has a lifecycle, from collection to deletion. It's imperative to consider the privacy and data protection implications at each stage of this lifecycle. We will discuss this further below under "Ensuring Data Quality and

Integrity". Labadie and Legner have created a reference model for data lifecycles that incorporates GDPR requirements.[11]

Non-personal data implications

> C5. Did you consider the privacy and data protection implications of the AI system's non-personal training-data or other processed non-personal data?

When data does not relate to humans, it would not be regarded as personal data. Yet, such data may still have impact on humans. Imagine a pollution management system in a factory, that calculates the optimal moment for releasing polluting substances into the atmosphere. If the system releases pollutants at times when people are most active outdoors, it could lead to increased health issues, from respiratory problems to allergic reactions. While this does not involve personal data processing as such, there are still privacy implications.

General-purpose AI and its implications

General-purpose AI models (previously also sometimes called foundation models) are designed to optimize for generality and versatility of output, using extremely large and diverse datasets to be able to accomplish a wide range of downstream tasks, including some for which they were not specifically developed and trained.94 Today's most famous AI systems – GPT-4, DALL-E and BERT – are all general-purpose models. The lightning speed with which they overtook society's attention has caused various hastily-drafted amendments to be inserted into the AI Act.

Introduction to general-purpose models

As defined by the AI Act, a general-purpose model is an AI system that is trained on broad data at scale, is designed for generality of output, and can be adapted to a wide range of distinctive tasks. This definition clearly shows the original frame of mind of the European AI regulators: clearly delineated AI systems that perform specific tasks, from insurance claim assessments to security monitoring, food quality management and so on. General-purpose models can do each of these things – and more – but not out-of-the-box.

The evolution of AI has always seen a trajectory from narrow, task-specific models to more versatile and general models. While the concept of a general AI has been around for some time, general-purpose models represent a significant leap in this direction. They are not just an extension of the general AI idea but are a culmination of advancements in machine learning techniques, computational power, and the availability of vast datasets. The emergence of general-purpose models can be seen as a response to the increasing demand for AI systems that can handle a wider range of tasks without the need for building application-specific systems.

The significance of general-purpose models

At the heart of general-purpose models lies the principle of training on extensive and diverse datasets. This broad training data is not just about volume but also about variety. By exposing the model to a myriad of scenarios, languages, contexts, and nuances, the model learns to generalize across tasks and domains. This vast training landscape is what gives general-purpose models their unique adaptability. Instead of being confined to a narrow task, they can flexibly adjust to a wide range of applications. The richness of the data ensures that the model has seen a bit of everything, allowing it to make informed predictions or generate relevant outputs even in unfamiliar territories.

The training methodology plays a pivotal role in determining the capabilities of an AI system. Unimodal training focuses on one type of data, be it text, images, or sound. For instance, GPT-3, primarily a language model, is a result of unimodal training on text. On the other hand, multimodal training involves integrating multiple types of data. CLIP, for example, is trained on both images and text, allowing it to understand and generate content across both domains. While unimodal models excel in their specific domain, multimodal models bring a holistic understanding, bridging gaps between different data types.

Central to the widespread adoption of these models is the way they are made available to users and developers. Many providers offer these models through what is known as an API, or Application Programming Interface. To put it in non-technical terms, think of an API as a menu in a restaurant. Just as you would order a dish from a menu, developers can "order" specific functions or tasks from the general-purpose model using this API. It serves as a bridge, facilitating communication between the general-purpose model and the developer's application.

This API-driven approach has democratized access to these powerful models. By providing a subscription-based access system, it has become incredibly straightforward for businesses, researchers, and developers to tap into the prowess of general-purpose models. They can effortlessly integrate these models into their own platforms or craft specialized third-party applications tailored to specific needs. This ease of access and adaptability has further solidified the indispensable role of general-purpose models in today's technological landscape.

Ethical and societal considerations

Being AI systems, any of the ethical considerations discussed in this book would equally apply to general-purpose models. However, general-purpose models do introduce a unique set of ethical considerations given their scale and broad applicability:

1. Bias and Fairness: General-purpose models are trained on vast amounts of data sourced from the internet, which means they can inadvertently learn and perpetuate societal biases present in that data. While all AI models can exhibit bias, the sheer scale and general-purpose nature of these models mean that their biases can manifest in a wide range of applications, potentially affecting many sectors of society.

2. Transparency and Interpretability: The complexity of general-purpose models makes them inherently difficult to interpret. Understanding why a particular output was produced can be elusive. Due to their size and the vast amount of training data, these models are often seen as "black boxes," making it harder to dissect their decision-making processes compared to smaller, more specialized models.

3. Environmental Impact: Training general-purpose models requires significant computational resources, leading to substantial energy consumption and carbon emissions. The scale at which these models operate means their environmental footprint is considerably larger than that of smaller models. Their training not only demands powerful hardware but also extended periods of runtime.

4. Economic and Competitive Implications: The development and maintenance of general-purpose models require substantial resources, potentially leading to a concentration of power in a few tech giants that can afford such investments.[13]

5. Dependency and Generalization Risks: Over-reliance on general-purpose models can lead to a lack of diversity in AI solutions, as different tasks might start depending on a single model or a few popular models. Their versatility can be a double-edged sword. If too many applications lean on a single general-purpose model, it might lead to systemic risks if that model has an unforeseen flaw or vulnerability.

Compliance obligations specific to general-purpose models

At its core, the AI Act applies just as much to a general-purpose model as to a 'traditional' AI system. Complications arise when qualifying a foundation AI system, as most provisions of the AI Act assume the system is designed with a specific task or goal in mind. For instance, the qualification of an AI system as high-risk requires a determination of a field of application and a risk assessment of the specific activity in that field. A language model such as GPT-4 does not have either, so does that mean it can never be high-risk?

The main focus of the AI Act's provisions regarding general-purpose models relates to their unique capabilities and corresponding risks. Data quality and integrity – the subject of our next section – is paramount, as is availability of proper documentation and fair terms for API access to foundation models as services.

Intellectual property and AI systems

With more and more data being fed into data sets for training purposes of AI systems, protests from intellectual property (IP) rights holders have become louder and louder. While certain parallels can be drawn to earlier IP conflicts such as the Napster and Pirate Bay-era, the unique nature of the usage by AI providers raises fundamental questions.

The scope of IP protection

The main tool in the IP protection arsenal is copyright: a work is automatically protected against copying, modification and offering to the public, except in some limited cases such as quotations, home copying or parodies. To qualify for copyright, a work only needs to pass the limited bar of being the author's "own intellectual creation" (as the European Court of Justice put it). Without a doubt, the vast majority of data harvested today – texts, images and video – from the internet is protected by copyright.

Even when data is not protected by copyright, e.g. lists with factual information, another IP right may be in play. Since 1996, the European Union has had the so-called database right, a separate legal right that protects a database if "there has been qualitatively and/or quantitatively a substantial investment in either the obtaining, verification or presentation of the contents". Thus, a dataset containing measurements of weather sensors in a particular province for a period of 10 years would be protected as a database, even though this dataset contains no copyrighted material.

Copyright and database rights both are not unlimited. The freedom of information necessitates certain exception: scientific research for instance would not be possible without the right to quote or cite from earlier work, and parodying a well-known work or trend requires the ability to use parts of that work. In 2019 the European Union introduced a new exception for what then was known as *text and data mining* or TDM: it should be legal to make "reproductions and extractions of lawfully accessible works and other subject matter for the purposes of text and data mining."

TDM, ML and AI

At the time, text and data mining or TDM was mostly a scientific effort: researchers would harvest large corpuses of texts to identify linguistic developments, for instance. The biomedical research community in particular has benefited from TDM for a long time. However, the language of this TDM exception allows for data mining for commercial purposes,[14] a fact machine learning and AI providers have quickly grasped on when copyright holders became more threatening in assertion of their legal rights against those who would do wholesale copying to train AI models.[15]

The TDM exception provides an escape for IP holders. They can make an "express reservation" or opt-out to prevent any TDM on their content, but must do so in "an appropriate manner, such as machine-readable means in the case of content made publicly available online". The law does not provide any guidance of what an 'appropriate' manner would be. Many have pointed to the 'robots.txt' protocol, where site operators can exclude search engines from indexing their site. Adding the robots that feed AI systems would be a logical step.[16] However, this protocol was designed in a different era and mainly serves to avoid *specific* robots by name. This is hardly compatible with the vast army of startups and other newcomers that create new robots by the week to harvest the internet.

There's also the anticompetition aspect to consider. Most of the AI giants already have the entirety of the internet in their dataset, and are thus able to build new AI systems with little need to re-crawl their sources. Supporting one opt-out protocol or another thus costs them very little. A newcomer on the other hand would be significantly curbed by widespread opt-out notices. Arguably, an incumbent supporting TDM opt-out would therefore harm their competition and leave themselves in a comfortable position. This can hardly be the point of copyright law.

Meanwhile independent artists have started to assert themselves against widespread harvesting of their content. Next to political lobbying, some have devised technological countermeasures such as Glaze. Images processed with the Glaze algorithm contain imperceptible pertubations that are designed to throw generative AI off the mark: newly created content closely based on such images will contain significant distortions. Even more disruptive is the Nightshade algorithm, that causes the entire generative AI model to produce erroneous or corrupted images.[18] These are examples of data poisoning attacks (see chapter 3). With good data governance practices (see chapter 5) their impact should be limited.

Reasonable royalties

A second step in the debate has focused on the issue of royalties. If usage by AI cannot be stopped, or even should be permitted in the interest of innovation, then at least rightsholders should be fairly compensated.[17] Collective societies (such as the German GEMA, the Dutch BUMA and French SACEM) have already expressed interest in collecting and dividing such royalties, but so far no one has been able to formulate any reasonable criterion for allocating royalties to a particular author.[20]

The core of the issue is that with traditional copying, the copyist sought to enrich himself with copies of the original work. The line from profit to infringing copy is then easy to draw. AI providers do not sell or otherwise offer access to copies: they split these works into their constituent elements and perform advanced statistical techniques to make totally new predictions, texts or other outputs. There is no reasonable connection between any such output and any given particular input work.

One area of particular concern is known as the "style of"-debate. Users of generative AI systems may order the creation of particular works, adding "in the style of" as a parameter referring to a particular artist, who may or may not be alive and in the business of creating such works. While "Man's landing on Mars in the style of Vincent van Gogh" may simply be a whimsical flair, asking for "a horror short story in the style of Stephen King" seems to be an entirely different thing. However, legally it is unclear whether famous author Stephen King would be able to act against new works that merely follow his *style* of writing, as long as no existing characters or settings are copied. Referring to his name may be a trademark infringement, but that is an entirely different matter.

IP governance steps

The debate on TDM, royalties and the like is far from settled, and it is very much unclear which rules will be settled on. The AI Act does not provide any specific guidance, and the Guidelines for Trustworthy AI leave IP out of scope. A few recommendations however can be made:

1. Document copyright/database ownership of any data sources used.
2. Document any opt-out references in source databases or websites. When none can be found[18], document the content of common sources (e.g. the robots.txt file and copyright notice) to demonstrate their absence.
3. Look for AI providers that offer indemnification for third-party copyright claims.
4. Evaluate royalty-allocation options for future implementation. While it's too soon to recommend paying royalties, it's worth keeping one's options open.
5. Allow content creators to indicate an opt-out from the data set, either by following a voluntary standard set by creator websites (e.g. the "NoImageAI" tag used by visual artist site DeviantArt) or by offering an easy-to-use form of your own.
6. Limit or block "in the style of" and other input options that would make it too easy to create copyright violations or plagiarism.

Ensuring Data Quality and Integrity

The quality and performance of AI systems hinges not just on advanced algorithms, but predominantly on the caliber of the data that powers them. Foundation models have only served to underline this message. Prioritizing data quality is not merely a best practice – it's a strategic decision that will define the trajectory of AI advancements and their transformative potential in the coming years.

Data sets and data processing

A dataset or data set is the general term for any collection of data from which an AI model is created. A simple example is reproduced in the following table:

Sepal Length (cm)	Sepal Width (cm)	Petal Length (cm)	Petal Width (cm)	Species
5.1	3.5	1.4	0.2	Setosa
4.9	3.0	1.4	0.2	Setosa
6.7	3.0	5.2	2.3	Virginica
6.3	2.5	5.0	1.9	Virginica
6.5	2.8	4.6	1.5	Versicolor
5.7	2.8	4.5	1.3	Versicolor
5.8	2.7	5.1	1.9	Virginica
6.0	2.7	5.1	1.6	Versicolor
5.4	3.4	1.7	0.2	Setosa
5.6	2.9	3.6	1.3	Versicolor

This table provides a snapshot of the well-known 1936 Iris dataset,[19] showcasing 10 **data items** from all three species of the iris flower: Setosa, Virginica, and Versicolor. Each row represents a unique iris flower, and the columns detail the **features** of the dataset: sepal length, sepal width, petal length, petal width, and the species. In machine learning, the species will be the **target feature**, the label to be predicted given the other features.

When working with data sets in AI systems, three key terms will make frequent appearances:

❶ Training Data: The training data is that set of data on which the machine learning algorithms perform analysis, deriving key insights and criteria with which new outputs can be generated. It's imperative that this data is not only vast but also diverse and representative of the real-world scenarios the model will encounter. A model trained on a narrow or biased dataset will inevitably produce skewed results. Ensuring a broad spectrum of patterns in the training data is crucial for models to learn and adapt effectively, capturing the nuances and complexities of varied inputs.

❷ Validation Data: Once a model is trained, validation data steps in to refine it further. This dataset plays a crucial role in fine-tuning the model, helping it generalize well to scenarios it hasn't been explicitly trained on. Without a robust validation set, there's a risk that the model might overfit to its training data, becoming too specialized and failing to perform well in real-world applications.

❸ **Testing Data:** The final litmus test for any AI model is its performance on testing data. This dataset provides an unbiased evaluation of the model's readiness for deployment, assessing its accuracy, reliability, and overall performance. It's the checkpoint that ensures the model not only has learned well but is also prepared to deliver consistent results in diverse operational environments. Both testing and validation data should not overlap with the training data, as this will significantly affect the AI model's quality.

On data processing pipelines

In today's data-driven world, the concept of a data processing pipeline has become prevalent. The phrase refers to a set of processes and tools used to move data from one system to another, typically involving stages of data collection, processing, storage, and analysis. Think of it as a conveyor belt for data, where raw information enters at one end and emerges as actionable insights or processed data at the other. Just as an industrial pipeline carries fluids through a series of processes, a data pipeline transports data through various stages of transformation and validation.

A data pipeline for a typical machine learning (AI) system involves several stages, each of which processes and transforms the data to make it suitable for model training and deployment, as illustrated in the figure below.

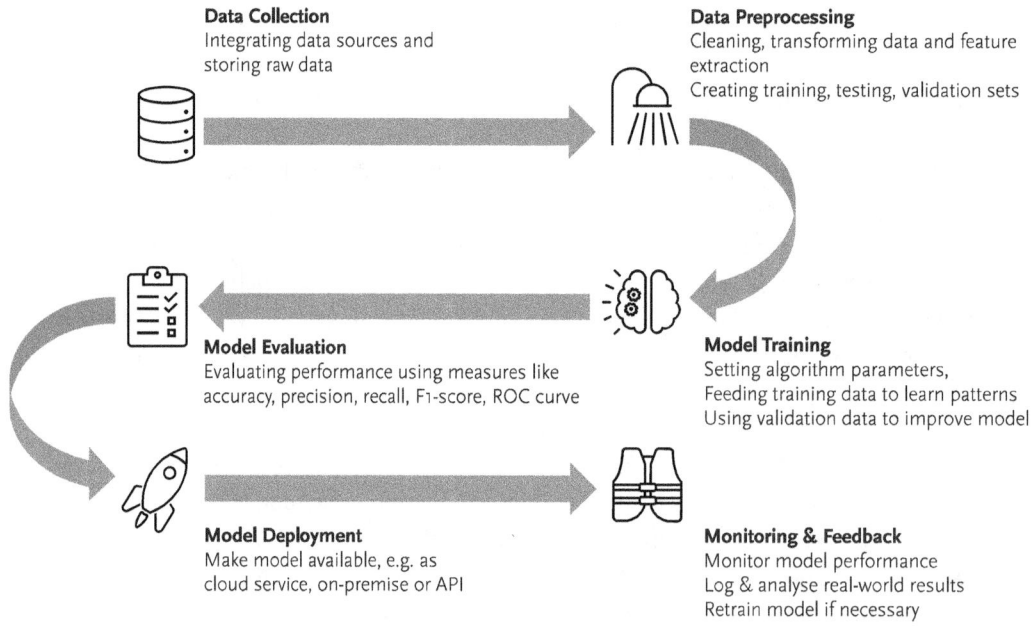

Towards high quality datasets

The data that is fed into AI systems plays a pivotal role in determining their efficacy and reliability. Data quality is an upper bound to the system's quality. The need for growth has however generally won in the past years: a system improves as much, if not more, with a large addition of low- or medium quality data than with the addition of a small highly curated set. The internet offered vast amounts of low-quality data, thus seemingly obviating the need for high-quality datasets. The tide is turning however.

Still, there is much work to do. While, as noted above, good data processing pipelines are available to streamline the process of creating an AI system, the curating of the data that goes into such a system is still very much bespoke manual labor. Often, this work is outsourced to unskilled freelance operators, e.g. through the Amazon gig platform *Mechanical Turk* where workers are available to label data for a fraction of a cent per data point. Needless to say, the quality and consistence of their work is often heavily criticized.[20] Similarly, creating data sets by harvesting large quantities of data from the internet – a key practice for foundation models – is also prone to risks.[21] Curated public datasets have long been hailed as the solution, but independent research often reveal significant biases or other errors.[22]

Given the impact of AI based on such low-quality data, it is understandable that the AI Act heavily leans on the quality of data sets. However, what exactly *is* 'quality' in terms of data? The Act refers to "high quality" data, and requires "appropriate data governance and management practices" to ensure that "appropriate statistical properties" are present, in particular to avoid negative bias or discrimination towards certain groups. Nowhere are any of these terms defined, leaving it up to implementers to work out quality criteria and processes.[23]

In the previous chapter, we discussed statistical measures (accuracy, F1 and ROC). However, a dataset with the highest accuracy or F1 score may still be of low quality. Typical causes include:

- ❶ Overfitting: Overfitting occurs when a statistical model or machine learning algorithm is focused too much on the precise properties of the training data, rather than all possible data. Any anomalies and outliers in the training data are treated as ordinary occurrences instead of discarded as the noise they properly are. As a result, while it may have high accuracy on the training data, it performs poorly on new, unseen data.
- ❷ Underfitting: Underfitting, on the other hand, is the opposite problem. It arises when the model is too simple to capture the underlying structure of the data. In this case, the model fails to capture important patterns in the training data, leading to a poor fit.
- ❸ Class Imbalance: This occurs when the classes in a dataset are not represented equally. For instance, in a binary classification task, if 95% of the data belongs to Class A and only 5% belongs to Class B, a model might achieve high accuracy by

simply predicting Class A all the time. However, this would not be a good representation of its ability to correctly classify instances of Class B.

❹ Data Leakage: This happens when information from the test set inadvertently gets used during the training of the model. It can lead to overly optimistic performance metrics, as the model has, in essence, already seen the test data during training.

The work of Budach et al. provides a complete and well-tested set of factors allowing an objective measure of quality for data:[24]

❶ Consistent representation: A dataset is consistent in its representation if no feature has two or more unique values that are semantically equivalent. For example, in a column listing countries, France should not be also represented as FR, La France or French Republic.

❷ Completeness: A dataset is complete if no items in the set have missing values. For instance, a temperature sensor that had a failure between 7 and 8 o'clock would have missing values for that time period. The completeness of the dataset is an explicit AI Act requirement.

❸ Feature accuracy: A feature is an element in a dataset, e.g. city and number of inhabitants. Real-world data tends to have errors in such features, which directly affects the quality of predictions. The AI Act requires the minimization of such errors.

❹ Target accuracy: The target is that feature for which the AI system makes predictions or other output. Target accuracy thus is the feature accuracy of this particular feature.

❺ Uniqueness: Often, large datasets contain duplicative data, which does not improve learning and may even introduce errors (e.g. if one of the duplicates is slightly different). While exact duplicates are easy to remove, the similar-but-not-identical category is much harder to identify.

❻ Target class balance: In determinative AI, the target feature is a member of a class, e.g. the class 'animals' with labels such as 'cat', 'dog' or 'capibara' or the class 'approved' with labels 'yes' and 'no'. Many ML systems perform best if the dataset has an approximately equal number of labels per class, and may make mistakes if classes are highly imbalanced. For instance, if 98% of labels for 'approved' are 'yes', the system may simply always output 'yes' without further analysis and report a 98% accuracy in predicting approvals.

The quality dimensions with the largest impact are completeness, feature accuracy and target accuracy. The dimensions uniqueness and target class balance show little impact, and consistent representation has impact as soon as the new representations outweigh the old one.

Liang et al propose a new approach to creating high-quality datasets. Rather than the traditional model-centric approach, where the data set is treated as a given and effort is put mainly in optimizing the system's performance, a data-centric approach should be taken where the data pipeline is continually used to improve the data.[25] As the figure below illustrates, the process has three main steps: data design, data sculpting and model testing. The considerations mentioned in the paper are a valuable recommendation for any organization deploying a data pipeline.

Data design for AI
- Data sourcing
- Data coverage
- Engaging community
- Data documentation

Data sculpting for AI
- Data valuation
- Data programming
- Data assertion
- Data augmentation

Data strategies for model testing
- Data ablation
- Error discovery
- Subgroup bias
- Data stream

Data policies: data agency, privacy and balancing regulation with needs of trustworthy AI

The data-centric approach for high-quality data pipelines (source: Liang et al. 2022)

Confronting and addressing data biases

One of the most pressing challenges in AI today is the presence of biases in data, which can lead to skewed, unfair, and even harmful outcomes. Addressing these biases is not just a technical necessity but an ethical and legal imperative: the AI Act identifies bias as a key risk and risk management therefore must put explicit attention towards combating any potential bias. Bias in an AI system can have many causes, which we will address more generally in chapter 7. In the context of data governance we can identify a few specific sources of bias that are worthy of attention:

❶ **Sample Bias:** This occurs when the input data does not accurately represent the situation that is being modeled. A traffic prediction system trained primarily on urban traffic patterns might not accurately predict traffic in rural areas.

❷ **Association Bias:** This type of bias arises when the system incorrectly links unrelated aspects together. An advertising algorithm might associate buying sports equipment with a specific gender, leading to skewed product recommendations.

❸ **Incompleteness Bias:** This happens when the input data lacks certain crucial information. A property valuation model might not have data on recent infrastructure developments in an area, leading to undervalued property predictions.

④ **Precision Bias:** This bias emerges when an AI's statement or prediction is mistakenly viewed as objective or of significant importance, in particular because its manner of presentation appeared very precise and accurate. A weather prediction tool might forecast a 90,6235% chance of rain, leading an event planner to cancel an outdoor event, only to find the day remains sunny.

⑤ **Prejudice Bias:** This occurs when measurements or inputs are conducted or collected in a biased manner. A hiring tool might favor candidates from certain universities based on historical data, overlooking potentially qualified candidates from lesser-known institutions.

Such biases in datasets can arise from a myriad of sources. Historical prejudices, for instance, can leave lasting imprints on data. If an AI model is trained on historical data that reflects past societal biases, it can inadvertently perpetuate those biases. Skewed data collection methods, where certain groups are overrepresented or underrepresented, can also introduce biases. Additionally, unrepresentative sampling, where the data doesn't accurately reflect the broader population, can lead to models that are biased towards specific subgroups.

Combatting data biases requires a multi-faceted approach. Fairness-enhancing interventions can be employed to adjust models and ensure they make fair decisions across different groups. Adversarial testing, where models are deliberately challenged with data designed to expose biases, can help in identifying blind spots. Furthermore, sourcing data from diverse and representative sources can reduce the chances of biases creeping in. Continuous monitoring and feedback loops, where the outputs of AI models are regularly checked for biases and the models are adjusted accordingly, can also play a pivotal role in ensuring fairness.

Technical Measures for Data Security

Given the above, the imperative to ensure data security and privacy becomes more and more pronounced. While foundational security practices – like robust password protocols, timely software patches, and firewalls – are essential, they do not fully address the unique challenges of data privacy in machine learning contexts. The process of collecting, preprocessing, training, and deploying models introduces multiple unique points of vulnerability.

Adherence to data management standards

> C6. Did you align the AI system with relevant standards or widely adopted protocols for (daily) data management and governance?

Aligning an AI system with relevant standards or widely adopted protocols for data management and governance is paramount to ensuring the system's integrity, reliability, and compliance with best practices. One of the most recognized standards in this domain is the ISO/IEC 27001, which pertains to information security management. This standard provides a systematic approach to managing sensitive company information and ensures that robust security measures are in place to protect data from breaches and unauthorized access.

In addition to adhering to such standards, it's essential to establish a daily protocol for data management within the AI system. A typical protocol might involve routine data audits to identify and rectify any inconsistencies or errors, regular backups to prevent data loss, and periodic reviews of access controls to ensure that only authorized personnel can access sensitive data. This protocol not only ensures the smooth operation of the AI system but also reinforces trust among stakeholders by demonstrating a commitment to data protection and governance best practices.

In the research field of machine learning, many data management protocols have been developed from the perspective of ethical and reproducible experimentation.[26] Their lessons can easily find applications in today's AI environments.

Data processing techniques

Securing data during processing and ensuring data privacy of the persons affected by that data is not just a desire from lawmakers, it's also a technical challenge. Over the years, researchers have created many advanced technologies to foster better security while being able to create AI systems. Let's look at a few:

❶ Differential privacy is a mathematical framework that ensures the results derived from a dataset do not reveal specific information about any individual within that dataset. By introducing calibrated noise to the data or the output of a query, it guarantees that the presence or absence of a single record doesn't significantly affect the outcome. This is particularly crucial when training machine learning models on sensitive datasets, ensuring that the model's predictions don't inadvertently leak individual data points.

❷ Homomorphic encryption is a groundbreaking cryptographic technique that allows computations on encrypted data without requiring decryption first. In the context of machine learning, this means that models can be trained and make predictions on encrypted data, ensuring data privacy throughout the entire processing pipeline. The resultant encrypted output can then be decrypted by the data owner, ensuring that sensitive information remains concealed from potential adversaries, including the model operators.

❸ Federated learning is a decentralized approach to training machine learning models. Instead of centralizing data from various sources into one location, the model is trained at the data source itself, be it a mobile device or a local server. Only model updates or gradients are shared and aggregated centrally, ensuring raw data remains at its source, significantly reducing the risk of data breaches or unauthorized access.

❹ Secure Multi-Party Computation is a cryptographic technique that allows multiple parties to collaboratively compute a function over their inputs while keeping those inputs private. In machine learning, this can be employed to train a model on combined data from multiple sources without any party revealing their individual data. The data remains partitioned, and intermediate computations are encrypted, ensuring data privacy is maintained throughout the collaborative process.

❺ Data masking involves obscuring specific data within a database, rendering it inaccessible for unauthorized users. It ensures that sensitive data remains confidential and is especially useful in development and testing environments. Tokenization, on the other hand, replaces sensitive data with non-sensitive substitutes or tokens. These tokens can then be processed without exposing the underlying data, ensuring that machine learning operations, especially in cloud environments, don't compromise data integrity or privacy.

Data storage measures

Storing data isn't just about finding a place for it; it's about ensuring that this data, whether at rest or in transit, remains inaccessible to unauthorized entities. In this section, we will explore advanced storage solutions that not only house data but also fortify it against potential breaches and unauthorized access.

❶ In the realm of data security, tokenization stands out as a robust method to protect sensitive information. It involves replacing sensitive data elements with non-sensitive equivalents, termed as "tokens." These tokens retain essential data characteristics without disclosing the underlying data value, ensuring that even if a breach occurs, the exposed tokens have no exploitable meaning or value.

❷ Data masking is another pivotal technique that aims to protect the original data. It works by concealing the actual data with altered content, yet the structure remains similar to the original. This ensures that while the data can still be used for testing and development purposes, any unauthorized access will not reveal the true sensitive information.

❸ As data breaches become more sophisticated, the need for advanced protection mechanisms has never been higher. Encrypted databases rise to this challenge by employing encryption techniques to safeguard data when it's at rest. By encrypting the actual data values in a database, unauthorized access will only yield indecipherable content, ensuring data remains confidential and secure.

Data access control

Securing data doesn't end once it's stored. Equally vital is the manner in which this data is accessed and utilized. Access control mechanisms serve as the gatekeepers, ensuring that data is only available to those with the right permissions, thereby preventing misuse or unauthorized access. Three organizational measures are important:

1. Role-Based Access Control (RBAC): **In large organizations, where myriad users require data access, RBAC plays a crucial role. It operates on the principle that not everyone needs access to all data. By assigning roles within the organization, RBAC ensures that individuals can only access data pertinent to their specific role, thereby minimizing the risk of unauthorized data manipulation or exposure.**
2. Attribute-Based Access Control (ABAC): **While RBAC focuses on roles, ABAC takes data access control a notch higher. It defines access levels based on a combination of attributes, such as the user profile, device used, and even the time of access. This granularity ensures a more dynamic and context-aware access control, adapting to various scenarios and requirements.**
3. Audit Trails: **Transparency and accountability are pillars of robust data security. Audit trails provide this by maintaining comprehensive logs of all data access and modifications. This is well understood as a general security measure, but becomes more prevalent in the context of AI systems: the AI Act requires logging (audit trails) of *outputs* of the AI system, allowing reconstruction of potential mistakes and ensuring a paper trail for ensuring and demonstrating compliance with the Act.**

Key takeaways

As we've navigated through the multifaceted landscape of AI systems, GDPR implications, foundation models, intellectual property concerns, data quality, and technical security measures, one thing becomes abundantly clear: the sanctity of data stands at the heart of trustworthy AI. Ensuring data integrity, security, and respect for privacy rights is not just a legal or ethical imperative but a cornerstone for the broader acceptance and success of AI in society.

Now that we've established the importance of good data, let's turn our attention to promoting transparency in AI operations.

6
Emphasizing Transparency in AI Operations

In this chapter, we explore the foundational importance of transparency in building trust and the challenges surrounding its definition. The chapter examines traceability as a means of ensuring accountability, including quality of input and output and the required practices under the AI Act. We further look at the significance of explainability in AI decisions, and the ethical considerations of automated decision-making. The latter subject of course requires an examination of the GDPR and its relationship to the AI Act. We also discuss the pivotal role of communication in bridging the gap between AI systems and users, emphasizing the need for clarity and ethical interactions.

Introduction to Transparency in AI

As is widely recognized, transparency is crucial for building and maintaining users' trust in AI systems.[1] In fact, the concept is the single most common principle in the vast number of ethical guidelines addressing AI on a global level.[2] Yet, there is no agreement on the actual meaning of the term. Some use 'transparency' as the opposite of the well-known "black box" AI, others see transparency as a documentation requirement or refer to the need for traceability in evaluation and decision-making.

The growing need for transparency

In the initial stages of AI development during the mid-20th century, AI systems were relatively simple. Early AI systems, such as rule-based expert systems, were designed with clear, predefined rules. These systems made decisions based on a set of explicit guidelines, making their reasoning processes transparent and interpretable. However, this changed dramatically after the rise of deep learning models, in particular neural networks. Being based on statistical models, they are great in making accurate predictions but do not have any meaningful underlying guidelines or rules to justify them. "The data says so" is an apt summary of their working.

As AI systems began to play crucial roles in sectors like healthcare, finance, and criminal justice, this so-called *black box* issue became more than just a technical challenge.[3]

By the end of this chapter, you'll be able to ...

- Explain the concept of transparency as it applies to AI systems.
- Apply best practices to establish traceability, explainability and communication.
- Address automated decision-making and work with legal limitations.

It raised ethical and legal concerns. The inability to understand why an AI made a particular decision became problematic, especially when these decisions had real-world consequences. Hence the urge for transparency in AI systems.

The "what" and the "how"

Generally speaking, transparency can take two forms: transparency on the *outcome* and transparency on the *process* of getting at that outcome.[4] The first form relates to the clarity and interpretability of the results or decisions produced by an AI system. Stakeholders, especially end-users, often need to understand the "what" behind an AI's decision. For instance, if an AI system denies a loan application, the applicant would want to know the reason for this decision. The concept of "explainable AI" (to be discussed below) relates to this aspect of transparency.

Transparency on the process refers to the clarity in understanding the mechanisms, algorithms, and data that the AI system uses to arrive at its decisions. Knowing the "how" is crucial for developers, regulators, and other stakeholders. For instance, understanding the process can help in identifying biases in the system, ensuring fairness, and making necessary adjustments. This is where documentation becomes key. Registering the entire AI development lifecycle, from data collection to model training and validation, can enhance process transparency. Additionally, using interpretable models or model-agnostic explanation techniques can shed light on the inner workings of complex models.

Three aspects of transparency

Transparency can be broken down further into three aspects:

- ❶ Traceability: Traceability refers to the ability to track the decision-making process of an AI system. This includes understanding the data sets used, the algorithms applied, and the various processes that culminate in the AI system's final decision. By ensuring traceability, we can document and understand the journey of an AI decision, from the initial data input to the final output. This is especially vital when errors or unexpected outcomes arise. Being able to trace back to the root cause allows for corrective measures, continuous improvement, and accountability.
- ❷ Explainability: Explainability is about making the AI's decision-making process understandable to humans. It's not enough for an AI system to make a decision; it must also be able to explain its decision in a manner that is clear and comprehensible, especially when its decisions have significant impacts on individuals or society. This can be challenging, especially with complex models like deep neural networks, often termed as "black boxes" due to their opaque nature. However, the goal is to strike a

balance between the accuracy of a model and its explainability, ensuring that users, regulators, and stakeholders can understand and trust the AI's decisions.

- **Communication:** Communication is about being forthright about the AI system's capabilities and, equally importantly, its limitations. Every AI system, no matter how advanced, has its strengths and weaknesses. Communicating these openly ensures that users are aware of what the system can and cannot do. This includes informing users when they are interacting with an AI (as opposed to a human) and providing clear instructions and disclaimers about the system's use. Open communication builds informed trust, where users are not just relying on the AI blindly but are aware of its scope and potential pitfalls.

In the following sections, we will delve deeper into each of these elements, addressing specific questions and providing actionable insights to ensure the transparent and trustworthy deployment of AI systems.

Traceability: Ensuring Accountability in AI Systems

Traceability is key to the principle of accountability. This principle, further discussed in chapter 9, means that every decision made by an AI system can be attributed to a specific process or action within the system. By ensuring traceability, we are essentially creating a documented pathway that can be followed to understand how a particular AI decision was reached. This not only bolsters confidence in the system but also ensures that when things go awry, there's a clear trail to follow, pinpointing where and why a mistake occurred.

Traceable lifecycle

> D1. Did you put in place measures that address the traceability of the AI system during its entire lifecycle?

The lifecycle of an AI system is intricate, and traceability plays a pivotal role at every stage. From the initial data gathering to the final decision output, each step should be rigorously documented. This includes the processes of data labeling and the specific algorithms employed. Such comprehensive documentation ensures that if an AI system's decision is called into question, there's a clear record of how the decision was derived.

For high-risk AI, this is a legal requirement: technical documentation must be drawn up prior to release of the AI system, and be of such quality that compliance with the

Act's requirements can be easily demonstrated. This documentation should include at the very least:

① The AI system's intended purpose, the person/s developing the system the date and the version of the system;
② How the AI system interacts or can be used to interact with hardware or software that is not part of the AI system itself, where applicable;
③ The versions of relevant software or firmware and any requirement related to version update;
④ The description of all forms in which the AI system is placed on the market or put into service;
⑤ The description of hardware on which the AI system is intended to run;
⑥ Where the AI system is a component of products, photographs or illustrations showing external features, marking and internal layout of those products;
⑦ Instructions of use for the user and, where applicable, installation instructions;

This documentation can take the form of so-called model cards, more on which in chapter 9.

Input data quality

> D1a. Did you put in place measures to continuously assess the quality of the input data to the AI system?

Of particular attention is a continuous assessment of the quality of input data. It's not just about having vast amounts of data; the quality of this data is equally crucial. Regular automated quality assessments can help in identifying issues like missing values, data gaps, breaks in data supply, or even instances where the data is erroneous or mismatched in format. For instance, consider sensor calibration, a process that refines sensor performance by rectifying inaccuracies in sensor outputs. In legal processes, an issue may be that feedback on decisions is not obtained until years later, when an appeal or objection is finally confirmed by the courts.

Several best practices in this area include:

① **Data Validation Frameworks:** Frameworks like TensorFlow Data Validation and the Python Pandera library generate descriptive statistics, detect anomalies, and ensure data consistency from datasets. This can greatly contribute to adequate data governance (chapter 5) and help traceability.
② **Monitoring Data Drift:** Data drift (also known as covariate shift) is the concept that distribution of values within features may shift over time.[5] For instance, a spam detection filter trained on email from the previous decade will not perform well on today's AI-crafted unsolicited e-mail.

- **Data Versioning:** Data versioning permits keeping track of different versions of datasets. This allows for reproducibility and easier identification of when and how data might have changed. Such a process would typically be part of what's called MLOps or machine learning operations.[6]
- **Regular Data Audits:** A periodic review of data sources and collection methods to ensure they remain relevant and reliable. We refer back to chapter 5 on data governance.
- **Data Annotation Quality Control:** For AI systems that require annotated data (supervised and semi-supervised AI), quality control measures should be in place for the annotation process. This could include periodic reviews, inter-annotator agreement checks, or using multiple annotators for the same data. As with item 3, this would be part of a good MLOps setup.
- **Historical Data Backtesting:** Regular testing of the AI system historical data may reveal inconsistencies, indicating the need for further steps to address quality and relevance of the input data.
- **Documentation and Metadata:** Comprehensive documentation of data sources, collection methods, preprocessing steps, and any known issues or limitations can help in quickly identifying potential data quality concerns.

Tracing back decisions

> D1b. Can you trace back which data was used by the AI system to make a certain decision(s) or recommendation(s)?
>
> D1c. Can you trace back which AI model or rules led to the decision(s) or recommendation(s) of the AI system?

Traceability doesn't end with input data. It's equally vital to be able to trace back the specific data that influenced a particular AI decision or recommendation. This involves understanding which AI model or rules were at play and how they interacted with the data to arrive at a conclusion. This is particularly relevant under the AI Act as well as the GDPR, both of which require explainability of decisions – which just isn't possible if the data and model used is not available in the form used at the time.

The work of Mora-Cantallops et al provides a good review of available tooling for traceability, including backtracing of data.[7] A common measure is to attach metadata referring to source data to every step of the AI process. Unfortunately, this requires a lot of work as most AI pipelines are not designed by default to accommodate this, and may even discard the metadata as irrelevant noise.

A related best practice again is versioning: ensure that the introduction of new datasets or models is clearly separate from earlier models, using names or sequence numbers to allow easy identification. Using the practices from the previous subsection, maintain logs that record every decision made by the AI, the data it used, the model version, and other relevant parameters. This creates a clear audit trail.

Output quality

> D1d. Did you put in place measures to continuously assess the quality of the output(s) of the AI system?

Furthermore, the output of the AI system should also be under continuous scrutiny. Standard automated assessments can ensure that prediction scores align with expected ranges and anomalies in outputs are promptly detected. If an anomaly is identified, it's crucial to reevaluate the input data that led to the unexpected output, ensuring that the system remains reliable and trustworthy.

Three key principles underscore the importance of output quality:[8]

1. Repeatability: This refers to the ability to obtain consistent measurements under identical conditions. In the context of AI systems, it implies that an investigator can consistently reproduce a particular prediction or other output, using the same procedures and systems, across multiple trials.
2. Replicability: This principle emphasizes that a different group, given the same experimental setup, should be able to achieve results from the AI system with the stated precision.
3. Reproducibility: Perhaps the most stringent, this principle dictates that even with a different team and a different experimental setup, consistent measurements should be achievable. For AI systems, it signifies that an independent group should be able to obtain the same results from the same source data, even if they develop their tools and artifacts from scratch.

At the very least, an AI Act-compliant system should follow the principle of repeatability. The other principles are best practices to ensure high quality operations.

Output of generative AI

A particular concern with AI output is that of generative AI. As the quality of such system rapidly increases, it becomes harder and harder to distinguish AI-generated content and real-world images, audio or movies. This is a cause for concern, especially when dealing with newsworthy events; the issues of fake news, disinformation and so-called deepfakes have been widely discussed.[9] Various solutions have been proposed, all of which boil down to watermarking generative AI output with invisible yet indelible

Chapter 6 – Emphasizing Transparency in AI Operations

markers to allow detection, even when the image is significantly modified.[10]

One such initiative, with more than 1200 companies behind, it is Content Credentials, introduced by image editing software giant Adobe. Content Credentials (CC) serve as tamper-evident metadata, allowing creators to embed additional information about themselves and the actions taken on content directly into that content. The information is tamperproof and hard to remove. What's more, CC are also stored using Adobe cloud services and thus are traceable even if an image is itself manipulated to remove it. The below image provides an example. The CC are displayed on the right of the image as a summary. Examination reveals that the image has been edited using AI tools, and that certain assets (e.g. a lamppost) have been imported from elsewhere. This is not to say that the image was manipulated for nefarious purposes; CC is a neutral scheme designed to allow identification of modifications. Human judgment is still required to determine the authenticity of the image and its usefulness in e.g. legal proceedings or information gathering.

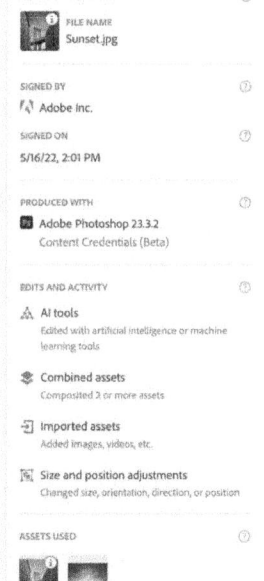

A sample image with Content Credentials (source: Adobe)

Logging practices

> D1e. Did you put adequate logging practices in place to record the decision(s) or recommendation(s) of the AI system?

By maintaining a detailed record of the AI system's decisions and recommendations, an AI provider creates a robust framework that not only enhances transparency but also serves as a foundation for future improvements and refinements. The practice of logging is an integral component of software engineering and system administration. When done right, logging provides a clear, chronological account of events, aiding in debugging, monitoring, and understanding the behavior of a system.

Best practices in logging emphasize the importance of clarity, consistency, and relevance.[11] Logs should be clear and concise, avoiding verbosity that can clutter and obfuscate the essential information. Consistency in log format ensures that logs can be easily parsed and analyzed, while relevance ensures that only pertinent information is logged, avoiding the pitfalls of information overload. Furthermore, sensitive information should never be logged, ensuring that user data and system secrets remain secure.

There is no single standard for logging quality, as it depends highly on the application, its intended purpose and expected risks what information should be logged. However, common logging frameworks and libraries are widely available for almost every programming language or development environment. Examples include the log4j Java and Logrus Golang logging frameworks. Other languages, such as the Python language widely used in machine learning, have built-in logging capabilities. Logging frameworks specific to machine learning environments are also available, a common example is TensorBoard.

Logging is not just a good software development practice, it's the law: the AI Act explicitly requires high-risk AI systems to have state of the art logging facilities, enabling the monitoring of operations and events that may pose a risk to fundamental rights. Research on best practices for logging machine learning operations is still ongoing.[12]

Explainability: Making AI Understandable

> D2. Did you explain the decision(s) of the AI system to the users?

Explainability is often cited as a key factor for adoption of AI systems in a wide range of contexts. This includes the legal context: the GDPR contains a right to obtain *"meaningful information about the logic involved"* – commonly interpreted as a "right to an explanation". Yet, defining what an explanation is remains a still open research question.[13] The AI Act nor the GDPR provide concrete guidance in this regard, other than stipulating that the explanation should be understandable and in clear language.

Balancing technical explainability and human decisions

Explainability of a machine learning model is usually inverse to its prediction accuracy – the higher the prediction accuracy, the lower the model explainability.[14] This fundamental issue is illustrated in the figure below, which is based on DARPA research.

For instance, decision trees have an excellent degree of explainability but exhibit the worst prediction accuracy among the listed learning techniques. In the other extreme, Deep Learning methods are better in predictive capacity than any other learning methods but they are least likely to be explicable.

The requirement for explainability has been criticized as being overly limiting to innovation. For instance, in the field of credit scoring in the USA there is a stringent legal requirement that credit risk predictions must be maximally accurate and come with the highest transparency and auditability. This leaves developers with only very simple predictive models, which actually harms the quality of predictions.[15] In the medical field, it is generally accepted that evidence is needed *that* medication or treatment works but not *why* that medication works. From this, arguably explainability in medical AI would be unnecessary if the effectiveness of the AI can be proven through standard clinical trials.[16] A more general criticism is that an AI outcome may be based on millions of features taken in combination. It is then simply unrealistic to expect a comprehensible and easy to follow explanation in layman's terms.

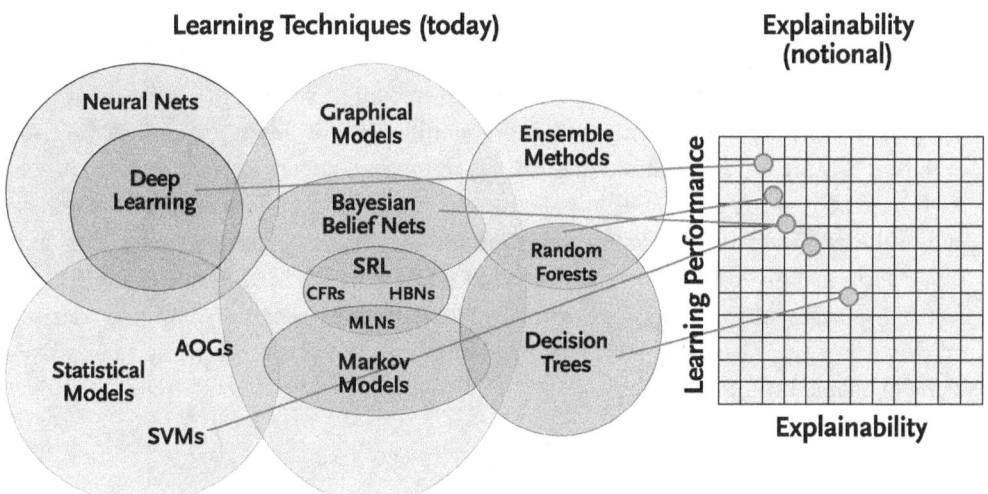

Explainability versus quality (source: Xu et al., 2019)

Still, this does not help to answer the question of what constitutes an 'explanation'. Neither the GDPR nor the AI Act define this term. Psychologists and social scientists however have long investigated how humans evaluate explanations. The consensus is that choosing one explanation over another is often an arbitrary choice heavily influenced by cognitive biases and heuristics. The primary criterion appears to be whether the explanation helps to understand the underlying cause.[17] This is not sufficient: for instance, humans are more likely to accept explanations that are consistent with their prior beliefs, and prefer explanations that are simpler and more generalizable.[18] It therefore seems likely that each individual AI system's output must be evaluated on expected character and level of explanation.

Explaining Deep Learning

As noted in chapter 5, datasets used to train machine learning (ML) models contain a variety of features. For motor vehicles, features could for instance be number of wheels, engine power, maximum speed, and so on. In a loan application systems, factors such as past creditworthiness, savings and checking account balance would be features from which the system derives its decision-making model.

However, it's key to remember that a ML system does not derive a rule-based decision-making model: it creates a probabilistic model based on patterns and correlations found in the data. This means that while the system might recognize that individuals with higher savings balances are generally more creditworthy, this is not used as a *rule* or weighted against other rules. Instead, the data items in the set are divided into groups based on patterns spotted in the data – correlations, in statistical terms.

"Correlation does not imply causation" is an old maxim in statistics. The fact that two features go together does not mean that one is the cause of the other, or that the two even have a mutual relationship. For example, in the well-known *German Credit* dataset used for teaching basic statistics, one feature of loan applicant data relates to whether or not the applicant has a landline telephone.[19] This feature correlates well with the expectation that the loan will be paid back, but no human at a bank would ever cite this fact as a relevant reason to approve or reject a loan. Nevertheless, an AI system trained on this dataset will certainly spot the correlation and thus be more likely to approve loans to people having landlines.

XAI: Breaking the black box

The term "black box" and its synonym *opacity* have become synonymous with models that operate without offering clear insights into their decision-making processes. It is clear that under the AI Act, a high-risk AI system cannot be a black box. In the literature, several approaches have been proposed to add transparency to machine learning systems. This field of study has become known as "XAI", short for "eXplainable AI".[20]

- **Model Simplification:** Using simpler models that are inherently more interpretable, such as linear regression or decision trees. While these might not always achieve the same accuracy as complex models, they offer more transparency. In case the actual

AI system's and the simpler model's outcomes deviate significantly, human intervention may be needed to resolve the matter.
- Feature Visualization: Techniques that visualize the importance of different features in the model's decision-making process. However, as mentioned earlier, feature importance doesn't always equate to human reasoning. This approach therefore is only usable when feature importance is sufficient for transparency purposes.
- Post-hoc Explanations: Much research has been done on methods that provide explanations after the AI has made a decision. Techniques like LIME (Local Interpretable Model-agnostic Explanations) or SHAP (SHapley Additive exPlanations) fall into this category. The general approach is the identification of key features and their relevance to the output categorisation. For instance, in text sentiment classification LIME may highlight words that correlate strongly with the reported sentiment and words that strongly point to another sentiment.

A popular technique for post-hoc explanations is LIME. This system was introduced in 2016 as a general technique to add explanations to individual predictions.[21] The below image visually illustrates how LIME adds explanations to an image classifier. The original image on the left was classified as a 'frog'. LIME creates variations of the image called "perturbed instances", as seen in the middle. For each of these instances the original system is asked to make a new classification with probability. The relevance of each section is thus derived and a weighted conclusion is made. In this case, the conclusion is that the frog face in top middle of the image was the most pertinent factor in making the determination.

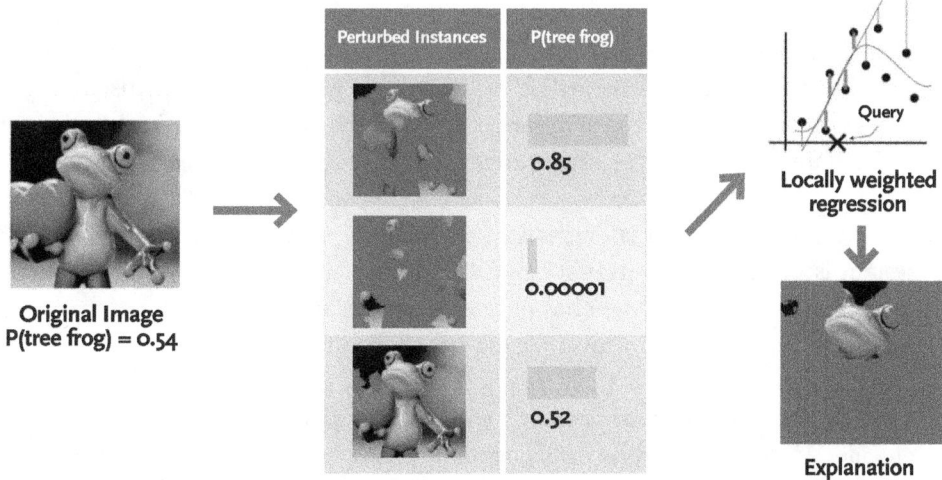

A demonstration of LIME in use on an image classifier (source: Ribeiro et al., 2016)

Post-hoc explanations, by design, offer insights into the AI's decision-making process after the fact. This approach is particularly beneficial in scenarios where the AI model is complex and not inherently interpretable. By translating the AI's decisions into natural language, post-hoc explanations make the outcomes more accessible and relatable to users, regardless of their technical expertise. This fosters a sense of transparency and can alleviate concerns or skepticism users might have about the AI's decisions.

However, there are several risks and downsides to relying solely on post-hoc explanations:

1. Over-reliance on Simplicity: While simplifying data-driven decisions into natural language is beneficial, there's a risk of oversimplifying the explanation to the point where it no longer accurately represents the AI's decision process. This can lead to misunderstandings or misconceptions about how the AI operates.
2. Potential for Misleading Explanations: Post-hoc explanations are generated based on the model's outputs, but these might not always capture the true underlying reasons for a decision. There's a risk that the explanation provided might be plausible but not entirely accurate.
3. Template Structure: Post-hoc explanations may follow a stringent format, and thus be very similar in structure and approach. This may cause the reader to gloss over the explanation and fail to notice subtle differences in a particular case.
4. Temporal Limitations: Since post-hoc explanations are generated after the AI's decision, they might not be timely enough for scenarios where real-time understanding is crucial. This can be problematic in situations where immediate human intervention is required based on the AI's decision.
5. Overconfidence in AI Decisions: While post-hoc explanations can enhance trust, they might also lead users to place undue confidence in the AI's decisions without critically evaluating the rationale provided. A well-known phenomenon for instance is that detailed textual explanations are seen as a sign of *competence of the AI system,* and therefore ignored as a specific justification.

A more general point of criticism against post-hoc explanations is that often the AI system is used in an adversarial context. Usually, a user who requests a decision or evaluation from the AI system has different interests than the provider of that system, such as with a loan applicant and a bank, a shopper and mall security or a patient and a healthcare provider. In each of these scenarios, the user seeks a favorable outcome, while the provider aims for accuracy, efficiency, and risk mitigation. It is not in the provider's interest to provide explanations that help users to their own disadvantage, e.g. by revealing that the application was denied due to the user's ethnicity.[22] This problem is hard to solve.

An alternative approach may be to offer explanations in the form of counterfactuals: "You were denied a loan because your annual income was €30,000 and your age is below 27. If your income had been €45,000 and your credit score above 0.65, you would have been offered a loan." This type of explanation avoids translating specific and perhaps hard-to-grasp features and their interaction into a complete explanation.[23] The counterfactual indicates what went wrong, what was missing and how this could (in theory) be rectified. Key to a good counterfactual is to present the smallest change that would lead to the desired result. Calculating a satisfactory counterfactual is technically feasible, and while the approach is new, initial results appear promising.[24]

User surveys

> D3. Do you continuously survey the users if they understand the decision(s) of the AI system?

Continuously surveying users to gauge their understanding of the AI system's decisions presents an alternative approach to post-hoc explanations. The focus on real-time feedback helps to ensure that the AI system's decisions are not just technically correct but also intuitively understood by its users. If users consistently indicate that they do not understand or trust the AI's decisions, it's a clear sign that the system's explanations, whether they are post-hoc or real-time, are not effective.

By continuously collecting feedback, organizations can dynamically adjust and refine the AI's explanatory mechanisms, ensuring that they align more closely with human intuition and reasoning.For instance, in a medical diagnosis AI tool, if patients consistently indicate through surveys that they don't understand why a particular treatment was recommended, the healthcare provider can take steps to improve the system's explanatory capabilities or provide additional training to medical staff to better communicate the AI's decisions.

However, there are challenges to this approach. Continuously surveying users can be seen as intrusive or burdensome, leading to survey fatigue. There's also the risk of receiving skewed feedback if only a subset of users, perhaps those with strong positive or negative feelings, choose to respond. Despite these challenges, when implemented thoughtfully, continuous user surveys can serve as a valuable tool in the quest for more understandable and trustworthy AI systems.

Transparency and Automated Decision Making

The AI Act takes a slightly different approach: products must meet pre-set conformity requirements during their lifetime, and providers must have compliance and risk assessment procedures in place.

Types of decision-making

The process of automated decision-making can be divided into four main categories based on the nature of human involvement:[26]

1. **Supporting:** Providing information to a human decision maker to help them make a decision about a case, but where they are just one source of information amongst others under consideration. This is clearly not 'solely' automated decision-making, unless the human were to blindly adopt the recommendation from the supportive AI system. A simple trick to avoid the latter is to not include a specific conclusion.
2. **Positive Triaging:** New cases are profiled and categorized. The categorization determines the future decision pathway that the case continues along: some category can be automatically processed, while other(s) require human review. The former category would typically constitute the 'positive', 'easy' or 'standard' cases, such as loan applications that clearly meet all requirements or an airplane passenger raising no red flags. Passengers that do raise flags are then selected for human review.
3. **Full Triaging:** Similar to positive triaging, but with only the unclear, low confidence or otherwise hard to automate cases being presented to humans. In the loan application example, both the applications that clearly meet the requirements and those that are clearly deficient are automatically processed.
4. **Summarizing:** Here the human decision-making occurs prior to the automated processing. One or more human decisions or assessments are recorded as structured data, and that data is summarized or consolidated automatically to generate an overall score or assessment which is used to make a decision. For instance, a teacher can review essays and assign scores on topics such as spelling, consistency and quality of work. The automated system would use the teacher's scores to create a full and motivated review for the student, including calculating the final grade.

Addressing automated decision making under the GDPR

In legal circles, the concept of automated decision-making is often connected to the GDPR, which contains a long-standing provision against automated decision-making. According to its article 22, humans "shall have the right not to be subject to a decision based solely on automated processing, including profiling, which produces legal effects concerning him or her or similarly significantly affects him or her." Note the word 'solely': if there is a certain level of human oversight, the decision is not 'solely' automated. However, this must be more than a token human gesture such as rubberstamping the computer's recommendation. The European Data Protection Board uses the term "meaningful human involvement".[27]

Further, the decision must be produce legal effects or otherwise significant effects. A legal effect is one that affects one's legal rights, e.g. by cancelling a contract, denying access to elections or refusing admission to enter the country. This definition is somewhat muddy – is refusing to enter into a contract a legal effect, considering that no one has a right to demand a contract? For this type of case, the second prong of the article is relevant: denying a contract application has a similarly significant effect to cancelling a contract and is therefore also covered by article 22. The effect must be significant and long-lasting. For instance, denying an employment opportunity is covered, but a profile-based decision to hide certain content on social networks is not.

A second GDPR demand is that the person subject to such a decision is provided with 'meaningful information about the logic involved' (art. 13 GDPR). This corresponds to the transparency requirements of the AI Act discussed above. The AI Act has a similar requirement: persons faced with AI-generated decisions must get a detailed explanation. This means an application of the facts and circumstances to this particular case, not just a general explanation as to what factors would be relevant. This creates an interesting interaction between the GDPR and the AI Act.

The prohibition on automated decision making is not absolute, however. The GDPR has certain exceptions, such as where the automated decision is necessary for the performance of a contract or where other regulations permit it. In the Schufa case (C-634/21) the European Court of Justice applied a low bar for "automated decision making". Automatically determining a risk factor (in that case: a credit score) which is used by other parties more or less without further analysis is sufficient. While the credit score was provided by credit risk assessor Schufa to other parties (loan agencies) who acted upon it, the ECJ held that it was Schufa itself that provided the decision – the credit score as such.

Automated decision-making under the AI Act

The AI Act does not declare automated decision making as such a high-risk endeavour, with a few exceptions. The main exception is when the decision is based on profiling. And generally speaking, decision-making is high-risk if it occurs within the realm of judicial authorities or law enforcement. Indirectly, decision making plays a role in various other high-risk use cases, such as evaluating potential hires or denying benefits to citizens.

The AI Act confirms that in such a case, the AI would still be subject to the GDPR's requirements even when all the AI Act's own requirements have been fulfilled. This also applies when the AI system does not qualify as high-risk yet takes solely automated decisions, although it is harder to imagine what type of decision this would be given the requirement of a "legal right" being affected or a "similar significant effect". Conversely, an AI system where the automated decision-making has been amended to involve meaningful human involvement may still qualify as high-risk.

Decision-making and the Platform Work Directive

Complementing the GDPR and in parallel to the AI Act, the European Commission is working on a Proposal for a Platform Work Directive (2021/0414) which aims among others to promote fairness, transparency and accountability in algorithmic management in platform work.[28] Its provisions on algorithmic management are supposed to cover both the "automated decision making" of the GDPR, as well as "automated monitoring systems which are used to monitor, supervise or evaluate the work performance of platform workers through electronic means". It provides various specific requirements on transparency, appeal to a human review and an explanation of the underlying criteria.

The legal position of the Platform Work Directive (PWD) versus the AI Act is yet unclear. It seems logical that, in case of inconsistencies, the PWD would prevail given its specific area of application, but in the European legal systems Regulations (such as the AI Act) override national legislation and Directives (such as the PWD).[29] The status of the PWD is currently unclear, after a negative vote in the Council of Ministers. It will take at least until 2025 before a new draft will be available.

In all these categories, there is some form of automated decision-making at play. Generally, this occurs only for the 'easy' or 'clear' cases, where the decision seems favourable to the humans involved: receive a loan, be allowed on the plane, receive a passing grade. This may however be an oversimplification: an application for a building permit is not merely a question of meeting certain requirements, as such a permit would also affect the neighbours. Automatic approval of such a permit would therefore put them at a disadvantage without meaningful human intervention. For this reason, the GDPR does not limit its restriction on automated decision-making against only *negative* decisions.

Another concern with solely automating straightforward cases and delegating complex ones to humans is the potential for bias. By quickly processing the 'simple' cases using automated decisions, there's a risk that 'simple' might inadvertently align with specific ethnic or socio-economic factors. For instance, an AI system may be optimized to streamline job applications from candidates who don't add special requests or explanations. This would unintentionally favor fully able job applicants over those who might need wheelchair access or other accommodations, overlooking equally qualified candidates with disabilities. Additionally, when humans consistently handle only ambiguous or challenging cases, they might develop a skewed perception, assuming that most of these cases have negative outcomes since they always appear doubtful.

Communication: Bridging the Gap between AI and Users

The final aspect of transparency to be discussed is communication. AI systems are very novel and users are generally expected to be unfamiliar with them. The onus therefore is on AI producers, distributors and deployers to provide the information users need to be able to work with the systems.

Recognizing the AI Interface

> D4. In cases of interactive AI systems, do you communicate to users that they are interacting with an AI system instead of a human?

Distinguishing between human and machine interactions is crucial, as already discussed in earlier chapters. This distinction ensures that users can set appropriate expectations regarding the nature and limitations of the responses they receive. For instance, while chatting with customer support, knowing that one is communicating with an AI can help users tailor their queries more precisely, understanding that they might not pick up on nuances or emotions in the same way a human would.

Clarity on purpose and criteria

> D5. Did you establish mechanisms to inform users about the purpose, criteria, and limitations of the decision(s) generated by the AI system?

Every AI system is designed with a specific purpose in mind, and it operates based on certain criteria. Users have a right to understand the primary objective of the AI they're interacting with. For example, a recommendation engine on a streaming platform aims to suggest shows or movies based on a user's viewing history and preferences. Being aware of this can help users appreciate why certain content is being recommended to them and can guide them in refining their preferences if needed.

The AI Act puts the 'intended purpose' of AI systems front and center. Any testing and risk evaluation is done with the intended purpose in mind, and the intended purpose must be disclosed in the documentation (see next section). The Act defines this term as "the use for which an AI system is intended by the provider, including the specific context and conditions of use" and confirms that what it says on the box is what the system is supposed to do – the small print cannot change that.

Highlighting the benefits

> D5a. Did you communicate the benefits of the AI system to users?

While AI systems bring numerous advantages, it's essential to communicate these benefits clearly to the users. This not only fosters trust but also ensures that users can make the most of the technology. For instance, a predictive text feature can speed up typing and improve accuracy, but users might only fully utilize it if they understand its potential benefits.

One of the most effective ways to communicate the benefits of an AI system is through interactive demonstrations. By allowing users to engage with the AI in real-time, they can directly experience its advantages. For instance, a photo editing software with AI-enhanced features could offer a side-by-side comparison where users can upload an image and see the before and after effects of the AI's enhancements. This hands-on approach can be more impactful than merely reading about the benefits.

Addressing technical limitations

> D5b. Did you communicate the technical limitations and potential risks of the AI system to users, such as its level of accuracy and/ or error rates?

As part of the transparency obligations, the AI Act requires producers of high-risk AI to disclose the levels of accuracy and the relevant accuracy metrics of their systems in documentation. The previous chapter goes into more detail on the various options and trade-offs. What's important is to also look beyond the metrics as such: a 98% accuracy in voice recognition software is great, but does that apply across all languages or only American-accent English?

Training and disclaimers

> D5c. Did you provide appropriate training material and disclaimers to users on how to adequately use the AI system?

Providing users with adequate training materials and clear disclaimers can ensure that they know how to interact with the AI optimally. For instance, a medical diagnostic AI tool might be highly efficient, but without proper training on inputting patient data correctly, its predictions might be off. The system can also caution users against over-relying on the AI and remind them to use their judgment in critical situations.

The term 'disclaimer' may call up the image of small print written by a lawyer to address a variety of situations. It is well-known that such disclaimers have little to no practical effect. Disclaimers should be user-centric: they should help the user if and when they approach problematic situations. Sensitive content warnings on social networks are a prime example of user-centric disclaimers. These alert users about potentially distressing content, such as graphic images or discussions on sensitive topics. By giving users a heads-up, they can choose whether or not to engage with the content, ensuring they have control over their digital experience. In an AI system, such a warning can serve to alert the user that he or she is about to generate graphic or otherwise sensitive outputs.

Another effective use of disclaimers is the mandatory acknowledgment before accessing specific features. For example, software applications with advanced functionalities might present a warning that requires users to click "I Understand" before proceeding. This ensures that users are aware of the potential risks or complexities of the feature they're about to use. In an AI system this could be used when the user requests an action or output that would exceed the intended use of the AI system.

Moreover, tutorial pop-ups in applications can also be seen as a form of disclaimer. They guide users through new features, ensuring they understand the functionality and potential implications before diving in. If the user goes too fast, the action could be refused and the user redirected to an earlier step or simpler procedure. This proactive approach not only educates users but also reduces the likelihood of misuse or unintended actions.

Clarity out of the box: the CE logo

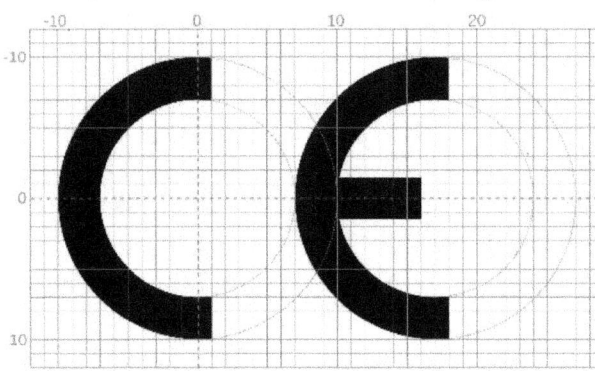

The AI Act is part of the New Legislative Framework of the EU, which aims to improve the internal market and boost the quality of conformity assessments. The old Conformité Européenne (CE) marking, which translates to "European Conformity" is given a new life. Since the 1980s, this distinctive symbol signifies a product's compliance with European Union (EU) health, safety, and environmental protection standards and thus is an early example of transparency, the subject of this chapter.

The AI Act applies the CE logo into the domain of AI systems. Providers of high-risk AI systems must undertake a conformity assessment, compile a technical dossier with all relevant documentation, and sign an EU Declaration of Conformity. Only after this step can the CE logo be affixed to the system – and without the logo, the system may not be deployed in the European Economic Area. This way, the European citizens' trust in the CE marking can also apply to the use of high-risk AI systems. The advantage of the marking for producers, importers and distributors of AI systems is that they enjoy the freedom of movement; Member States should not create unjustified obstacles to the placing on the market or putting into service of high-risk AI systems that comply with the AI Act and bear the CE marking.

Key takeaways

We have seen the paramount importance of transparency in fostering trust and ethical interactions. We've dissected the intricacies of traceability, the nuances of explainability, and the profound implications of automated decision-making. Furthermore, the emphasis on clear communication highlighted the necessity of distinguishing between human and AI interactions, ensuring users are well-informed and can set appropriate expectations. These takeaways are foundational in understanding the ethical deployment of AI systems. Next, we'll look at how AI can be fair, diverse, and non-discriminatory.

Chapter 6 – Emphasizing Transparency in AI Operations

7

Fostering Fairness, Diversity, and Non-Discrimination

Chapter 7 – Fostering Fairness, Diversity, and Non-Discrimination

The quest for fairness, diversity, and non-discrimination stands at the forefront of ethical considerations. Ensuring fairness and diversity involves both substantive and procedural approaches. This chapter will review robust fairness measures and explain the importance of diversity and how to ensure it. Further, we will review the imperative of accessibility and the principles of Universal Design, fostering AI systems that are universally usable and inclusive. By prioritizing inclusivity and engaging with diverse stakeholders, we can pave the way for AI systems that are not only efficient but also ethically sound and universally beneficial.

Introduction to Fairness, Diversity, and Non-Discrimination in AI

Fairness is paramount in the development and deployment of AI systems. While interpretations of fairness vary, it encompasses both substantive and procedural dimensions. Substantively, fairness mandates an equitable distribution of benefits and costs, ensuring freedom from bias, discrimination, and stigmatization. Procedurally, decisions by AI should be contestable, with clear accountability and explainable processes. Let's start with a closer look at these concepts.

The imperative of fairness

In the context of AI, the term 'fairness' has its roots in statistics. Statistical fairness exists when an AI system's outcomes do not disproportionately favor or disadvantage any subgroup of a dataset based on attributes that are independent of the selection criterion.[1] For example, in the context of creditworthiness a statistical model would be called unfair if its predictions were influenced by a person's gender or ethnicity rather than solely their financial history and current financial status, as such features have no relevance in such an analysis. However, in a study analyzing the prevalence

By the end of this chapter, you'll be able to ...
- Understand and implement fairness measures.
- Prioritize accessibility and inclusivity.
- Apply the principles of Universal Design in creating inclusive and accessible AI systems.
- Engage and collaborate with stakeholders.

of certain genetic diseases, ethnicity would be a relevant selection criterion due to the known genetic variations and predispositions among different populations.

In society, fairness is a fundamental right: the equitable treatment of all individuals regardless of their inherent or acquired characteristics, ensuring that every person has equal access to opportunities and resources, and is protected from unjust discrimination, bias, or prejudice in all spheres of life. In Europe, these values are reflected in art. 21 of the Charter and art. 14 of the European Convention on Human Rights. The AI Act and the Guidelines recognize fairness as a building block for trustworthy AI: a fair AI system fosters trust among its users, promotes equitable outcomes, and paves the way for a more inclusive digital future.

The concept of 'bias'

Discussions on fairness go hand in hand with the concept of 'bias'. Again, this term originates from the field of statistics, where it refers to systematic errors in estimates or inferences.[2] Bias occurs when a model's predictions consistently deviate from the actual values it's trying to estimate. For instance, if a machine learning model consistently underestimates the wear on a car tire, it exhibits bias. Common forms of bias in statistical models include:

- ❶ Measurement bias: Arises when data is consistently measured incorrectly. This could be due to faulty equipment or human error. In the car tire example, this could be a defective sensor that fails to count one in ten wheel revolutions.
- ❷ Sampling bias: Occurs when the sample collected is not representative of the entire population. For instance, if the car tire data is obtained from measurements in taxis, this would not be representative of the entire population of car drivers.
- ❸ Model bias: Introduced when the assumptions made by a model do not align with the real-world data. For example, if the car tire model assumes that tire wear is solely based on distance driven and neglects factors like road conditions or driving style, it would exhibit model bias by not accurately predicting wear in scenarios with frequent hard braking or rough terrains.
- ❹ Confirmation bias: This occurs when data is selectively chosen, consciously or unconsciously, to confirm a pre-existing belief or hypothesis. For instance, if a researcher believes that car owners would obviously swap tires according to the manufacturer's recommended driving distance, they might be inclined to ignore measurements that exceed such recommendation.
- ❺ Selection bias: This type of bias arises when the data used to train a model is not representative of the broader population. For example, if a tire wear estimation model is trained only on data from cars driven in summer conditions, it might not perform well when estimating wear for tires used in winter conditions.

The difference between sampling and selection bias in particular can be subtle. As an example, if the car tire model only sampled cars from a single neighborhood, it would exhibit a sampling bias if that neighborhood has unique driving conditions not representative of the entire city. In contrast, the model would exhibit selection bias if all all car owners in the city were invited to participate in the data gathering, but only infrequent drivers chose to respond and participate (e.g. because the date and time of the data gathering was particularly inconvenient for frequent drivers). In this case, the voluntary participation of a specific group with distinct driving habits would skew the results, making them not representative of the average car owner in the city.

Bias and discrimination in AI and algorithms

In everyday language, 'bias' is often equated with 'discrimination', which refers to the unjust or prejudicial treatment of individuals based on attributes like race, age, or gender. It's important to note that the term 'discrimination' carries a heavy connotation, suggesting malicious intent or hate towards certain groups. Usage of this term can therefore derail discussions, as the vast majority of AI developers and businesspeople might feel unjustly accused and act defensively.[3] The term 'bias' is perceived as more neutral.

That's not to say AI systems never exhibit forms of bias that negatively affect groups of people.[4] In fact the opposite is true. Gender biases have been identified in word embeddings in natural language processing systems, e.g. associating male terms more closely with career-oriented words and female terms with family-oriented words.[5] Facial recognition systems often have difficulty recognizing non-white skin, notably Google Photos mistakenly labeling African American faces as "gorillas".[6] Algorithmically chosen job advertisements often present higher-paying jobs to men rather than women.[7] And the list goes on.

The potential for bias in AI was starkly highlighted by the 2016 COMPAS controversy. That year investigative journalism collective ProPublica revealed that an algorithm used by U.S. courts for reoffender risk assessment for probationary release was found to be biased against African-American defendants.[8] For most of the general public, as well as most politicians, this was the first time the real-life consequences of a highly complex technologies were laid bare like this. Ever since, any application of AI in judicial and legal systems has earned a heightened focus on ensuring fairness and eliminating biases. Next to the general prohibitions on discrimination, fairness in data processing in particular is enshrined in article 8 of the European Charter of Fundamental Rights and article 5 of the GDPR.[9]

Inclusive engineering

Inclusivity is about ensuring that all individuals, regardless of their background, identity, or ability, are included, considered, and actively sought to participate in a process or system. In the context of AI or product design, inclusivity means designing systems, interfaces, or products that are usable by as many people as possible, including those with disabilities or those from diverse backgrounds.

While AI systems are rooted in technical intricacies, it's essential to recognize that addressing fairness and inclusivity goes beyond mere code adjustments. Simply put, ensuring diversity and inclusion isn't just about tweaking algorithms or removing certain data columns like gender or ethnic background. It's a holistic endeavor that encompasses understanding societal nuances, ethical implications, and the broader human experience.

Relying solely on an engineering-centric approach can inadvertently simplify and even misrepresent the profound ethical challenges at hand.[10] Engineers, designers, and product managers, while experts in their domains, might sometimes view challenges through a lens that emphasizes abstraction and formalization. This can lead to a scenario where vital concepts like diversity and inclusion are treated as mere technical parameters or checkboxes to be met. Moreover, an overly technical mindset might shift the ethical onus away from AI developers and providers. Instead of taking full ethical responsibility, they might perceive their role as merely offering a set of tools or configurations for users to navigate. However, the AI Act underscores that every entity in the AI value chain, be it producer, distributor, or deployer, bears the responsibility for the ethical and legal integrity of the AI systems. A strategic approach is therefore necessary.

Establishing Strategies and Procedures to Avoid Bias

> E1. Did you establish a strategy or a set of procedures to avoid creating or reinforcing unfair bias in the AI system, both regarding the use of input data as well as for the algorithm design?

To ensure that AI systems are both fair and effective, it's crucial to adopt a comprehensive strategy that addresses potential biases at every stage of the model development process. The CRISP-DM (Cross-Industry Standard Process for Data Mining) process model provides a structured framework that can be adapted to this end.[11] While the model dates from the late 1990s, its approach is still very much sound, assuming the project is goal-directed and process-driven. More exploratory applications of AI may benefit from other techniques, such as the Data Science Trajectories (DST) framework.[12]

Chapter 7 – Fostering Fairness, Diversity, and Non-Discrimination

The CRISP-DM model can be visualized as follows:

Step 1: Business understanding

The process starts with a clear definition of the business objectives for the AI model. This involves understanding the potential risks associated with biases, especially in sectors where decisions can have significant real-world consequences, such as healthcare or finance. By identifying potential areas of concern early on, teams can be more vigilant in subsequent stages.

We will use two running examples in this section to illustrate application of the process. The first focuses on predicting patient risk in healthcare, and the second on improving anti-theft surveillance in a supermarket. The business objectives and risks could be formulated as follows:

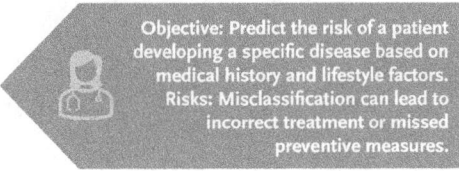
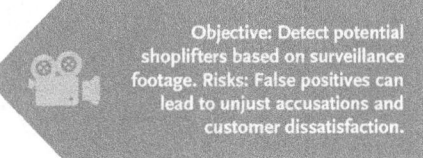

Step 2: Data understanding

Next, a good understanding of the data to be used is needed. This second step therefore involves examining data sources for potential biases or gaps, including a verification that the data is representative of the broader population or the specific context in which the model will be deployed. This requires a study of the historical context of the data, as past biases can propagate if not addressed.

Some work has been done on creating statistical techniques to identify bias. The key principle is to generate a large number of outcomes, which are then correlated with gender or other features where bias is suspected. If a correlation can be found, bias should be investigated further. This does require processing of gender or other special categories of personal data, which triggers stringent GDPR requirements. However, the AI Act provides an explicit legal basis for this particular processing, as it is in the public interest to have bias-free AI systems. A DPIA with clear justification on why the special personal data is strictly needed is a key requirement.

Specific statistical techniques commonly used for this purpose are:
❶ Disparate Impact Analysis: This technique measures the difference in outcomes between different groups. For instance, in a hiring algorithm, if one demographic group has a significantly lower selection rate than another, it may indicate potential bias. The "four-fifths rule" is a common threshold used in disparate impact analysis: if the selection rate for a particular group is less than 80% (or four-fifths) of the selection rate for the group with the highest selection rate, it may be evidence of potential bias.
❷ Odds Ratio: The odds ratio is a measure used to compare the odds of an event occurring in one group to the odds of it occurring in another group. In the context of bias detection, if the odds ratio is significantly different from 1, it might indicate a potential bias between the two groups. For example, in a credit scoring model, if the odds of being classified as a high-risk borrower are three times higher for one demographic group compared to another, it suggests potential bias.
❸ Residual Analysis: In regression models, residuals (the differences between observed and predicted values) can be analyzed to detect potential biases. If residuals are systematically higher or lower for specific groups, it may indicate that the model is not fitting well for those groups, suggesting potential bias. For instance, if a model consistently underestimates the performance of certain demographic groups, it might be biased against them.

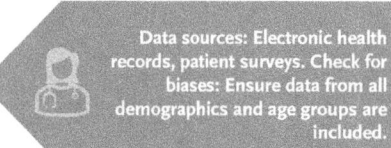

Data sources: Electronic health records, patient surveys. Check for biases: Ensure data from all demographics and age groups are included.

Data sources: CCTV footage, past incident reports. Check for biases: Ensure data is not biased towards specific demographics or times of the day. For instance, are small-scale thefts (a young teen stealing eyeliner) also included?

Step 3: Data preparation

Once data is collected, it needs to be prepared for modeling. This involves handling missing values, outliers, and other anomalies that can introduce bias, and balancing datasets, especially if certain classes or groups are underrepresented. Typical steps include

1. Data cleaning, e.g. by replacing missing values with approximations, normalizing and standardizing features, e.g. ensuring they are all on a scale from 0 to 100, and identifying and handling outliers.
2. Feature engineering, deriving new features from existing ones to better represent the underlying patterns, using techniques like correlation analysis, recursive feature elimination, or feature importance from tree-based algorithms to select relevant features.
3. Handling imbalanced data, through oversampling (replicating minority samples or generating synthetic samples using methods like SMOTE, Synthetic Minority Oversampling Technique), undersampling (randomly removing samples from the majority), or deploying cost-sensitive learning (assigning higher misclassification costs to the minority class).
4. Data splitting, creating training, testing and validation sets to validate model performance, using techniques like k-fold cross-validation to ensure the model's robustness and reduce overfitting.

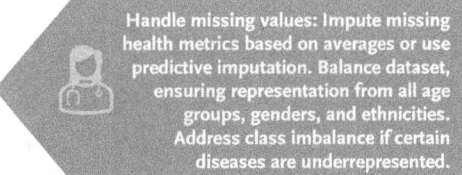

Handle missing values: Impute missing health metrics based on averages or use predictive imputation. Balance dataset, ensuring representation from all age groups, genders, and ethnicities. Address class imbalance if certain diseases are underrepresented.

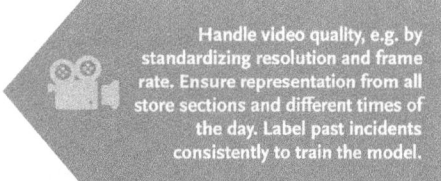

Handle video quality, e.g. by standardizing resolution and frame rate. Ensure representation from all store sections and different times of the day. Label past incidents consistently to train the model.

Step 4: Modeling

The choice of a machine learning algorithm plays a pivotal role in determining the fairness of the resulting model. Different algorithms have varying sensitivities to biases present in the data, and their inherent design can also introduce or amplify biases. Evaluating multiple algorithms thus is a clear necessity.

Today, few AI developers create their own models or algorithms from scratch. Many general models – pre-trained models, or foundation models in AI Act terminology – are available to quickly start with classification, content generation, recommendation and so on. As training a model from scratch requires significant computational resources and time, using foundation models can drastically reduce these costs.

However, foundation models are typically trained on general datasets that aim to capture a broad spectrum of information. To tailor these models to specific applications, developers often fine-tune them using their own datasets. This allows for customization and can improve performance for the task at hand. Yet, the general data they are trained on might carry inherent biases from the sources they were collected from. There are also the issues of transparency and explainability to consider. Foundation models, especially deep learning models, can be complex and not easily interpretable. This can pose challenges in applications where understanding the decision-making process of the model is crucial. At the same time, creating an own model from scratch may exhibit similar problems.

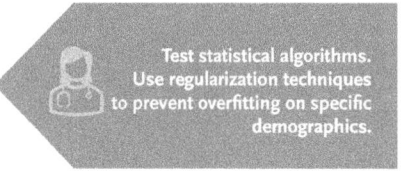
Test statistical algorithms. Use regularization techniques to prevent overfitting on specific demographics.

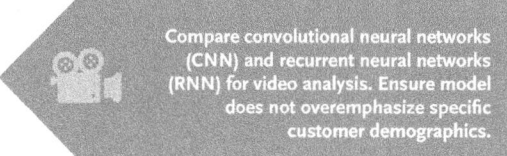
Compare convolutional neural networks (CNN) and recurrent neural networks (RNN) for video analysis. Ensure model does not overemphasize specific customer demographics.

Step 5: Evaluation

After modeling, the AI system should be rigorously evaluated for both performance and fairness. This involves using metrics that specifically measure bias and fairness, in addition to traditional performance metrics. Stakeholder consultations are key to gather feedback on potential real-world implications. Both are used to iteratively refine the model based on evaluation results.

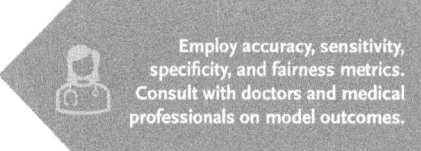
Employ accuracy, sensitivity, specificity, and fairness metrics. Consult with doctors and medical professionals on model outcomes.

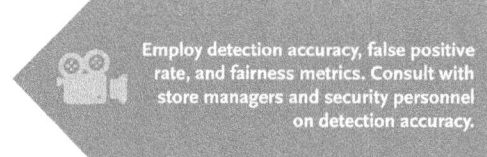
Employ detection accuracy, false positive rate, and fairness metrics. Consult with store managers and security personnel on detection accuracy.

Step 6: Deployment

Once deployed, continuous monitoring of the AI system is crucial. Real-world data can change, and new biases can emerge. Strategies for this phase include setting up automated bias detection mechanisms, regularly updating the model with fresh data to ensure it remains relevant and fair and engaging in periodic stakeholder consultations to stay informed about changing contexts and needs.

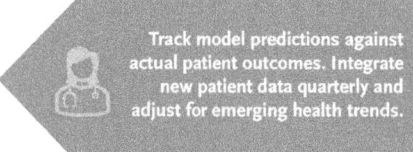
Track model predictions against actual patient outcomes. Integrate new patient data quarterly and adjust for emerging health trends.

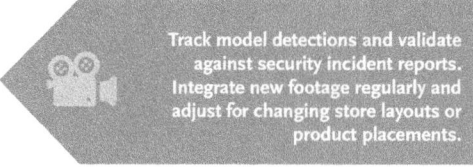
Track model detections and validate against security incident reports. Integrate new footage regularly and adjust for changing store layouts or product placements.

Ensuring diversity and representativeness

> E2. Did you consider diversity and representativeness of end-users and/or subjects in the data?
>
> E2a. Did you test for specific target groups or problematic use cases?
>
> E2b. Did you research and use publicly available technical tools, that are state-of-the-art, to improve your understanding of the data, model, and performance?
>
> E2c. Did you assess and put in place processes to test and monitor for potential biases during the entire lifecycle of the AI system (e.g., biases due to possible limitations stemming from the composition of the used data sets (lack of diversity, non-representativeness)?
>
> E2d. Where relevant, did you consider diversity and representativeness of end-users and or subjects in the data?

Considering the diversity and representativeness of end-users and subjects in the data is crucial. An AI system trained on a diverse and representative dataset is more likely to produce fair and unbiased results. This involves ensuring that the data encompasses various demographics, backgrounds, and scenarios to reflect the real-world diversity. Unfortunately, research on methodologies for data collection and annotation with the purpose of ensuring diversity and representativeness is scarce.

Lessons on improving diversity and representativeness may be drawn from archive data collection and management practices.[13] These focus on user consent, crowdsourcing models to collect open-ended responses from participants, explicit mission statements delineating the dataset's purpose, forming data consortia for the purpose of sharing and focus on transparency, ethics and privacy. In the context of AI datasets, these elements serve to prove compliance with the AI Act's requirements for establishing data provenance and sufficient representation of subjects in the dataset.

Testing for specific target groups or potentially problematic use cases is essential to identify and rectify biases. By simulating scenarios where the AI system might be prone to biases, developers can proactively address these issues before deployment. This involves actively seeking out diverse data sources and ensuring that the data collection process is inclusive.

Continuous monitoring for biases is vital. This involves setting up processes that regularly test the AI system for biases, especially those that might arise due to the composition of the datasets used. Regular assessments ensure that the system remains fair and unbiased even as it evolves and learns over time. Leveraging state-of-the-art technical tools can enhance the understanding of data, model behavior, and overall performance. These tools can help in visualizing data distributions, understanding model decisions, and detecting potential biases.

Education and Awareness Initiatives

> E3. Did you put in place educational and awareness initiatives to help AI designers and AI developers be more aware of the possible bias they can inject in designing and developing the AI system? The design and development stages of AI system?

The design and development stages of AI systems are particularly susceptible to bias, as these are the phases where human influence is most pronounced. It's here that the inadvertent introduction of biases can occur, stemming from the designers' and developers' own perspectives, experiences, and preconceptions.

To counteract this, the emphasis on education and awareness cannot be overstated. By equipping AI designers and developers with the knowledge and tools to recognize and mitigate biases, we can take a proactive stance against the unintentional skewing of AI outputs. Comprehensive training programs that delve into the nuances of biases, their origins, and their potential impacts are instrumental. These programs not only illuminate the pitfalls to avoid but also foster a culture of continuous learning and self-reflection. A typical program could look like this:

1. Introduction to Bias in AI
2. Sources of Bias
3. Bias Detection and Measurement
4. Bias Mitigation Strategies
5. Ethical Considerations in AI Design
6. Hands-on Workshops and Simulations
7. Continuous Learning and Reflection
8. Community Engagement and Collaboration
9. Evaluation and Feedback Mechanisms
10. Future Directions and Challenges

Moreover, awareness initiatives play a pivotal role in keeping the issue of biases at the forefront of AI discussions. Regular workshops, seminars, and discussions can serve as platforms for professionals to share experiences, challenges, and best practices. Unfortunately it is hard to provide concrete examples of how to create awareness, as it depends very much on the application and the organizational context. Much work remains to be done.[14]

Mechanisms for Flagging Issues

> E4. Did you ensure a mechanism that allows for the flagging of issues related to bias, discrimination or poor performance of the AI system?
> E4a. Did you establish clear steps and ways of communicating on how and to whom such issues can be raised?
> E4b. Did you identify the subjects that could potentially be (in)directly affected by the AI system, in addition to the (end-)users and/or subjects?

A robust mechanism should be established that allows stakeholders, users, and even the broader public to flag issues related to bias, discrimination, or subpar performance of the AI system. For instance:

1. Bias Detection Toolkits: Implementing software toolkits that allow users to test the AI system's outputs against various demographic groups. By comparing results, these toolkits can highlight disparities in outcomes, indicating potential biases. An example could be a toolkit that analyzes facial recognition software's accuracy across different ethnicities, pointing out if certain groups are misidentified more frequently than others.
2. Feedback Portals with Bias Categories: Creating dedicated online feedback portals where users can report perceived biases. These portals can have specific categories or tags related to common bias concerns, such as gender bias, racial bias, or age-related bias. By categorizing feedback, it becomes easier to analyze and address specific areas of concern.
3. Stakeholder Review Panels: Organizing periodic review panels consisting of diverse stakeholders who evaluate the AI system's decisions in real-world scenarios. These panels can assess if the AI system's decisions are favoring certain groups over others and provide recommendations for adjustments. For example, a panel reviewing a hiring AI tool can assess if the tool is consistently ranking certain demographic groups lower than others for no justifiable reason.
4. Clear Guidance: Providing step-by-step guidance on the reporting process ensures that individuals know exactly how and to whom they can voice their concerns.

Beyond the immediate users of the AI system, it's essential to recognize that the ripple effects of AI decisions can impact a broader audience. The AI Act recognizes this by defining "affected person" as anyone who could be indirectly affected by the AI system's outcomes. This includes not just end-users but also individuals or groups who might be influenced by the decisions, predictions, or actions of the AI system. For instance, in autonomous car design any person participating in traffic is affected by the car's decisions, not just the driver or passengers.

Any affected person should be able to flag issues if he or she is affected by the system. This is not trivial: often, feedback mechanisms are only available to customers. Outside parties often face impregnable walls before being able to find contact points, or are directed to general customer service representatives with no particular connection to the AI developers.

A solution could be found by borrowing inspiration from the field of IT security. In this realm, companies often employ 'bug bounty' programs, where they incentivize external experts to find and report vulnerabilities in their systems. Just as these programs reward individuals for identifying weak spots that could be exploited by malicious actors, imagine a 'bias bounty' system for AI. In this system, organizations would reward individuals or groups who identify and report biases in AI models and algorithms. Just as bug bounty programs have become a cornerstone in ensuring software security, a bias bounty system could be a revolutionary step in ensuring fairness and transparency in AI. By tapping into the collective expertise of a diverse community, organizations can benefit from a wide range of perspectives, ensuring that AI systems are as unbiased and equitable as possible.

Defining and Measuring Fairness

E5. Is your definition of fairness commonly used and implemented in any phase of the process of setting up the AI system?

E5a. Did you consider other definitions of fairness before choosing this one?

E5b. Did you consult with the impacted communities about the correct definition of fairness, i.e. representatives of elderly persons or persons with disabilities?

E5c. Did you ensure a quantitative analysis or metrics to measure and test the applied definition of fairness?

E5d. Did you establish mechanisms to ensure fairness in your AI system?

Ensuring fairness is not just about selecting a particular metric or definition but involves a holistic approach that considers various stakeholders, especially those who might be impacted by the system's decisions. Settling on a particular definition helps align those involved in the development.

There are many definitions of fairness, each tailored to address specific challenges and scenarios. Common metrics for fairness include:

- **Equalized Odds (EO):** This metric ensures that the AI model's predictions are equally accurate for different groups, especially in scenarios where false positives and false negatives have different consequences. For instance, in a loan approval system, EO would require that both the qualified and unqualified applicants have an equal chance of being mistakenly approved or denied across all demographic groups.

- ❷ Equality of Opportunity: This metric focuses on ensuring equal true positive rates across different groups. In the loan approval example, this metric would require that all qualified individuals, regardless of their group, have an equal chance of being correctly identified by the model as either approved or rejected.
- ❸ Demographic Parity: Under this metric, the selection rate (the rate at which individuals are positively classified) should be the same across different groups. For instance, in a job hiring scenario, if 30% of male applicants receive job offers, then 30% of female applicants should also receive offers to achieve demographic parity (sometimes also called statistical parity)
- ❹ Predictive Parity: This metric requires that, for any given group, the probability of a positive outcome (as predicted by the model) is the same as the actual rate of positive outcomes for that group. In a system predicting loan defaults, if it predicts a 20% chance of default for a set of young borrowers, then, in reality, 20% of those borrowers should actually default.
- ❺ Individual Differential Fairness: This metric ensures that similar individuals receive similar outcomes, regardless of their group membership. It requires that for any two individuals who are similar in terms of their relevant characteristics, the difference in their expected outcomes should be small. This metric is particularly useful in scenarios where individual fairness is more critical than group fairness.
- ❻ MDFA (Multi-Dimensional Fairness Assessment): This is a more comprehensive metric that considers multiple dimensions or attributes simultaneously to assess fairness. Instead of evaluating fairness based on a single attribute (e.g., gender or race), MDFA takes into account multiple attributes to ensure that the AI model is fair across various intersections of attributes. This is particularly relevant in real-world scenarios where individuals belong to multiple marginalized groups, and fairness needs to be ensured across all these dimensions.

Before settling on a particular definition, it's crucial to explore various fairness metrics. Each metric has its strengths and limitations, and the choice often involves trade-offs.

For instance, consider fraud detection. The positive class (fraudulent transactions) is typically rare, but the consequences of false negatives can be severe. Here, a metric like Predictive Parity might be appropriate. This would mean that the proportion of actual fraudulent transactions among those flagged should be consistent, whether the transactions are from corporate accounts or individual accounts. A problematic choice would be Demographic Parity. This metric would flag transactions from all demographic groups at the same rate. This could be misleading if one group genuinely has a higher rate of fraudulent activity.

In situations where there's a roughly equal distribution of outcomes, ensuring fairness becomes especially critical to avoid systemic biases. A metric like Equal Opportunity would then be more appropriate. Using Predictive Parity would actually hide biases, if one group genuinely has more false negatives. Then maintaining the same precision across groups might lead to unequal outcomes.

In scenarios like content recommendation systems (e.g., news articles, videos, or music), there's often an imbalance in representation. Mainstream or popular content might overshadow niche or minority interests, leading to a potential echo chamber effect. In such cases, a metric like Exposure Fairness can be particularly useful. Using Equalized Odds on the other hand would mean that content from different niches has the same likelihood of being correctly or incorrectly recommended. If indie music is already underrepresented, ensuring equalized odds would still lead to mainstream content dominating the recommendations, further marginalizing niche content.

Merely defining fairness is not enough; it's equally important to measure it. This involves a quantitative analysis where the chosen fairness metric is rigorously tested against the AI system's outputs. For instance, if Equalized Odds is the chosen metric, the system's false positive and false negative rates should be analyzed across different groups to ensure consistency.

Accessibility and Universal Design

> E6. Did you ensure that the AI system corresponds to the variety of preferences and abilities in society?

It is no longer sufficient for AI to be merely functional; it must be inclusive, catering to the diverse tapestry of human experiences and needs. This does not just mean in the dataset; users from a variety of backgrounds should gain the same experience and use from the AI system. So let's examine some of the best practices for ensuring diversity, universal access and usability.

Ensuring accessibility in AI system design

If AI systems are not designed with a broad spectrum of users in mind, they risk excluding or disadvantaging certain segments of the population. For instance, individuals with visual impairments might struggle with AI-driven visual content platforms that lack alternative text descriptions or voice-over functionalities. Similarly, those with hearing impairments could be left out if voice-activated AI assistants don't provide visual feedback or captioning. Physical disabilities might limit the use of touch or gesture-based interfaces, and neurodivergent individuals might process information differently, requiring a more straightforward and less metaphorical interaction.

Designing a system usable by all has been a challenge throughout the history of computer systems, and designing AI systems has been no different. The field of Human-computer interaction (HCI) has been focusing on the design of computer technology and, in particular, the interaction between humans (the users) and computers for a long time. Already in the 2000s, the field focused on product design incorporating dilemmas on automation versus human control, expanding in the early 2010s towards incorporating the impact machine learning.[15]

In the European Union, accessibility is not merely a commendable design principle; it's a binding legal requirement. The European Accessibility Act (Directive 2019/882) mandates a wide range of products and services to be accessible by all. This includes ticketing machines, check-in machines, computers, telephones, televisions, banking services, e-books, and e-commerce.[16] The EAA emphasizes the importance of harmonized standards for products and services. A key standard is EN 301 549, enabling organizations to measure the accessibility of websites, electronic documents and non-web software such as native mobile apps, against documented success criteria for all people, including those with disabilities.[17] For public sector bodies, stricter rules follow from the earlier Web Accessibility Directive (2016/2101).

Making user interfaces usable by all

> E7. Did you assess whether the AI system's user interface is usable by those with special needs or disabilities or those at risk of exclusion?
> E7a. Did you ensure that information about, and the AI system's user interface of, the AI system is accessible and usable also to users of assistive technologies (such as screen readers)?
> E7b. Did you involve or consult with end-users or subjects in need for assistive technology during the planning and development phase of the AI system?

As with all computer systems, the user interface (UI) of an AI system serves as the primary bridge between the technology and its users. Ensuring that this bridge is sturdy, welcoming, and inclusive is paramount. Every individual, regardless of their abilities or needs, should be able to navigate, understand, and benefit from AI systems. Accessibility by all has always been a key issue, whose importance everyone agrees with; unfortunately industry – at large – has not embraced proactive approaches.[18] A potential reason is that although the total number of persons having specific accessibility needs is large, each individual need represents only a small portion of the population, making it impractical to design everything so that it is accessible by everyone regardless of their limitations.[19] This however is a misconception: there is no need for a "one-size-fits-all" design.

Assistive technologies have long acted as vital tools in bridging the gap between AI systems and users with specific needs. Screen readers, for example, vocalize digital content for those with visual impairments. Voice recognition software allows users to command and control systems without the need for traditional input methods. Braille displays transform digital text into tactile braille characters. They however often served as afterthoughts: a UI is designed for on-screen interaction with a mouse, and then voice interaction is added to accommodate impaired users.

Today, multimodal interaction presents a different paradigm. Systems should be designed to be interacted with in multiple ways. For example, consider a smart home assistant device. A user might use voice to ask the device to play their favorite song or provide the weather update, tap on the device's screen to adjust settings or browse through options, wave their hand in front of the device to skip a song or mute an alarm and receive information through on-screen visuals, like a dynamic weather map or a video clip.

To ensure AI systems are accessible to all:
- Developers should adhere to established accessibility standards, such as the Web Content Accessibility Guidelines (WCAG) which is recommended to establish EAA compliance.[20]
- Systems should be designed with adaptive interfaces, offering multiple modes of interaction.
- Regular testing with assistive technologies should be conducted to identify and rectify potential compatibility issues.
- End-users, especially those relying on assistive technologies, should be actively involved to acquire insights that can shape the trajectory of AI development.

Universal Design principles in AI development

> E8. Did you ensure that Universal Design principles are taken into account during every step of the planning and development process, if applicable?

Universal Design (UD) is an approach that seeks to create products and environments that are inherently accessible to both people with disabilities and those without. The concept is also known under names such as inclusive design, Design for All and especially in an EU context as eInclusion and eAccessibility.[21] The seven principles of Universal Design are:

- Equitable Use: The design should be useful and marketable to people with diverse abilities. For example, a voice-activated virtual assistant that can understand and respond to a wide range of accents, speech patterns, and languages, ensuring that users from different linguistic backgrounds can use it effectively.

❷ Flexibility in Use: The design should accommodate a wide range of individual preferences and abilities. For example, an AI-driven learning platform that offers content in multiple formats – videos, text, audio descriptions, and interactive simulations – allowing users to choose the mode that suits their learning style best.

❸ Simple and Intuitive Use: Use of the design should be easy to understand, regardless of the user's experience, knowledge, language skills, or concentration level. An AI system should thus uses simple, clear language and visual aids to explain complex terms or procedures appropriate to the target audience.

❹ Perceptible Information: The design should communicate necessary information effectively to the user, regardless of ambient conditions or the user's sensory abilities. For instance, an AI traffic navigation system should provide both auditory directions and visual maps, ensuring that drivers can receive information through their preferred sensory channel.

❺ Tolerance for Error: The design should minimize hazards and the adverse consequences of accidental or unintended actions. An AI photo editing tool for example should permit multiple undo levels and confirms potentially irreversible actions, reducing the chance of users making unintended changes.

❻ Low Physical Effort: The design should be usable comfortably and with a minimum of fatigue. The use of voice commands is a common way to achieve this, e.g. in an AI-powered home automation system.

❼ Size and Space for Approach and Use: Appropriate size and space should be provided for approach, reach, manipulation, and use, regardless of the user's body size, posture, or mobility. For example, an AI-driven virtual reality game that adjusts its interface and controls based on the user's height, arm length, and mobility, ensuring an immersive experience for all.

Assessing AI system impact on end-users

E9. Did you take the impact of the AI system on the potential end-users and/or subjects into account?

E9a. Did you assess whether the team involved in building the AI system engaged with the possible target end-users and/or subjects?

E9b. Did you assess whether there could be groups who might be disproportionately affected by the outcomes of the AI system?

E9c. Did you assess the risk of the possible unfairness of the system onto the end-user's or subject's communities?

The development and deployment of AI systems have profound implications for end-users and subjects. As already stressed elsewhere in this book, this requires a holistic approach to AI development, involving not just the technical team but also the potential users of the system. It's essential to ask:

- Were the target end-users consulted during the development phase?
- Did the development team actively seek feedback from a diverse set of potential users?
- How were the insights and concerns of these users addressed in the final product?

For instance, an AI system designed for elderly care should involve feedback from seniors, caregivers, and medical professionals to ensure it meets the unique needs and challenges of its target audience. The strategies above to mitigate bias should also go a long way to address disproportionate impact on specific target groups.

Stakeholder Participation

> E10. Did you consider a mechanism to include the participation of the widest range of possible stakeholders in the AI system's design and development?

Engaging a diverse range of stakeholders ensures that the AI system is designed with a holistic understanding of its potential impacts and applications. This participation can lead to more robust, ethical, and effective AI solutions. The involvement of key stakeholders is an AI Act requirement for high-risk AI systems, and a recommended option for other AI systems.

Working with stakeholders

In the context of computer systems, a "stakeholder" refers to any individual, group, or organization that has an interest in or is affected by the design, development, deployment, and operation of the system. This can include end-users, developers, business owners, investors, regulatory bodies, and even communities where the system might be deployed. Stakeholders can influence or be influenced by the system's objectives and outcomes.

The field of Human-Computer Interaction (HCI) in particular has always emphasized the importance of understanding and designing for the end-user. An early start was made with the advent of personal computers in the 1980s, which caused a shift towards making systems more user-friendly. Of particular note is the concept of co-design or participatory design, which emphasizes the active involvement of users in the design process (rather than, say, merely giving feedback on the almost-finished prototype). Today, with the rise of complex socio-technical systems, stakeholder participation has become even more critical. Issues like privacy, ethics, and societal impact have brought a wider range of stakeholders into the design and decision-making process.

Chapter 7 – Fostering Fairness, Diversity, and Non-Discrimination

While in the field of AI design there is a strong and growing consensus that end-users and stakeholders should participate, there is still an enormous divergence on what this actually means. Tools such as workshops and feedback rounds are often employed, but without standardization or frameworks often appear to be mere afterthoughts or symbolic gestures.[22] In the literature, five key questions have been identified as key to stimulating participation at the key decision points in an AI design process. They are illustrated in the figure below.[23]

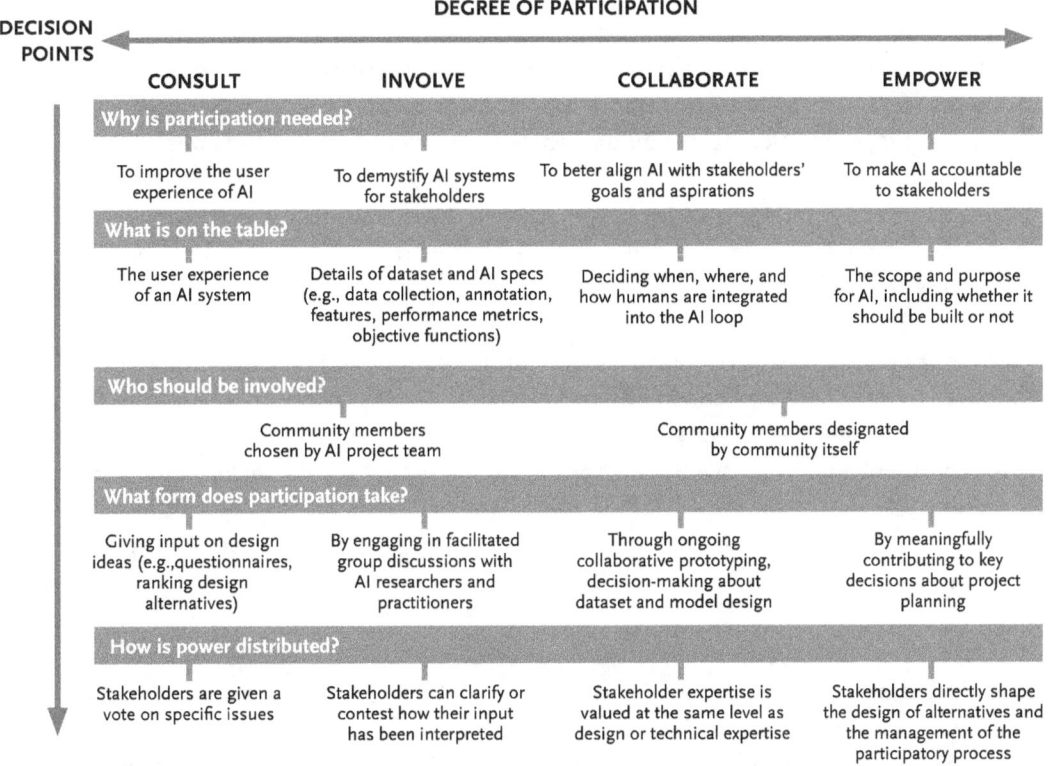

Tactics for increasing stakeholder participation in designing AI, from consulting to empowering (source: Delgado et al., 2021).

The five questions are:
① **Is participation needed?** This requires a good understanding of the necessity and benefits of involving stakeholders in the design process.
② **What is on the table?** This step involves determining the specific issues, topics, or decisions that are open for discussion and input.
③ **Which stakeholders should be involved?** This requires identification of all relevant individuals, groups, or entities that should be part of the process.
④ **What form does their participation take?** The method or approach of involvement is of crucial importance. For instance, using a Social Choice Theory approach, AI practitioners might poll stakeholders and then aggregate their preferences. However, this might not address power imbalances between AI researchers and stakeholders. Alternatively, participatory democracy research suggests more collaborative methods, like bringing stakeholders together to discuss and negotiate design decisions.
⑤ **How is power distributed among the participating stakeholders and between stakeholders and technology designers/engineers?** Assessing the balance of influence and decision-making authority among all involved parties is key to understanding what the stakeholders actually bring to the table.

There exists a notable disparity between idealistic aspirations and practical limitations. Two primary considerations emerge from this context:
① What defines the baseline for substantial participation, especially when determining the efficacy of human and algorithmic proxies in representing stakeholder values and preferences?
② At which juncture does the enhancement of stakeholder involvement yield diminishing benefits?

It's imperative for businesses to address these considerations to optimize stakeholder engagement in AI design and development. We recommend conducting a thorough evaluation to establish clear benchmarks for meaningful participation and to determine the optimal level of stakeholder involvement to ensure both efficiency and inclusivity.

Toolkits for participation

To foster creation of ethical or trustworthy AI, a plethora of tools, resources, guides, and kits is available from many sources.[24] Such toolkits often promise to also address participation, but in practice do little more than recommending that stakeholders participate or their voice is heard. For instance, the Microsoft Azure Application Architecture Guide recommends that implementers "seek more information from stakeholders that you identified as potentially experiencing harm". This is little more than hand-washing akin to legal disclaimers.

A useful approach is the stakeholder-first framework by Bell, Nov and Stoyanovich.[25] Their framework (illustrated below) puts the 'technologists' or those who work on the AI system on equal footing with policymakers, users (humans-in-the-loop), compliance officers and affected individuals (the stakeholders, in the terminology of the previous subsection). Assuming algorithmic transparency is intended to improve the understanding of a human stakeholder, AI designers must first consider the stakeholders of the system, before thinking about the system's goals or the technical methods for creating transparency.

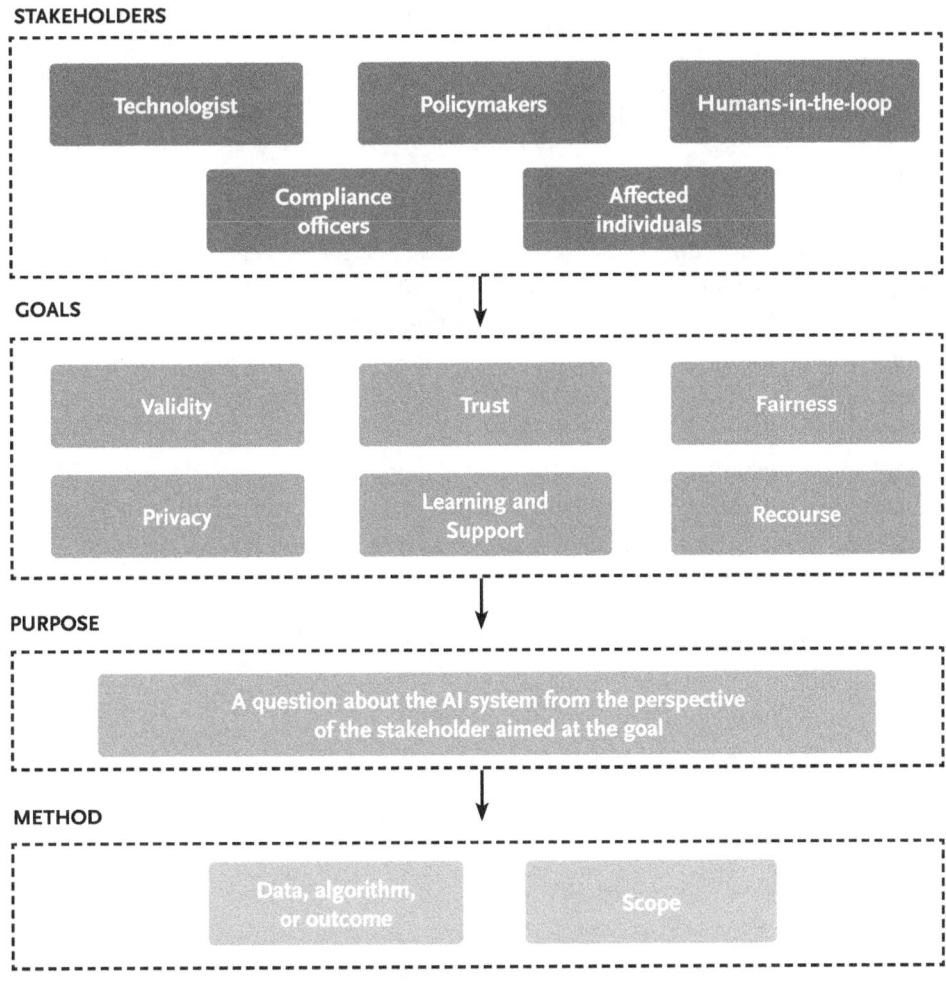

A stakeholder-first approach for creating transparent AD
(source: Bell, Nov and Stoyanovich 2023).

Next, the goals of desired transparency or fairness are defined. These can be put in one of six categories: validity, trust, learning and support, recourse, fairness, and privacy. From here the purpose question – what does the stakeholder want from the AI system aimed at their specific goal – can be formulated. Only then is it possible to select the methods: data, algorithm, outcome and scope.

Key takeaways

In this chapter, we've seen that both substantive and procedural dimensions of fairness are crucial. AI systems should ensure equitable distribution of benefits and costs, and their decisions should be transparent and accountable. Implementing comprehensive strategies, such as the CRISP-DM process model or the DST framework, can help in addressing biases throughout the AI model development process. Here, ensuring that AI systems are trained on diverse and representative datasets is essential for producing unbiased results.

Next to the data and model design, AI systems should be designed to cater to a wide range of users, ensuring both functionality and inclusivity. This aspect of human-computer interaction is a challenge given the high-tech nature of these systems. Engaging with a diverse set of stakeholders can lead to more ethical and effective AI solutions.

As we move forward, it's essential to consider the broader implications of AI. The next chapter will delve into the impact of AI systems on societal and environmental well-being, exploring how these technologies can shape our world for the better.

Chapter 7 – Fostering Fairness, Diversity, and Non-Discrimination

Societal and Environmental Implications of AI Systems

Chapter 8 – Societal and Environmental Implications of AI Systems

A I has the potential to revolutionize our world in positive ways, but it's crucial to understand the societal and environmental implications. The deployment of AI will intersect with global sustainability, societal constructs, and environmental implications. In this chapter we'll explore both the bright prospects and the challenges that lie ahead. Moreover, we'll analyze AI's potential impact on democratic processes and its significance and discuss strategies for mitigating its societal and environmental risks.

Aligning environmental impact with global goals

> F1. Are there potential negative impacts of the AI system on the environment?
>
> F1a. Which potential impact(s) do you identify?

The deployment of AI systems can carry environmental implications. While AI can optimize processes and reduce waste in certain applications, the computational infrastructure powering advanced AI models demands significant energy resources. This raises the question of how to align AI with sustainable development.

Environmental impact of AI

AI systems, especially those at the cutting edge of technology, rely on vast computational power. The immense energy demands of these computations, particularly during the training phase of large-scale models, result in significant CO2 emissions.[1] For instance, training the generative AI model GPT-3 consumed 1,287 megawatt hours of electricity, leading to carbon emissions equivalent to 123 cars driven for an entire year. While data on the carbon footprint of individual AI queries is limited, it's believed to be up to five times that of a typical search engine request.

> **By the end of this chapter, you'll be able to ...**
> - Understand the intersection of AI with global sustainability, societal constructs, and environmental implications.
> - Analyze the potential impact of AI on democratic processes and its role within ESG and CSR considerations.
> - Develop strategies for mitigating societal and environmental risks.

The water footprint of AI models, often overlooked, is significant.[2] Training GPT-3 in Microsoft's advanced U.S. data centers uses 700,000 liters of freshwater, equivalent to the water needed to produce 370 BMW cars. While smaller than energy production's water consumption, the water usage by AI systems merits attention.

In addition to the carbon emissions and water usage, the AI industry contributes to electronic waste.[3] The rapid pace of technological advancements in AI necessitates frequent hardware updates. This results in the quick obsolescence of previous generation hardware, leading to considerable amounts of discarded electronics. These discarded components often contain hazardous materials, which, when not properly recycled or disposed of, can leach into the environment, posing threats to soil, water sources, and ecosystems.

To mitigate these environmental impacts and to ensure AI's alignment with broader global objectives, it's imperative to turn our attention to the Sustainable Development Goals (SDGs). These goals provide a framework for integrating environmental sustainability with the continued progression of AI technology.

The Sustainable Development Goals (SDGs)

Sustainable development is the practice of meeting present needs without compromising the ability of future generations to meet their own, ensuring a balance between economic growth, environmental protection, and social well-being for long-term societal prosperity.

The Sustainable Development Goals (SDGs) have their origin in the global community's recognition of the intertwined nature of economic, social, and environmental challenges. In 2000, world leaders adopted the United Nations' Millennium Development Goals (MDGs), setting clear targets for reducing poverty and other sources of human deprivation. However, by their end date in 2015, it became clear that more holistic and ambitious goals were needed to address the range of pressing global challenges.

Building on the foundation of the MDGs, the SDGs were adopted in September 2015 as part of the UN's 2030 Agenda for Sustainable Development, which provides a shared blueprint for peace and prosperity for people and the planet. The SDGs comprise 17 interconnected goals, which reflect the socio-economic, environmental, and governance dimensions of development. One of the most notable initiatives championing the union of AI and sustainable goals is the 'AI for Good' project.[4] This initiative is rooted in the belief that targeted AI solutions can accelerate progress towards the SDGs. It has set up a range of projects from tackling climate change to improving health and education.

The use of Social Impact Assessments

A useful tool in the context of SDGs is the formal process of a Social Impact Assessment (SIA). A SIA is a systematic process used to analyze and manage the social consequences of projects or decisions in general. They emerged in the 1970s as a way to understand and manage the social consequences of development projects, particularly in sectors like infrastructure, mining, and energy. With its origins tied to environmental impact assessments, the SIA soon carved out its own niche by focusing on the human dimension of projects.

The European Union (EU) has consistently advocated for rigorous impact assessments to ensure that its policies and practices meet social, economic, and environmental objectives. For instance, the EU's commitment to the Sustainable Development Goals (SDGs) underscores the need for assessments that consider societal well-being. The EU's approach towards impact assessments is holistic, aiming to anticipate potential impacts across various dimensions – economic, social, and environmental. Thus, while a SIA can be carried out independently from other assessments (such as a GDPR data protection impact assessment or an AI Act human rights assessment), the preferred approach is to integrate the assessments into one analysis. The SIA would address potential social changes, challenges, and benefits. It examines aspects like public health, education, employment, social cohesion, and inequality. While it's a component of the broader assessment, its methodologies and focus areas remain distinct.

Structured approach towards SIA

The Social Impact Assessment (SIA) for AI systems necessitates a structured approach. This methodology involves:

- **Scoping:** Identify the scale and nature of potential social impacts by focusing on the specific domains the AI system will influence.

- **Data Collection:** Gather relevant qualitative and quantitative data, ensuring diverse stakeholder input, which aids in capturing a comprehensive view of potential impacts.

- **Impact Analysis:** Analyze the data to discern direct and indirect social effects, both positive and negative, the AI system may introduce or exacerbate. To mention a few:

    - Employment: The introduction of a new technology platform in a region can lead to job creation in tech support, maintenance, and administration roles, enhancing local employment opportunities.

- Social Isolation: Over-reliance on virtual communication tools can decrease face-to-face interactions, contributing to feelings of loneliness and reduced community bonding.

- Education: Implementing a new online learning system can increase accessibility to education for remote areas, bridging the urban-rural education gap.

- Social cohesion: Launching a community-based social media app can strengthen neighborhood ties and foster a sense of belonging among residents.

- Job Displacement: Rapid automation and adoption of AI in various sectors can lead to significant job losses, particularly in roles that involve repetitive tasks, affecting economic stability for many workers.

④ Mitigation and management: Develop strategies to minimize negative impacts and maximize positive ones, always keeping stakeholders' well-being at the forefront.

⑤ Monitoring and review: Establish continuous feedback loops to monitor the AI system's social effects post-deployment, making necessary adjustments as societal contexts and needs evolve.

Mitigating the environmental impact of AI

> F2. Where possible, did you establish mechanisms to evaluate the environmental impact of the AI system's development, deployment and/or use (for example, the amount of energy used and carbon emissions)?
>
> F2a. Did you define measures to reduce the environmental impact of the AI system throughout its lifecycle?

Conducting a SIA is a general way to identify and mitigate potential negative impacts of the AI system on the environment. There are however various other, more practical ways to mitigate the concrete impact of AI on the environment:

① Energy and water consumption monitoring: Implement tools and software that can accurately measure the energy and (cooling) water usage of AI operations. These tools can track the energy consumed during the training, deployment, and usage phases of the AI system, giving an understanding of its environmental footprint. Using advanced cooling technologies like liquid immersion cooling or air-side economization is a quick way to reduce the reliance on water-based cooling systems.

② Model efficiency: Developing and deploying more efficient AI algorithms can reduce computational needs. Techniques like model distillation, pruning, and quantization can produce smaller, faster models without sacrificing much in terms of accuracy.⁵ Similarly, instead of training new models from scratch, transfer learning techniques can adapt pre-trained models to new tasks, reusing a lot of the computational effort from the initial training.

③ Transition to green energy: Migrate to data centers and infrastructure that are powered by renewable energy sources, such as solar, wind, or hydroelectric power. Many leading tech companies offer 'green cloud' services, which ensure that the energy-intensive processes of AI are backed by renewable energy sources. Utilize energy-efficient computing systems that produce less heat. Adopt advanced cooling techniques, like liquid cooling, to manage heat more efficiently.

④ Offsetting environmental impact: Address the carbon footprint by investing in projects that either reduce or capture equivalent emissions. This includes initiatives like afforestation, renewable energy installations, and carbon capture technologies. Offset water consumption by supporting projects that either save, replenish, or purify equivalent water volumes. Key strategies encompass reforestation (integral to water cycles), water purification for underserved communities, and sustainable agricultural practices optimizing water use.

⑤ Invest in sustainable technology: Invest in sustainable mining practices and support recycling and upcycling of old devices. Opt for manufacturers that prioritize sustainable sourcing and responsible mining. Implement and promote responsible e-waste recycling programs. Encourage extended producer responsibility where manufacturers are accountable for the entire life cycle of their products.

AI in the work environment

> F3. Does the AI system impact human work and work arrangements?

The integration of AI into the workplace has been rapid, transforming many sectors from manufacturing to the service industry. As work for many people is a key part of their lives, including the assurance of their livelihood, there's a significant social impact to consider.

The Good: Productivity enhancements

AI systems can automate repetitive tasks, allowing employees to focus on more complex and value-added activities. For instance, AI-powered analysis tools can review standard applications or questions, reducing the workload of human advisors, legal counsels and so on. And with the ability to analyze vast datasets quickly, AI aids in making informed decisions. This can be particularly beneficial in areas like finance, where AI models can predict market trends, or in healthcare, where they can help diagnose diseases with high accuracy.

Of particular note are AI-driven platforms that allow workers to choose when and where they work. The system's predictive analytics can also suggest the best times to work to maximize earnings. Famous examples are taxi platforms and food delivery services, but a great many freelance operators in other sectors have significantly benefited from such platforms.

The Bad: Job insecurity

As noted earlier, automation might lead to job losses in certain sectors, especially for routine and repetitive roles. For instance, administrative tasks, data entry roles, and even some blue-collar jobs in manufacturing may see reductions. The rapid integration of AI demands new skill sets. Those unable to adapt or learn these new skills might find themselves marginalized in the job market.

Another aspect of job insecurity is the replacement of management, rather than workers, with AI tooling. This may cause depersonalization and loss of attachment to the job: as human supervisors, who can understand and empathize with employee circumstances, are substituted by algorithmic systems, there's a risk of reduced morale and engagement. Such AI-driven management tools may lack the nuance and emotional intelligence of human managers, leading to decisions that might be technically efficient but lacking in human touch. Over time, this can erode the sense of belonging and loyalty employees feel towards their organization, potentially increasing turnover rates and reducing overall job satisfaction.

In the area of platform work, workers are already largely managed by algorithms, which make decisions on job allocation, performance assessments, and even terminations. Further, AI algorithms also can dynamically adjust pay rates based on demand. This can result in unpredictable earnings for workers, with no guarantees of a minimum wage or even a job next week. For this reason, the EU is introducing a Directive on improving working conditions in platform work. Its implications for automated decision making in the workplace is discussed in more detail in chapter 5.

Mitigating negative impact of AI

> F4. Did you pave the way for the introduction of the AI system in your organisation by informing and consulting with impacted workers and their representatives (trade unions, (European) work councils) in advance?
>
> F5. Did you adopt measures to ensure that the impacts of the AI system on human work are well understood?
>
> F5a. Did you ensure that workers understand how the AI system operates, which capabilities it has and which it does not have?
>
> F6. Could the AI system create the risk of de-skilling of the workforce?
>
> F6a. Did you take measures to counteract de-skilling risks?
>
> F7. Does the system promote or require new (digital) skills?
>
> F7a. Did you provide training opportunities and materials for re- and up-skilling?

The inherent risks associated with AI's integration into the workplace demand a proactive approach. This is particularly complicated by two factors. First, AI often is introduced in a piecemeal fashion, which means its inherent risks become less immediately noticeable, making proactive mitigation more challenging. Second, when AI's primary introduction serves cost-cutting motives, addressing its potential negative consequences might appear counterintuitive to management's initial goals.

Here are four concrete steps that employers can take to mitigate negative impacts AI on the workforce.

❶ Foster understanding and clarity on AI systems

- To make certain that the impacts of AI systems on human work are comprehensible, companies should conduct thorough assessments prior to implementation. This involves not only understanding the capabilities of the AI system but also grasping the potential implications for the workforce.

- To address knowledge gaps, regular training sessions can be arranged, which focus on how employees can effectively use the AI system. This empowers employees to not just work alongside AI but to also leverage it to enhance their individual roles.

❷ Avoid de-skilling of the workforce

- While automation can handle repetitive tasks, it's essential to strike a balance and ensure that employees don't lose touch with core competencies. Regular skill assessments and the creation of 'manual operation' opportunities can help maintain a workforce that's adept both with and without AI assistance.

- As AI systems evolve and take over certain tasks, opportunities should be created for employees to acquire new skill sets. Institutions can offer training materials, courses, and workshops that align with emerging industry demands. This not only helps in avoiding the risk of de-skilling but also ensures that the workforce remains competitive and future-ready.

- Encourage an environment where employees can learn from each other. Those adept at using AI tools can guide their peers, fostering a culture of collective growth.

❸ Ensure career progression and security

- As some roles may diminish due to automation, companies should design new job profiles that tap into the human potential to manage, supervise, or work in tandem with AI.

- Employees should be kept in the loop regarding AI implementations, its potential impact on job roles, and the company's plans to manage transitions. This can mitigate fears and apprehensions tied to job security.

- By partnering with universities and training institutes, businesses can ensure a steady flow of talent equipped with the latest skills, ready to navigate an AI-integrated work environment.

❹ Involve works councils.

- Works councils can facilitate open dialogue between employees and management about AI deployments. Such conversations allow both parties to express concerns, ask questions, and collaboratively strategize on best practices.

- In many countries, introducing automated employee performance monitoring systems requires the involvement or even prior permission of the works council.

- As AI systems are deployed and updated, councils can establish feedback mechanisms to monitor the real-time effects on employees. This iterative process can catch unforeseen challenges or areas of friction, allowing for timely modifications.

- Given that a major challenge with AI is its 'black box' nature, councils can advocate for transparent algorithms, especially in cases where AI systems are used in decision-making roles affecting employee careers and well-being.

AI in healthcare

The healthcare and caregiving sectors have always been at the forefront of technological innovation, and AI is no exception. From robots designed to care for the elderly to AI-driven medical triage systems and personalized treatment recommendations, these tools promise better, more efficient care. But their adoption is not without societal concerns.

The Good: More effective care

Care robots, often termed "carebots", are increasingly being designed to assist the elderly or those with special needs. Their capabilities range from offering medication reminders to detecting falls. Carebots can provide consistent care, ensuring that tasks are not missed and are done on time. And with sensors and alert systems, they can quickly detect anomalies such as falls and inform caregivers or medical personnel.

AI-driven systems are increasingly used to triage patients in emergency settings or virtual health platforms, predicting the urgency of medical issues based on the symptoms. These systems can quickly process information and prioritize patients, potentially reducing waiting times.

Using AI to analyze a patient's medical history, genetic makeup, and even lifestyle can lead to highly personalized treatment plans. Recommendations can be precisely tailored to the individual, potentially leading to better outcomes. AI can identify risk factors and recommend preventive measures early on.

The Bad: Depersonalization

As with social AI in general (see chapter 3), there's a risk of elderly individuals becoming emotionally attached to robots, potentially at the cost of human interaction. For instance, while carebots can perform tasks, they lack genuine human touch and empathy, which are vital in caregiving. Initial human interaction in medical settings can be comforting and insightful; an AI interface might lack this warmth and miss non-verbal cues.
There's also the risk of over-reliance: Sole reliance on AI can miss nuanced human symptoms or rare conditions that a trained human eye might catch. And more generally, those with more comprehensive data or access to sophisticated AI-driven care might receive better recommendations, potentially widening healthcare disparities.

Mitigating negative impact of AI

Key to a deployment of AI in healthcare is understanding that AI should act as a complementary tool rather than a replacement. Continual training for medical professionals on AI's capabilities and limitations ensures informed decision-making, reducing over-reliance. Moreover, establishing ethical guidelines and oversight for AI usage, particularly in critical areas like triage, is essential to ensure that patients' best interests are always prioritized. Concrete steps to take are:

❶ Implement an integrated feedback loop for AI Decisions

- Allow for real-time input from both healthcare providers and patients, ensuring that AI recommendations align with human expertise and patient experience.

- Continuously refine the AI system by identifying and correcting inaccuracies or biases based on diverse patient outcomes and feedback. Focus particularly on the risk of AI perpetuating outdated or biased medical practices.

❷ Periodically assess for carebots' effectiveness

- Evaluate whether carebots are fulfilling both the emotional and physical requirements of patients, ensuring they add value to the caregiving process.

- Identify areas of improvement or adjustment, ensuring carebots complement rather than replace essential human interactions.

❸ Provide continuous training and education for medical staff

- Equips healthcare professionals with up-to-date knowledge on the capabilities and limitations of AI tools, fostering informed clinical decisions.

- Encourages the optimal use of AI, ensuring it serves as an enhancement to, rather than a replacement for, human expertise.

❹ Promote Equitable Access to AI-Driven Healthcare Tools

- Ensures that AI's benefits in healthcare are not limited to a specific demographic, reducing potential healthcare disparities.

- Encourages healthcare institutions to offer AI-driven treatments and tools to a wider patient base, ensuring uniform quality of care.

❺ Involve patients in AI oversight

- Create a platform for patients, caregivers, and family members to voice concerns, share experiences, and provide feedback on AI tools and practices in healthcare settings.

- Educate and involve the patients' council or its ombudsman, to establish clear points of contact for AI-related patient issues.

ESG, CSR, and AI

With the rise of Artificial Intelligence, the corporate landscape has witnessed a paradigm shift. This rapid transformation has raised the bar for Environmental, Social, and Governance (ESG) and Corporate Social Responsibility (CSR) considerations. This section will briefly consider both in the context of compliance management.

Environmental, Social, and Governance (ESG) considerations

Environmental, Social, and Governance (ESG) refers to the three central pillars in measuring the sustainability and ethical impact of an investment in a company or business. Over recent years, ESG considerations have taken center stage in the corporate landscape, evolving from peripheral concerns to integral components of business strategies. As investors, consumers, and regulators increasingly prioritize sustainable and responsible business practices, ESG factors have become vital in assessing a company's performance, risks, and future potential.

Artificial Intelligence presents a promising avenue for corporations to achieve their ESG objectives with precision. However, it isn't devoid of challenges. Issues related to data privacy, transparency in algorithms, or AI's energy consumption can deter ESG achievements. Furthermore, without proper oversight, AI can unintentionally perpetuate biases, leading to skewed ESG results and outcomes. Thus, AI compliance processes can significantly contribute to improving a company's ESG achievements.

Adding AI to the ESG

One structured way to embed AI within a company's ESG initiatives is the protocol proposed by Henrik Sætra.[6] The protocol delineates a structured approach for companies aiming to embed AI within their ESG initiatives. The elements are illustrated in the figure below:

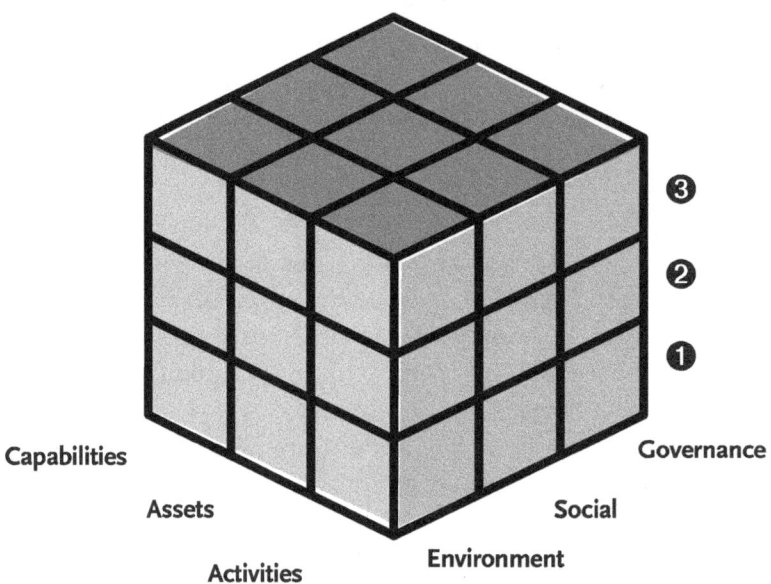

Capabilities Governance
Assets Social
Activities Environment

In brief, the protocol uses the following approach:

❶ Initial Descriptive Statement:

- Furnishes a holistic understanding of AI's position and role within an organization.

- Details on AI operational control, responsibility, relevant strategies, plans, and governance are documented.

- Ethical policies, anchored on trustworthy or responsible AI principles, are highlighted.

❷ Main Impact Statement:

- The Impact Statement methodically maps the ESG impacts through qualitative and quantitative data.

- It also points out known data constraints and areas lacking clarity.

- For each topic, a qualitative statement is given together with items such as quantitative data on relevant indicators, links and references to relevant indicators from other standards and framework, links to policies, assessments, processes, the person/department responsible and any relevant external sources of information (suppliers, partners, etc.).

❸ Risks and Opportunities Statement:

- Synthesizing insights from the initial description and impact statement, this segment lays out potential risks and prospects tied to AI.

- Employing risk matrices, materiality analysis, and an AI readiness assessment ensures comprehensive evaluation.

❹ Action Plan:

- The action plan should describe which topics are addressed, what should be done, when it should be done, and describe in detail who oversees implementation and who controls progress on the initiatives described.

- It is highly recommended to include a roadmap and a discussion of where the entity is currently at in its "AI ESG journey."

Corporate Social Responsibility (CSR) considerations

Corporate Social Responsibility (CSR) is a self-regulating business model that holds companies accountable for their impact on social, environmental, and economic dimensions. It involves practices that go beyond the requirements of regulations, emphasizing voluntary actions that a business can take to make a positive impact on society.

The advent of AI has revolutionized CSR by enhancing methodologies, refining measurement techniques, and streamlining management processes. Their data-driven approach allows for more precise tracking of CSR initiatives, ensuring they align with stated goals and adapt to changing conditions. Furthermore, machine learning models can predict the potential societal and environmental impact of business decisions, helping firms align better with their CSR objectives.

Integrating AI in a company's framework of Corporate Social Responsibility (CSR) is an oft-quoted desire of management boards. Generally speaking, employing AI systems compliant with the regulations and ethical considerations discussed in this book should not interfere with CSR considerations. Key issues, rephrased in concrete CSR-focused action points, would be:

- Stakeholder Engagement: It's vital for businesses to involve a wide range of stakeholders (employees, customers, communities, shareholders, etc.) in discussions about AI deployment. This ensures diverse perspectives are considered and the technology serves the broader good, not just business interests.

- Digital Inclusion: As part of their CSR initiatives, companies should work to minimize the digital divide by making AI-driven solutions accessible and usable for all, irrespective of their socio-economic background, physical abilities, or digital literacy levels.

- Ethical Data Sourcing: Beyond just data privacy, ethical sourcing of data means ensuring that the data used to train AI models is acquired consensually, without exploiting vulnerable populations, and with respect to indigenous and local knowledge.

- Transparent Governance of AI: Companies should establish clear guidelines, protocols, and oversight mechanisms for AI projects. This includes ethical reviews, transparency reports, and third-party audits, all of which ensure AI projects align with CSR objectives.

- Environmental Footprint of AI: Consider the environmental costs associated with AI processes, especially in terms of energy consumption. Companies should work towards greener AI, optimizing algorithms, and sourcing sustainable energy for AI computations.

- Crisis Management Protocols: Since AI systems can sometimes behave unpredictably or be exploited in malicious ways, companies should have robust crisis management protocols in place. These should be geared towards swiftly mitigating any negative societal impacts resulting from their AI deployments.

- Collaboration for Ethical Standards: Companies can join industry-wide efforts to set ethical standards for AI. Collaborative approaches can lead to more universally accepted and robust ethical guidelines.

- **Continuous Review:** Given the rapid pace of AI development, companies should commit to regularly reviewing and updating their AI-related CSR strategies, ensuring they remain relevant and effective in addressing emerging challenges and harnessing new opportunities.

AI and Democracy

> F8. Could the AI system have a negative impact on society at large or democracy?
>
> F8a. Did you assess the societal impact of the AI system's use beyond the (end-)user and subject, such as potentially indirectly affected stakeholders or society at large?
>
> F8b. Did you take action to minimize potential societal harm of the AI system?
>
> F8c. Did you take measures that ensure that the AI system does not negatively impact democracy?

One of the areas where AI can have the most fundamental impact is where AI and the fundaments of democracy intersect. From shaping public opinion to streamlining political processes, the impact of AI in this realm has raised many questions.

Influence on political decision-making

The attraction of AI in the political realm has been clear for over a decade now. With advanced data analytics and predictive modeling capabilities, politicians and policymakers can gain invaluable insights. By analyzing vast datasets—from social media interactions to economic metrics—AI can forecast public reactions to policy decisions, identify emerging societal concerns, and even predict geopolitical shifts.

However, this also introduces the risk of basing crucial decisions on algorithmic recommendations, which may lack nuanced human judgment or be based on biased data. If policy is set based on AI predictions, other factors may be ignored or treated as less important than they deserve. AI-driven algorithms to filter public comment on new legislation may favor one position over another due to unintended factors. Furthermore, the opacity of some AI models can obscure the rationale behind certain policy recommendations, reducing public trust and transparency in the decision-making process.

From a different perspective, the impact of AI on society has put regulation of AI on many a politician's radar. The European AI Act and its related legislation is a prime example. Specific instances of AI misuse, bias or other harm caused by AI may cause politicians to jump to new legislative efforts or urge supervisory authorities to intervene.

An example is the regulation of deepfakes: AI-generated imagery that purports to depict real situations. While general legislation should be sufficient to address the downsides of this type of technology, many countries have specific laws in the pipeline to specifically regulate deepfakes. This touches on a general point of laws and regulations: it is not so much the number of laws on the books, as it is the budget for the supervisory authorities that determines how well a technology is regulated.

Influence on political discourse

The rapid advancement of AI technologies has given birth to novel tools capable of generating highly convincing fake multimedia content, be it deepfake videos, AI-generated texts, or synthetic personas. While these technologies have legitimate uses in fields such as filmmaking and virtual reality, their potential misuse in the political realm raises significant concerns. To name a few:

1. Voter Manipulation: Deepfakes can depict political figures saying or doing things they never did, leading to false perceptions and misleading narratives. An impeccably timed release of a deepfake video days before an election, for instance, could severely damage a candidate's reputation, altering the course of the election. AI-generated text, on the other hand, can create fabricated news stories or quotes, further swaying public opinion. Such falsehoods, when shared and amplified on social media, can misinform vast segments of the electorate.
2. Hijacking Political Debate: The infiltration of AI-generated content can divert genuine political discourse. For example, synthetic personas can flood online forums or social media platforms with extremist views or disruptive comments, overshadowing genuine human perspectives and derailing meaningful conversations. They can also be used to amplify fringe opinions, making them seem more popular and mainstream than they truly are.
3. Issues of Censorship and Free Speech: Addressing the menace of AI-generated misinformation is not straightforward. Any attempt to regulate or remove such content walks a fine line. Political speech, even if controversial or unpopular, is strongly protected under free speech laws as it's a cornerstone of democratic societies.

The 2019 European Parliamentary elections serve as a concrete example. Avaaz, a global web movement that brings people-powered politics to decision-making, conducted an extensive study ahead of the elections. Their findings were alarming: they discovered hundreds of fake news stories on Facebook that had amassed millions of views across France, Germany, Spain, Italy, the UK, and Poland.[7] These misleading posts were aimed at influencing voter behavior, promoting extremist ideologies, or delegitimizing the EU's democratic processes. AI played a double role: AI was used to generate parts of the fake content, and AI-driven algorithms on platforms like Facebook were responsible for surfacing and promoting content (sometimes misinformation) to users based on their behaviors and preferences. Yet AI was also leveraged by entities like Avaaz to detect, analyze, and report such content.

The EU's 2022 Digital Services Act aims to regulate the large online platforms that today manage and control the online discourse. The issue of desinformation and algoritmic manipulation plays a central role in its application. One key weapon is its requirement of transparency: researchers must be able to do Big Data-style analysis on posts and engagements on these platforms. AI and machine learning algorithms may thus be able to learn to recognize fake news before it does harm.

Influence on elections

Of particular attention is the role of AI and algorithms in influencing elections, a topic that came to the public's attention in the context of the 2016 US presidential election and the earlier Facebook–Cambridge Analytica data scandal. Cambridge Analytica, a political data analysis firm, harvested the personal data of millions of Facebook users without their explicit consent.[8] The company set out to work for Donald Trump's election campaign. Cambridge Analytica claimed to have the tools to identify the personalities of American voters and influence their behavior through what they termed "psychographic targeting". This meant categorizing individuals based on certain traits and tailoring messages that would resonate consciously and unconsciously most effectively with each category. The AI Act's declaration of manipulative AI as prohibited practice (see chapter 2) can be clearly linked to this approach.

One of Cambridge Analytica's main strategies involved targeting "persuadable" voters in crucial swing states with specific messages that would appeal to their emotions and beliefs. This didn't just mean promoting Donald Trump's policies but also included negative advertising aimed at his rivals. By micro-targeting these segments of the population with messages crafted to resonate specifically with them, Cambridge Analytica sought to magnify the impact of the campaign's advertisements. The actual extent of their influence on the election outcome remains a topic of debate among experts. Some argue that their tactics had a significant impact, while others believe the effect was marginal compared to other factors in the election.

Key takeaways

The environmental costs of AI, notably its energy consumption and e-waste, have highlighted the challenge of maintaining sustainable development alongside technological progress. The workplace, healthcare and other key parts of society are the first place where we can clearly see some of the profound societal shifts we're expecting. On the corporate front, the intersection of AI with ESG and CSR emphasizes the evolving responsibility companies bear in the age of intelligent machines. Finally, AI's influence on the democratic processing has been both empowering and troubling, drawing attention to its potential to shape political landscapes and the public's perception.

Having delved deep into these societal and environmental consequences, Chapter 9 beckons with a shift in focus. We've mapped the impacts; now, let's explore the avenues to ensure accountability and redress in AI systems.

Chapter 8 – Societal and Environmental Implications of AI Systems

Accountability and redress

Chapter 9 – Accountability and redress

Accountability is what makes an AI system reliable and trustworthy. Let's uncover how we can ensure it, with a focus on the learning goal of evaluating accountability mechanisms in AI systems. This chapter will discuss practical strategies and building blocks for accountability, and explore the complex relationship between accountability and trust. But first, we must understand the concept of accountability itself.

Understanding accountability

Accountability is often considered the bedrock of responsible and ethical AI deployment. But to understand what this means in the world of AI, let's dissect the multifaceted concept of accountability. A simple definition is that one must be able to justify their aims, motivations, and reasons.

The essence of accountability

Accountability, as outlined by the OECD, refers to "the expectation that organisations or individuals will ensure the proper functioning, throughout their lifecycle, of the AI systems that they design, develop, operate or deploy, in accordance with their roles and applicable regulatory frameworks, and for demonstrating this through their actions and decision-making process".[1] Thus, the concept acts both as a principle that ensures compliance with the key requirements for a trustworthy AI and as a set of practices and measures, e.g., audit, risk management, and redress for adverse impact. The latter is recognized in the AI Act as a legal requirement: one must have an adequate quality management and assurance system in place, including risk management, and add "an accountability framework setting out the responsibilities of the management and other staff" on top of it.

Accountability is one step above compliance. Merely following the law to the letter is one thing; being accountable means being able to justify the choices made in the compliance process, or being required to redress what went wrong. This provides a three-step accountability process:[2]

> **By the end of this chapter, you'll be able to ...**
> - Define key concepts underpinning AI accountability.
> - Develop practical strategies ensuring AI accountability.
> - Understand the relationship between AI accountability and societal trust.

- **Information:** The first step involves clearly outlining and providing knowledge about what the AI system does, its purpose, data it processes, algorithms it uses, and the decisions it makes.

- **Explanation or justification:** In the second step there's an onus on AI developers, managers, or deployers to offer reasons for why the AI behaves as it does. For instance, if an AI loan system denies an application, the system (or the organization deploying it) should be able to justify that decision. This is more than explaining *why* the decision was made (transparency, chapter 6) or ensuring the decision was fair (chapter 7). A justification means that the decision was right, legally and ethically – and with a clear up-front explanation rather than an after-the-fact excuse.

- **Consequences:** The third step relates to taking responsibility for AI outcomes. If an AI tool gives an incorrect or unjust output, there should be mechanisms for redress, which might include rectifying the mistake, compensating the affected person, or refining the AI model. There can be no accountability without consequences.

A framework of accountability

Accountability generally has four goals: compliance, report, oversight and enforcement. Compliance is usually the foremost goal. Holding the entity accountable for noncompliance creates a willingness to comply. The main tool for demonstrating compliance is reporting: proper documentation of actions and decisions is crucial for justifying them. Oversight is a key aspect that ensures continued compliance. Based on the findings from oversight, an enforcement agency may set appropriate consequences, such as sanctions or orders to cease the behavior.

The relation of answerability can be expanded into a number of features, as the table below shows.[3] Two examples are added for illustrative purposes. Example 1 refers to typical juridical or legal accountability; example 2 deals with accountability in the electoral context.

Chapter 9 – Accountability and redress

Features	Explanations	Example 1	Example 2
1. **Context** (what for?)	Fields in which an accountability relation is established	Juridical	Electoral
2. **Range** (about what?)	Tasks, like actions, services, decisions, and assessments taken by the accountable agent	Conducts, omissions, and decisions	Choices of political direction, laws, and recruitment
3. **Agent** (who?)	The entity who exercises the delegated powers, accepting to be blamed or praised	Natural persons, legal persons, states, and assets	Representatives, leaders, parties, governments, and institutional bodies
4. **Forum** (to whom?)	The entity engaged in actual interrogation and supervision and/or the bearer of the interests served through delegation of tasks (*principal*)	States, courts, supervisory authorities, arbitration bodies	Citizens, voters, taxpayers, political parties, and institutions
5. **Standard** (according to what?)	Principles, rules, and benchmarks against which the conduct of the accountable agent is assessed	Legal rules, principles, and precedents	Reliability, coherence, and ideology
6. **Process** (how?)	Procedures through which the agent is called to account	Judicial and extra-judicial review	Public debate (media), internal or external vigilance (e.g., judicial review), and elections
7. **Implications** (what follows?)	Consequences, formal or informal, triggered by the accountability assessment	Reparations, remands, detentions, fines, and prohibitions	Electoral outcomes, political reputation, careers, and funding

Internal and external accountability

Accountability in AI can broadly be categorized into two primary modalities: external and internal, each distinguished by who orchestrates the accountability process.

Internal Accountability, as the name suggests, is executed within the context of the entity deploying the AI system. It involves developers, internal auditors, and domain experts scrutinizing the AI processes to ensure alignment with standards, laws, and the organization's AI principles, including ethical benchmarks. An illustrative example is the Internal Audit Framework defined by Raji et al, shown below.[4] Gray indicates a process, and the colored sections represent documents. Documents in orange are produced by the auditors, blue documents are produced by the engineering and product teams and green outputs are jointly developed.

Scoping	Mapping	Artifact Collection	Testing	Reflection	Post-Audit
Define Audit Scope	Stakeholder Buy-in	Audit Checklist	Review Documentation	Remediation Plan	Go / No-Go Decisions
Product Requirements Document (PRD)	Conduct Interviews	Model Cards	Adversarial Testing	Design History File (ADHF)	Design Mitigations
AI Principles	Stakeholder Map	Datasheets	Ethical Risk Analysis Chart		Track Implementation
Use Case Ethics Review	Interview Transcript			Summary Report	
Social Impact Assessment	Failure modes and effects analysis (FMEA)				

External Accountability pertains to the evaluation and validation of an AI system by entities outside the deploying organization. This could involve regulators, users, or independent investigators who access parts of the system, for instance, via an API, and employ varied techniques like black box testing or input manipulation.

For the accountability process to be the most effective, external accountability is key.[5] In the European context, this means first and foremost the national supervisory authorities that oversee the enforcement of the AI Act. Other entities also play a role: affected persons can take legal action, including collective actions. Shareholders can hold management to account. Journalists can present their case before the court of public opinion. Research organizations may independently investigate the workings of the system and publish peer-reviewed papers on their findings, which may impact the market or value for investors.

A challenge in external accountability lies in balancing transparency with safeguarding proprietary information. Datasets, algorithms and related information used in the creation or deployment of AI systems are often closely guarded trade secrets of their creators. The AI Act contains various provisions requiring AI creators or deployers to disclose such proprietary information, with the requirement for supervisory authorities to treat the same in strictest confidence. No such right to disclosure exists for private parties.

An organization may choose to create an external accountability route, e.g. by having a research organization or university evaluate its AI system. Adopting a "controlled disclosure" approach, before sharing any proprietary data with external researchers or journalists, the organization would use non-disclosure agreements (NDAs) tailored specifically for the AI context. These NDAs would stipulate the boundaries of data usage and protect the intellectual property rights of the disclosing party. Another approach is to create a sandbox environment, where third parties can examine the AI model more closely (compared to the general public) without direct access to the underlying proprietary data or algorithms, can also be effective. This allows external entities to understand the model's behavior, test it, and report on its implications without exposing the system's inner workings.

Drawing a parallel to the cybersecurity domain, the concept of "responsible disclosure" can offer valuable insights. Responsible disclosure in cybersecurity pertains to the practice of notifying the software vendor about vulnerabilities before making them public, ensuring that they are rectified and don't pose threats. A similar mechanism can be instituted for responsible disclosure regarding issues with AI systems.

The use of model cards

An instrumental tool in internal accountability are offered by "Model Cards" or "System Cards". Introduced in 2019, Model Cards aim to provide a standardized framework to transparently communicate the specifications, performances, and intended uses of machine learning models to stakeholders, ranging from developers to end-users.[6] Such transparency can help reduce potential misuse and shed light on a model's limitations.

The essence of a Model Card is akin to a nutrition label on food products. Just as consumers can understand the contents and health implications of a food item through its label, users of an AI system can glean essential information about a model's design, strengths, and weaknesses through its Model Card. This approach aligns with the larger movement towards accountable and transparent AI, ensuring that potential biases, training data sources, and other critical aspects are accessible and understandable.

Typical elements of Model Cards are:
- Model Details: Name, version, date, and purpose.
- Intended Use: Specific use-cases and applications.
- Factors: Features used in the model, including data sources.

- **Metrics:** Performance metrics and evaluation criteria.
- **Training Data:** Description of data, sources, and preprocessing techniques.
- **Evaluation Data:** Data used to evaluate the model's performance.
- **Ethical Considerations:** Identification of potential biases and fairness implications.
- **Limitations:** Known constraints or shortcomings of the model.
- **Usage Constraints:** Guidelines on safe and appropriate use.
- **Licensing & IP:** Information on how the model can be used or distributed.
- **Contact Information:** Details for further queries or feedback about the model.

An example model card is shown below; it illustrates a Google ML system for face detection in images or video.

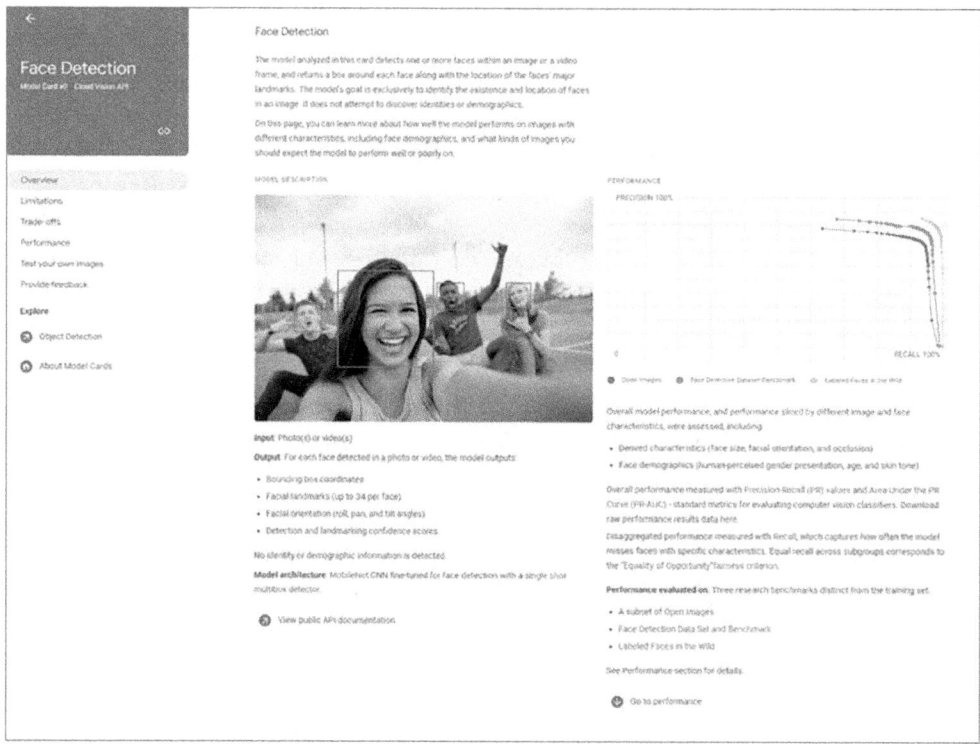

Source: Google

Building blocks of accountability

Translating the above into a practical approach means that mechanisms should be put in place to create accountability. This means during development but also during deployment and use. The key mechanism are auditability, compliance monitoring, reporting mechanisms, risk management, managing trade-offs and offering redress.

> G1. Did you establish mechanisms that facilitate the AI system's auditability (e.g. traceability of the development process, the sourcing of training data and the logging of the AI system's processes, outcomes, positive and negative impact)?
>
> G2. Did you ensure that the AI system can be audited by independent third parties?

An audit is a systematic evaluation of a system's or application's infrastructure, operations, and performance to identify potential issues, areas for improvement, and compliance with established standards or guidelines. In the context of an AI system, an audit encompasses a systematic review to ensure its accuracy, fairness, transparency, and adherence to business and ethical standards. This process involves scrutinizing the ML model's development, the traceability of its development processes, the sourcing and quality of its training data, and comprehensively logging the AI system's processes, outcomes, and both positive and negative impacts.

The Cross Industry Standard Process for Data Mining (CRISP-DM) model, created by IT audit association ISACA, provides a structured framework for auditing machine learning systems.[7] The CRISP-DM process comprises the following stages:

1. Business Understanding: This initial phase centers on the business problem the ML system intends to address. It defines the purpose of the model and outlines essential attributes for consideration. This includes establishing or constructing the traceability of the development process.
2. Data Understanding: A foundational understanding of data is vital for a robust model. Auditors delve into the nature, scale, sources, and potential biases of the data. Variables should be scrutinized to ensure they are devoid of conflicts and biases. Correlation and covariance matrices can shed light on the inter-relationships of variables. The sourcing of training data is primarily tackled in this phase.
3. Data Preparation: After understanding the data's nature, it needs to be processed and refined to be fed into the model efficiently. Logging the processes used to clean, transform, and enrich the data happens here.
4. Modeling: This stage involves crafting the actual algorithm. Data scientists tweak hyper-parameters, often utilizing grid search techniques, to achieve the best results.
5. Evaluation: This transcends traditional metrics like accuracy and generalizability. Auditors should ascertain that the model doesn't stray from business principles or induce inadvertent biases. Logging the AI system's outcomes, both positive and negative, is crucial at this stage. The models' results are assessed against business objectives set in the first phase, and the implications of the model's deployment in a real-world setting are considered, capturing any potential positive or negative impacts.
6. Deployment: The integration context of the algorithm is vital. Auditors need to ensure the algorithm's seamless operation within its intended environment, observing potential integration challenges and performance metrics.

> **G3.** Did you foresee any kind of external guidance or third-party auditing processes to oversee ethical concerns and accountability measures?
>
> **G3a.** Does the involvement of these third parties go beyond the development phase?

There are of course many firms professing to be able to perform such audits. Currently, there is no clear certification or accreditation, although the AI Act encourages the European Commission to work out suitable frameworks. In the meantime, here are some suggestions for selecting an auditor:

1. **Professional Services Firms:** Many of the large international professional services firms (often referred to as the "Big Four" — Deloitte, PwC, KPMG, and EY) offer audit and assurance services, including those related to technology, cybersecurity, and data. For instance, in April 2023, KPMG announced the availability of its Trusted Analytics service, which focuses on audits of AI systems.

2. **Specialized Technology Audit Firms:** These are firms specifically focused on auditing technology processes, systems, and implementations. These can provide specific deep-dive audits and reviews. Credentials such as ISACA's Certified Information Systems Auditor can help in the selection.

3. **Academic Institutions:** Some universities or research institutions have departments or experts that can offer third-party audit services, especially when it comes to assessing the technical and ethical aspects of AI and machine learning systems. As an example, the German Fraunhofer Institute for Telecommunications offers auditing and certification of AI systems.

4. **Non-governmental Organizations (NGOs) and Think Tanks:** These organizations, especially those focusing on digital rights, data privacy, or ethical AI, can offer independent audits or assessments. Their focus is often on ensuring public trust and ethical considerations. NGOs may be hesitant to audit or evaluate commercial offerings as it could be construed as an endorsement, which may interfere with their independent nature. Engaging an NGO to create ethical and trustworthy AI however may be a possibility.

5. **Standardization and Certification Bodies:** Organizations such as the International Organization for Standardization (ISO) and the European Committee for Standardization (CEN) have announced plans for standardized frameworks for AI quality, compliance and so on. Once these are available, any of the above may be able to help certify AI systems.

Compliance monitoring

To facilitate continuous monitoring and ensure compliance, a separate process can be set up to supervise the system's actions, especially during operations. This becomes particularly critical for AI systems with adaptive learning capabilities, as they can occasionally exhibit unpredictable behaviors. Drawing inspiration from the "sense-

> G4. Did you organise risk training and, if so, does this also inform about the potential legal framework applicable to the AI system?
> G5. Did you consider establishing an AI ethics review board or a similar mechanism to discuss the overall accountability and ethics practices, including potential unclear grey areas?
> G6. Did you establish a process to discuss and continuously monitor and assess the AI system's adherence to the ALTAI Assessment List?
> G6a. Does this process include identification and documentation of conflicts between the 6 aforementioned requirements or between different ethical principles and explanation of the 'trade-off' decisions made?
> G6b. Did you provide appropriate training to those involved in such a process anddoes this also cover the legal framework applicable to the AI system?

plan-act" cycle, it's crucial to integrate these requirements at every phase:

- **Sense:** The system should recognize all essential environmental factors to ensure requirements' adherence.
- **Plan:** During this phase, the AI should only develop plans that remain in line with the established requirements.
- **Act:** Every action the system takes should strictly adhere to behaviors that meet the set-out requirements. A best practice is to create "white lists" and "black lists" of desired and undesired behaviors.

The AI Compliance Officer

Maintaining the ethical integrity of AI systems requires a robust governance structure. Organizations need to implement both internal and external governance frameworks to ensure accountability at every stage, from development to deployment and use. One practical approach is appointing a dedicated individual responsible for ethical considerations related to AI systems. This individual – the AI Compliance Officer – would have a role similar to the GDPR's data protection officer. His or her role could encompass:

- Offering oversight to ensure legal and ethical standards are met.
- Providing advice on ethical dilemmas or decisions.
- Delivering appropriate training to those involved in the creation or deployment of the AI system.
- Taking the lead in carrying out the various impact assessments mentioned in this book.
- Engaging in regular communication with industry peers or public oversight groups, promoting the sharing of best practices and discussing potential challenges.
- Acting as the contact point for the supervisory authority.

Reporting mechanisms

> G7. Did you establish a process for third parties (e.g. suppliers, end-users, subjects, distributors/vendors or workers) to report potential vulnerabilities, risks or biases in the AI system?
>
> G7a. Does this process foster revision of the risk management process?

Identifying and mitigating potential negative impacts of AI systems, especially for those directly affected, is vital. The establishment of whistleblower protections and mechanisms for reporting concerns about an AI system is an integral part of this.

Given the number of stakeholders involved in the lifecycle of an AI system – from suppliers and end-users to workers and distributors – it's imperative to establish a clear, accessible, and responsive reporting process. This infrastructure should:

- Allow third parties to report perceived vulnerabilities, biases, or risks without fear of repercussions.
- Be designed with user-friendliness in mind, ensuring that even those with minimal technical knowledge can easily voice their concerns.
- Incorporate stringent whistleblower protections, guaranteeing that those reporting potential issues can do so anonymously and without fear of retaliation.

However, merely establishing a reporting mechanism is insufficient. The true value lies in how the gathered information is used. Hence, the process should ensure that all reported vulnerabilities, biases, or risks are meticulously evaluated, considering both the technical and ethical implications. This requires a culture of continuous improvement. In addition, a company should actively work on establishing communication channels with industry and/or public oversight groups, sharing best practices, discussing dilemmas and emerging issues of ethical concerns.

Managing trade-offs

Implementing requirements in AI often gives rise to complex scenarios where differing imperatives or interests compete with one another, necessitating methodological trade-offs. Properly navigating these trade-offs is fundamental to preserving the ethical foundations of AI systems.

Before delving into trade-off management, it's crucial to have a profound understanding of the different interests and values at stake. To achieve this, a mechanism should be established to regularly identify and review the interests and values implicated by the AI system. This can involve AI diagnostics, stakeholder interviews, and user feedback.

This in turn requires active monitoring of the AI system's operations and outcomes, identifying areas where ethical and operational imperatives might be at odds.

When conflicts between interests arise, a structured methodology is indispensable. Trade-offs should be evaluated in light of their risks to fundamental rights and ethical principles. This involves a multi-dimensional risk assessment that weighs operational efficiency, user experience, ethical implications, and legal considerations. Decisions regarding which trade-offs to make should be backed by solid reasoning. Decision-making frameworks, such as decision matrices or ethical impact assessments, can help guide this process. It is essential that every trade-off decision be properly documented, capturing not just the decision itself but also the rationale behind it. This ensures transparency and accountability.

Governance models play a pivotal role in ensuring trade-offs are made appropriately. A best practice is the integration of internal or external ethics experts or boards. Their specialized insight can spotlight potential conflict areas and offer resolutions. As noted in the previous section, engaging with industry and/or public oversight groups goes a long way in improving the management of trade-offs.

Offering redress

> G8. For applications that can adversely affect individuals, have redress by design mechanisms been put in place?

Redress refers to the provision of remedies or compensation for harm or injustice caused, often encompassing legal actions and payment of damages. In the AI landscape, it extends beyond traditional remedies to include rectifying algorithmic biases, adjusting decision-making processes, correcting flawed datasets, and ensuring transparent feedback mechanisms to prevent recurrent issues.

Providing avenues for redress isn't just ethical but vital to ensure that AI technologies garner trust and are used responsibly. They are also important for legal compliance. The AI Act mentions "effective measures of redress in relation to the risks posed by an AI system" explicitly as a factor to assess whether an AI system should qualify as high-risk AI. Fundamental rights impact assessments should discuss means of redress.

Redress, in AI applications, goes beyond mere acknowledgment of a problem. It involves:
- **Identification:** Recognizing when an individual has been adversely affected by an AI decision or process.
- **Rectification:** Taking steps to remedy the immediate issue, whether that means reversing a decision or compensating for a loss.
- **Amendment:** Adjusting the AI system to prevent the same issue from recurring.

For those impacted by AI, the path to redress should be transparent and accessible. Users should be informed about their rights to redress and the procedures to initiate a redress claim. Such redress procedures should be user-friendly, such as a simple online form or a dedicated helpline. Also important is a timely response: redress claims should be addressed promptly, ensuring that individuals don't face prolonged periods of uncertainty. Establishing an AI ombudsman as an impartial intermediary that can investigate complaints and recommend solutions can offer a more structured and trusted approach to handling grievances.

Redress by design goes further than merely having an easy-to-call helpline. Users should be able to incorporate the necessary information to help the deployer of the AI system understand the issue. The AI's interface should feature accessible feedback or complaint mechanisms, ranging from simple buttons to options that allow users to save the current state and submit a complaint. Additionally, it's crucial to have an automated audit trail, which captures the decision-making process at any given instance, providing a detailed view into how conclusions were drawn. Another mechanism could be a reverse-engineering module, allowing users or third-party experts to backtrack the AI's decisions to their origins, pinpointing areas of concern. In essence, redress by design ensures that the resolution of issues is as integral to the AI system as its primary functionalities.

In the context of AI decision-making systems, redress often translates into appealing the AI's decision. Such an appeal should be effective, with particular focus on the requirements of the GDPR as discussed in chapter 6. The focus on accountability gives these additional key features of the appeal process:

1. **Timeliness:** Quick response times are crucial. Parties seeking redress should not have to wait unduly long periods for a resolution. This ensures that any harms or issues arising from AI decisions are addressed promptly. In particular, any effects from the AI's decision should be suspended or postponed until the appeal has been resolved.

2. **Expert review:** Appeals should ideally be reviewed by a combination of technical and domain-specific experts. This ensures that both the technological and contextual nuances of the decision are considered. The presence of independent third-party reviewers is crucial to maintain trust.

❸ Protection for appellants: Individuals who appeal should be protected against any form of retaliation or discrimination for challenging the AI's decision. This ensures that users feel safe and encouraged to seek redress when necessary.

❹ Clear communication: At the end of the appeal process, the decision, along with the reasoning, should be clearly communicated to the appellant. This ensures understanding and trust in the process.

❺ Continuous monitoring and review: As AI systems and societal norms evolve, the appeal process itself should be periodically reviewed and updated to stay effective and relevant.

Accountability and trust

In the final part of this chapter, we will have a closer look at what the European Commission calls "trustworthy AI" and its relation to accountability. This pursuit of trustworthiness stems from a recognition that successful adoption and societal acceptance of AI technologies hinges on the establishment and cultivation of trust. Yet, signaling trustworthiness does not automatically translate to earned trust. In fact, past experiences, notably among historically discriminated populations, may color the perceptions of trustworthiness, leading to warranted skepticism even in the face of alleged trust signals.

Trust and trustworthiness

It's crucial to differentiate between the normative and empirical dimensions of trust and trustworthiness in AI. Normatively speaking, the Guidelines detail the ideal requisites for what constitutes trustworthy AI. Empirically, however, trust is subjective, varying depending on individual and societal experiences with AI. There exists an assumed correlation between trustworthiness and trust: a trustworthy entity, whether a person or technology, should rationally be trusted. Yet, historical context and biases can skew this correlation. Discriminated groups, for instance, may rationally distrust entities deemed trustworthy by the majority, underscoring the subjective nature of trust.

This misalignment between perceived trustworthiness and actual trust can have significant societal implications. When public institutions adopt AI systems believed to be trustworthy, and this erodes public trust, it can decrease institutional support and engagement.[8] The AI Act's approach to evaluating trustworthiness might further obfuscate the intricacies of trust. Trust, after all, isn't solely a product of rational thought. Psychological factors and the mere illusion of human involvement can boost trust, irrespective of the actual influence of human oversight on AI decisions.

Trust, trustworthiness and accountability

Trust is a multifaceted construct, especially in the realm of artificial intelligence. Trust in AI doesn't merely concern the accuracy or efficiency of an algorithm; it delves into the realm of transparency, fairness, and the system's capacity to act in ways that align with human values. It's an empirical sentiment, gauged by individual and collective experiences, and heavily influenced by the societal, cultural, and historical contexts of its users.

Trustworthiness on the other hand is a normative quality, representing the intrinsic attributes of an AI system that warrant the trust of its users. Central to this trustworthiness is accountability. An accountable AI system operates within a framework that not only complies with established laws and ethical guidelines but also possesses mechanisms for redress when failures occur. True accountability ensures that AI decisions can be traced, justified, and, if necessary, corrected. This transparent accountability, coupled with consistent performance, fosters trustworthiness. When users understand that an AI system is both responsible for its actions and can be held to account, the foundation for genuine trust is laid. The intertwined nature of trust, trustworthiness, and accountability in AI underscores the need for a holistic approach in AI design and deployment, one that prioritizes both technical excellence and ethical considerations.

The role of empathy

An unexpected role in the context of accountability and trustworthy AI may be played by the concept of empathy. Empathy is the ability to be sensitive to the needs of someone based on understanding their affective states and intentions, caring for their feelings, and socialization, which can help in addressing the social-technical challenges associated with accountability. Research across social science, organization science, and psychology show that by *regulating* empathy, it is possible to enhance accountability.[9]

Empathetic AI entails the infusion of human-like emotional and cognitive comprehension into machine algorithms, driving them to understand and respond to users in a more humane and considerate manner. This is an evolution beyond cold logic and data-driven decision-making; it represents a paradigm shift to integrate the subjective experiences and emotions of stakeholders into the equation. One key dimension that links empathy and accountability is responsibility. While accountability revolves around adherence to rules, regulations, and the consequent repercussions of a system's behavior, empathy requires a deeper, intrinsic responsibility that addresses the nuances of human experiences. This involves recognizing and addressing emotions, intentions, and societal norms. For instance, when considering AI-driven loan decisions, while accountability may focus solely on proper evaluation of credit scores or repayment histories, an empathetic system would factor in personal situations, long-term impacts, or unique challenges faced by the applicant.

An empathetic AI system inherently bridges several dimensions of accountability like justification, reporting, and redress. When an AI understands a stakeholder's perspective emotionally, it better explains its decisions (justification), transparently conveys the underlying logic (reporting), and works to mitigate any adverse consequences (redress). The alignment between empathy's facets, such as understanding and caring, with accountability's dimensions, such as responsibility and traceability, facilitates the creation of AI systems that are not only effective but also compassionate.

Potential pathways towards empathetic accountability

Incorporating empathy into AI systems enhances their accountability in multifarious ways. One avenue, especially in realms like healthcare diagnosis, is the emphasis on comprehensive patient well-being. Traditional diagnostic systems might base conclusions strictly on clinical test results, but an empathetic system would also consider the patient's mental and emotional well-being, lifestyle factors, and individual circumstances. By looking beyond just the clinical data and understanding the holistic health of a patient, an empathetic approach would potentially lead to more personalized and effective treatment plans. This holistic consideration not only promises better health outcomes but also fosters deeper trust between healthcare providers and patients..

Furthermore, the integration of subjective needs is crucial. Instead of blind adherence to data, considering the emotional and societal weightage of individual circumstances can lead to fairer outcomes. For instance, an AI system assessing loans for education might prioritize them over luxury items, understanding the broader societal impact of education. Lastly, empathy in AI doesn't necessarily need to be an intrinsic quality of the algorithm but can be fostered through external mechanisms. Incentive structures, for instance, can be designed to promote behaviors that reflect empathy and understanding. Cooperative schemes that focus on mutual understanding, negotiation, and consensus among stakeholders can also ensure that AI systems are not just effective but also compassionate and fair.

Accountability and sanctions

A final look at the AI Act must deal with the sanctions regime that it brings. Like the GDPR before it, the AI Act establishes a system of national supervisory authorities. These have various powers, including the ability to impose fines. Next to that, affected persons may have their own options for redress.

National supervisory authorities

Each Member State should designate a national supervisory authority for the purpose of supervising the application and implementation of the AI Act. Each national supervisory authority should act with complete independence in performing its tasks and exercising its powers in accordance with this Regulation. Mutual cooperation is ensured through the establishment of the European Union Artificial Intelligence Office, an independent body at the EU level that itself has no regulatory powers but can issue guidance.

Supervisory authorities primarily act as market surveillance powers, comparable to how abuse of competition law or financial services law is enforced. Authorities act on market signals, whistleblowers and reports and may initiate investigations with all the powers that national law grants to its enforcement authorities. Their scope may overlap with that of other authorities: a motor vehicle with AI self-driving mode is subject to specific, long-established supervision but would fall under the definition of high-risk AI. In such cases, the AI Act leaves primary responsibility with the sector-specific supervisor.

Powers of the authorities

The AI Act leaves open which powers the supervisory authorities have, as this is a matter of national law. A minimum requirement is the ability to impose fines, which can be significant as the table below shows. Further, investigative powers should be present: the AI Act only sets limits on these when the investigation would require access to raw model data or key parameters, which are the highest business secrets an AI provider can have. Only when a provider cannot sufficiently address the authority's concerns through documentation, experiments or other means would the power exist to demand access (in confidence) to these basic materials.

Under the AI Act, the penalties must be chosen to be effective, proportionate and dissuasive. To avoid stifling the market, they must take into account the interests of startups and SMEs. Supervisory authorities would have to draw up guidelines for administrative fines before being allowed to impose them. The table below summarizes the situations in which penalties may be imposed.

Practice	Administrative fine
Deploying unacceptable AI	Up to €35 million or 7% of worldwide gross revenue
Violating compliance provisions of high-risk AI	Up to €15 million or 3% of worldwide gross revenue
Violating requirements for general-purpose AI	Up to €15 million or 3% of worldwide gross revenue
Supplying incorrect, misleading or incomplete information	Up to €7,5 million or 1% of worldwide gross revenue

Civil damages

As mentioned in chapter 4, products and services employing AI must carry the European "CE" logo. This triggers a different aspect of EU law: a product that carries defects despite its bearing of the logo is considered noncompliant and its producer subject to civil claims for damages from purchasers. The burden of proof is reversed: if the purchaser can establish a reasonable link between damage and the apparent defect, the producer must show convincingly that no such link is in fact present. Otherwise, the producer will have to pay for the damages in full – and no small print or terms of service can prevent that.

Of course, damages suffered by an individual may be small or hard to quantify. A rising trend however is the use of the mass tort, which is well-known in the USA. An organization such as a foundation may represent a section of the population that collectively may have suffered from the AI system's unlawful behavior. Such an organization can then sue on behalf of this entire section, even when individuals in that group did not explicitly authorize them to do so. Moreover, the organization may have been established for the express purpose of the mass tort. We already see this effect with the GDPR, where the threat of mass claims is a significant incentive to drive companies towards compliance.[10]

Key takeaways

Accountability in AI serves as both a foundational principle and a set of actionable practices. Their building blocks include auditability, compliance monitoring, reporting mechanisms, risk management, managing trade-offs and offering redress. Establishing accountability thus becomes a practical matter, although not without its challenges.

Accountability however cannot be simply equated with trust. Trust must be earned, and no amount of compliance activity, transparency or other action can by itself force the earning of trust among those exposed to the effects of the AI system. Thus, the desired "trustworthy AI" of the European Commission requires more than merely executing compliance plans within governance frameworks and offering accountability mechanisms. A more comprehensive approach is needed. In the next and final chapter we'll bring it all together.

Chapter 9 – Accountability and redress

10

Bringing it all together

Weaving the threads of AI compliance

Chapter 10 – Bringing it all together

As the curtain falls on our exploration of AI ethics and law, let's revisit our journey, understand the importance of compliance, and learn how to navigate the complex landscape of AI with the tools we have gathered. In this chapter, we will delve into the intricacies of compliance, governance, and risk management, emphasizing their distinct roles in the AI landscape. We will also introduce the pivotal role of the AI Compliance Officer and explore the significance of the ALTAI Assessment in ensuring the trustworthiness of AI systems. Lastly, we will shed light on the importance of performing comprehensive impact assessments, ensuring that AI deployments align with societal values, ethical standards, and legal mandates.

Navigating the Nuances of Compliance, Governance, and Risk Management

In the business landscape, the terms "compliance," "governance," and "risk management" are often used interchangeably. However, while they are interconnected, each has distinct characteristics and purposes. Understanding the nuances between these concepts is crucial for professionals aiming to ensure that their organizations operate efficiently, ethically, and within the bounds of regulations.

Compliance: Playing by the book

At its core, compliance refers to the act of adhering to external laws, regulations, standards, and internal policies. For businesses, this means ensuring that operations, practices, and behaviors align with set guidelines, whether they are industry-specific regulations, international standards, or company policies. Compliance is reactive in nature; it responds to established rules and standards. Typical incentives to strive towards compliance are to avoid legal penalties, financial losses, and reputational damage.

By the end of this chapter, you'll be able to …

- Understand the comprehensive landscape of AI ethics and law.
- Navigate compliance using the ALTAI assessment tools and implement best practices.
- Stay adaptive and responsible in the ever-evolving AI domain.

In the realm of compliance, organizations often appoint dedicated officers or even entire departments to oversee adherence to laws, regulations, and internal policies. These individuals or teams are the gatekeepers of regulatory alignment, ensuring that the organization operates within the legal and ethical boundaries. Their role involves monitoring, reporting, and advising on compliance matters, and they serve as the primary point of contact for regulatory bodies. Their expertise is crucial in navigating the complex landscape of rules and standards that apply to the organization's operations.

Compliance
The act of adhering to external laws, regulations, standards, and internal policies.

Risk Management
The process of identifying, assessing, and prioritizing uncertainties that could impact an organization's objectives

Governance
The system of practices, processes, and policies by which a company is directed and controlled.

A prime example of a compliance officer is the role of the Data Protection Officer (DPO) under the General Data Protection Regulation (GDPR). DPOs are responsible for overseeing data protection strategy and implementation to ensure compliance with GDPR requirements. Their tasks include conducting audits, managing data protection impact assessments, and serving as the point of contact between the company and regulatory authorities.

The compliance officer holds a role distinct from that of the general counsel or corporate legal department. Lawyers provide essential legal counsel and representation, emphasizing the interpretation of laws and defending the organization's interests. However, their role is reactive: if a claim or legal issue arises, the lawyer or legal department responds to it. On the other hand, the compliance officer proactively ensures that the organization remains in line with regulations and standards, aiming to preemptively ward off potential legal complications.

Governance: Steering the ship

Governance encompasses the system of practices, processes, and policies by which a company is directed and controlled. It involves balancing the interests of a company's many stakeholders, such as shareholders, senior management executives, customers, suppliers, financiers, the government, and the community. Governance provides a framework for attaining a company's objectives and encompasses practically every sphere of management, from action plans and internal controls to performance measurement and corporate disclosure.

While governance is typically the responsibility of a company's board of directors, many organizations also have dedicated Governance Officers or committees. These individuals or groups are tasked with ensuring that the company operates with transparency, accountability, and integrity. They design and implement frameworks for decision-making, oversee management activities, and ensure that the interests of all stakeholders are considered. Their role is pivotal in shaping the strategic direction of the organization and ensuring that it adheres to its core values and principles.

A classic example in the corporate world is the Board of Directors, which provides oversight and direction to the company's management. Similarly, a diversity and inclusivity committee ensures that the organization promotes a culture of fairness, representation, and equal opportunity. This reflects the broader governance goal of acting in the best interests of all stakeholders, including employees, customers, and shareholders. As a counter-example, a product development group would not have a governance function as its primary role is operational.

Risk Management: Dodging the curveballs

Risk management is the process of identifying, assessing, and prioritizing uncertainties that could impact an organization's objectives, followed by coordinated efforts to minimize, monitor, and control the probability or impact of unfortunate events. It's about making strategic decisions to ensure the company's resilience in the face of challenges. While compliance might be seen as a part of risk management (non-compliance being a risk), risk management has a broader scope, considering various types of risks, from financial and operational to strategic and reputational. Examples include:

- ❶ Enterprise Risk Management: This is a holistic approach to risk management that considers risks across the entire organization, ensuring that risks are managed in a coordinated and strategic manner.
- ❷ Operational Risk Management: Focuses specifically on risks arising from day-to-day business operations, such as process failures, system breakdowns, or human errors.
- ❸ Financial Risk Management: Concentrates on risks related to financial markets, such as credit risk, market risk, and liquidity risk.
- ❹ Strategic Risk Management: Addresses risks that could impact the long-term strategic objectives of the company, such as competitive threats or regulatory changes.

Risk management often falls under the purview of Risk Managers or dedicated risk management departments. In some industries, especially finance, the role of the Chief Risk Officer (CRO) has emerged as a top-tier executive position, reflecting the critical importance of managing risks in today's volatile business environment. In companies heavily reliant on IT, the Chief Information Security Officer (CISO) is crucial in managing risks from security breaches. While this role is inherently tied to risk management—specifically, the risks associated with information security—it is not synonymous with the broader risk management function. However, in many organizations, the CISO collaborates closely with the risk management team or function and may even report to the CRO.

Similarities and interplay

While each of the three concepts has its unique focus, they are deeply interconnected. Good governance structures often facilitate better compliance and risk management. Governance sets the tone for an organization, ensuring that the right practices are in place, which in turn makes compliance more straightforward. Risk management, on the other hand, can inform governance structures by highlighting areas of vulnerability, while also ensuring that compliance risks are adequately addressed.

Integrated Governance, Risk, and Compliance (GRC) is a holistic approach to organizational management that seeks to align governance, risk management, and compliance activities across an enterprise.[1] This approach allows organizations to gain a comprehensive view of their risk landscape, streamline processes, and ensure that governance and compliance activities are aligned with the organization's risk appetite. By integrating these functions, organizations can more effectively identify and manage risks, ensure compliance with regulations, and drive better decision-making. The integrated GRC framework not only enhances efficiency by reducing duplicative efforts but also fosters a culture where governance, risk, and compliance are embedded into the daily operations and strategic planning of the organization.

Positioning AI in the triad

AI introduces a new dimension to the triad of governance, risk management and compliance. As AI systems become more integrated into business operations, their influence on these three pillars becomes increasingly significant. The AI Act presents many new compliance requirements, but as this book has demonstrated, merely following the law's demands is not sufficient: a governance function is essential to deploy AI lawfully, ethically and robustly. Given the risk-based approach to regulation in the AI Act, there will be significant overlap with risk management as well.

While lawyers, general compliance officers and risk managers each play vital roles in addressing the complexities of AI, their individual functions often remain too specific and siloed. Navigating the intricate web of AI's influence on compliance, governance, and risk management requires a more holistic approach. This brings us to the emergence of a new pivotal role in the organizational structure: the AI Compliance

Officer, a dedicated professional equipped to bridge these domains and ensure that organizations harness AI's potential both responsibly and effectively.

The role of the AI compliance officer

The AI Compliance Officer plays a crucial role in AI governance, ensuring that AI technologies are developed, deployed, and managed in alignment with ethical guidelines, legal requirements and best practices. The function echoes the role of the Data Protection Officer (DPO) under the General Data Protection Regulation (GDPR). Let's examine this new role more closely.

Position and significance of the AI Compliance Officer

An AI Compliance Officer should be strategically positioned to have a comprehensive view of the organization's AI initiatives, ensuring they have the authority and independence to oversee AI compliance effectively, much like the DPO's role in ensuring data protection compliance under the GDPR. The DPO focuses on data protection, ensuring that personal data is handled in compliance with GDPR and related laws. In contrast, the AI Compliance Officer's purview extends to the ethical, legal, and compliance challenges associated with AI technologies.

Many larger organizations have a general risk management function, whose role is to proactively manage and reduce risks, in particular through the creation and adjustment of business processes. This person's or department's role role is to identify, assess, and prioritize risks to the organization. While the AI Compliance Officer also deals with risk, especially those associated with AI, their role is more specialized, focusing on risks arising from the development, deployment, and use of AI technologies. Similarly, the Chief Information Security Officer (CISO) is crucial in managing risks from security breaches but operates from a different perspective than a general risk manager or an AI Compliance Officer.

Given the specialized nature of each role, it's essential for organizations to carefully consider whether the functions of the AI Compliance Officer can be combined with those of the DPO, CISO, or Risk Management officer. While there might be synergies, especially in organizations with limited resources, it's crucial to ensure that the distinct responsibilities of each role are not diluted. Combining roles might lead to potential conflicts of interest or gaps in oversight. However, in some settings, especially where AI is not the core business, a combined role might be feasible, provided the individual possesses the requisite expertise and the organization implements robust checks and balances.

Functions and responsibilities of the AI Compliance Officer

The primary role of an AI Compliance Officer is to operate as a cornerstone in the organizational structure, ensuring that the deployment and management of AI technologies align seamlessly with ethical, legal, and compliance guidelines. Drawing parallels with the responsibilities shouldered by Data Protection Officers under the General Data Protection Regulation (GDPR), the AI Compliance Officer's role is multifaceted and pivotal.

- At the forefront, the AI Compliance Officer is tasked with the duty to inform and advise. This entails keeping the organization and its workforce abreast of their obligations concerning AI ethics and compliance. By regularly updating and disseminating pertinent information, the officer ensures that all stakeholders remain cognizant of their roles and responsibilities.
- Monitoring compliance is another critical facet of the role. This involves a vigilant oversight of the organization's AI practices, ensuring they resonate with both internal policies and external regulations. Through regular audits and assessments, the AI Compliance Officer ensures that AI systems are in strict adherence to established guidelines and standards.
- Risk management is integral to the role. The AI Compliance Officer identifies, evaluates, and addresses potential risks embedded within the organization's AI operations. By facilitating comprehensive AI risk assessments, the officer ensures that potential pitfalls are not only identified but also effectively mitigated.
- The development, implementation, and oversight of policies related to the ethical and legal use of AI also falls under the officer's purview. Collaborative efforts with various departments are essential to draft, refine, and implement AI compliance policies that are both comprehensive and current.
- Cultivating a culture of AI compliance within the organization is paramount. Through training sessions, workshops, and awareness campaigns, the AI Compliance Officer ensures that the workforce is well-equipped with knowledge about AI compliance requirements and best practices.
- Serving as the primary liaison with regulatory authorities is another significant responsibility. The officer engages proactively with regulatory bodies, ensuring adherence to all external regulations and addressing any inquiries or investigations with promptness and precision. While the AI Act does not make this task explicit (unlike the GDPR), formally appointing a liaison officer in case of enquiries or investigations is nonetheless a good idea.
- Incident management is crucial. The AI Compliance Officer must have mechanisms in place to swiftly identify, report, and rectify any breaches or lapses in AI compliance. This requires a clear and swift cooperation with other functions, such as the DPO (in case of data breaches associated with the lapse), the CISO (security incidents) or the public relations management (to address publicity surrounding the lapse).

Given the AI Compliance Officer's pivotal role in monitoring and ensuring AI practices align with ethical and legal standards, a structured approach to evaluating AI systems becomes indispensable. The ALTAI Assessment, frequently referenced throughout this book, serves as a foundational tool in this regard. Let's delve deeper into its significance and application in the AI landscape. Next, we will also explore more comprehensive and formalized impact assessments, which provide a holistic view of the potential consequences and implications of AI deployments.

Applying the ALTAI Assessment

Throughout this book, we've referred to the ALTAI Assessment questions as specific points of attention. However, the Assessment List for Trustworthy Artificial Intelligence (ALTAI) is more than a collection of questions. It provides a framework for evaluating the trustworthiness of AI systems and thus aids organizations in navigating the complex regulatory landscape associated with AI.

Understanding the ALTAI Assessment

At its core, ALTAI provides a foundational framework for assessing AI's trustworthiness.[2] Its real-world application however requires organizations to adapt and contextualize the list to their specific operational environments. This means that rather than treating ALTAI as a static checklist, organizations should engage in continuous reflection and adaptation, taking into account the evolving nature of AI technologies and the diverse contexts in which they are deployed.

The first step to elevating the ALTAI results is to assign scores to each answer. This can be as simple as 1 for yes and 0 for no, but answers on a scale from 1 to 5 or any other system are also possible. One could even introduce weights: if diversity is a key ethical value, answers in this category (see chapter 7) would have higher weights than, say, human agency. The scores per category can then be added up and compared to a product- or organization-wide threshold. It is important however to remember that merely setting the threshold to a perfect 10 is not desirable: both the scores and the threshold must be set to meet realistic expectations.

ALTAI Assessments as spider charts

The designers of the ALTAI Assessment recommend to create a spider chart (also known as a radar chart or web chart) to visualize the results. This is a graphical method of displaying multivariate data in the form of a two-dimensional chart of three or more quantitative variables represented on axes starting from the same point.[3] Each category's score is plotted along its respective axis, and all the axes are arranged radially around a central point. The data points are connected, forming a polygon. This gives the chart a spider web-like appearance, hence the name. Spider charts can be created using commonly-available tools such as Microsoft Excel or LibreOffice Calc.[4]

The primary purpose of a spider chart is to visualize multiple quantitative variables simultaneously to understand how they compare. This makes it easier to see which variables have similar values or if there are any outliers. Thus, for ALTAI outcomes, this chart serves as an effective tool to visualize the outcomes of the assessment across its various categories. Given that ALTAI encompasses multiple dimensions of trustworthy AI, plotting these dimensions on a spider chart allows stakeholders to quickly grasp the areas where an AI system excels and where it might need improvement.

By scoring the outcomes per category and plotting them on the spider chart, organizations can get a holistic view of their AI system's trustworthiness. Each axis of the spider chart represents one of the seven categories of the ALTAI. The farther out the data point on an axis, the higher the score in that category.

The use of a spider chart in this context is beneficial for several reasons:
1. Visualization: It provides a snapshot of the AI system's performance across all categories, making it easier to identify strengths and weaknesses.
2. Comparative analysis: Organizations can compare multiple AI systems or the same system's performance over time.
3. Easy communication: It serves as a visual tool that can be easily understood by both technical and non-technical stakeholders, facilitating discussions around AI trustworthiness.

However, spider charts come with certain downsides or risks, especially when applied to the ALTAI Assessment:
1. Misinterpretation of relative importance: All axes on a spider chart are given equal visual weight, which might lead viewers to assume that all ALTAI categories are of equal importance. However, depending on the context or specific application of an AI system, some categories might be more critical than others. Without proper guidance, stakeholders might misinterpret the relative significance of each category.
2. Difficulty in comparing multiple AI systems: If an organization wants to compare the ALTAI scores of multiple AI systems on the same spider chart, it can become cluttered and challenging to interpret. Overlapping polygons can obscure details, making it hard to discern subtle differences between systems. Further, the impression may arise that a chart with a smaller area of coverage is somehow indicative of worse performance. This ties in to the issue regarding thresholds: there is no reason that any AI system should strive for a perfect 10 on each category axis.

Chapter 10 – Bringing it all together

- **Potential for Oversimplification:** The spider chart provides a high-level overview of the ALTAI scores across categories. However, there's a risk that stakeholders might focus solely on the chart and overlook the nuanced details and explanations behind each score. This could lead to oversimplified conclusions about an AI system's trustworthiness without a deeper understanding of the underlying factors.

To put the above into practice, we will now provide three fictional examples of AI systems that score very differently across the seven axes of the ALTAI Assessment, but would still have very good scores for their respective fields.

Medical diagnostic AI

This system analyzes medical data such as images, lab results, and patient histories to diagnose diseases or conditions. It aids healthcare professionals by providing insights based on patterns that might be challenging for the human eye to detect, ensuring early and accurate diagnosis.

Medical Diagnostic AI

- **High on:** Technical robustness and safety (because accurate diagnostics are crucial), Privacy and data governance (due to the sensitive nature of medical data), and Accountability (given the potential consequences of errors).
- **Variable on:** Transparency (some advanced models might be more like "black boxes"), and Diversity, non-discrimination, and fairness (depending on the diversity of training data).
- **Moderate on:** Human agency and oversight (doctors would likely review its outputs), and Societal and environmental wellbeing.

AI-driven Financial Trading System

Utilizing real-time market data, historical trends, and complex algorithms, this system predicts market movements and executes trades at optimal times. It's designed to maximize profits while minimizing risks, operating at a speed and precision beyond human capabilities.

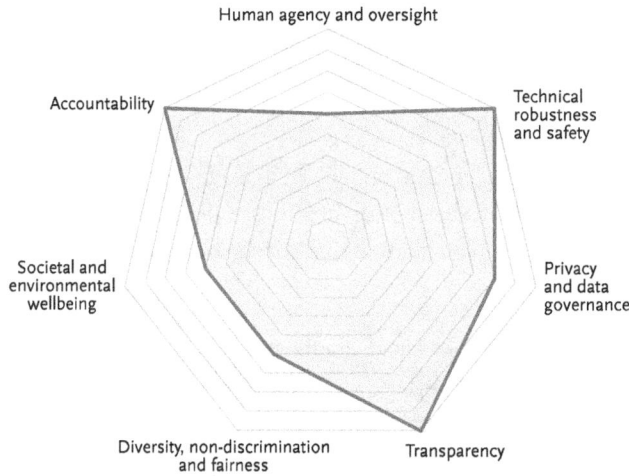

AI-driven Financial Trading System

- **High on:** Technical robustness and safety (to prevent financial losses), Transparency (to understand trading decisions), and Accountability (due to the financial implications of its actions).
- **Variable on:** Privacy and data governance (depending on the type of data it processes).
- **Moderate on:** Human agency and oversight (might operate autonomously within set parameters), Diversity, non-discrimination, and fairness (might not be a primary concern), and Societal and environmental wellbeing.

AI-powered Educational Tutoring System

Tailored to individual student needs, this system offers personalized learning experiences. It assesses students' strengths and weaknesses, adapts content accordingly, and provides real-time feedback, ensuring a more effective and engaging learning process.

Chapter 10 – Bringing it all together

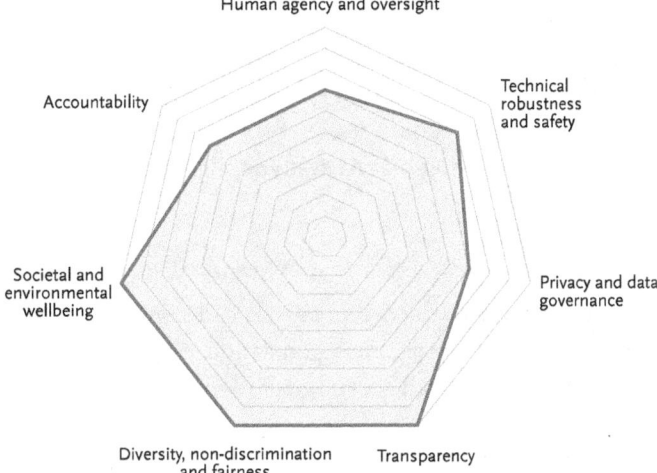

AI-powered Educational Tutoring System

- High on: Diversity, non-discrimination, and fairness (to ensure all students are treated equally), Transparency (so educators understand how it assesses and assists students), and Societal and environmental wellbeing (given its direct impact on education).
- Variable on: Technical robustness and safety (depending on its application, e.g., high stakes testing vs. casual learning).
- Moderate on: Human agency and oversight (teachers and parents might review its recommendations), Privacy and data governance (depending on age group and data collected), and Accountability.

As can be seen above, the spider chart for each of these AI systems is very different. Yet, the specific application of AI justifies the scores given. It is thus impossible to say that the medical diagnosis AI scores 'better' than the education system.

Effectiveness of ALTAI

As the Assessment List has only been available for a few years, scientific review on its effectiveness is scarce. A handful of studies is available on adapting ALTAI for specific applications, such as healthcare delivery[5] or driver-assistance systems.[6] A general study of the usefulness of ALTAI showed that next to this step of adaptation, a key factor to success is stakeholder involvement in the assessment process.[7] In essence, the practical application of ALTAI is about fostering a culture of continuous learning, adaptation, and stakeholder engagement to ensure the ethical and responsible development and deployment of AI systems. We will address this below.

The ALTAI Assessment is often thought of as an ex post tool: given an AI system, what is its score and where are the weaknesses that need to be addressed? However, a 2023 study underscores the value of ex-ante application of the ALTAI Assessment in proactively identifying and addressing ethical and social concerns associated with AI. By anticipating potential issues before they arise, organizations can implement preventive measures, ensuring that AI systems align with societal values and norms.[8]

Transforming ALTAI into a company-specific compliance tool

The ALTAI assessment, while comprehensive, is designed to be a general framework. For it to be effective within a specific organization, it needs to be tailored to align with the company's unique goals, values, and operational nuances. Customizing the ALTAI involves identifying which aspects of the assessment are most relevant to the company's AI applications and modifying or expanding upon them to address company-specific concerns. This ensures that the assessment is not just a generic checklist but a tool that resonates with the company's mission and objectives.

Most organizations already have some form of compliance mechanisms in place. A well-known example in the security world is the ISO 27001 compliance framework. Practitioners in the American health sector would have HIPAA (Health Insurance Portability and Accountability Act) compliance processes in place. And in the IT world the COBIT (Control Objectives for Information and Related Technologies) framework developed by ISACA provides tools for developing, implementing, monitoring, and improving IT governance and management practices. For organizations looking for ISO standards guidance, the ALTAI Assessment may be a good step towards ISO 42001 (AI Management) compliance.[9]

For organizations that already have established compliance frameworks, the challenge lies in seamlessly integrating ALTAI without disrupting existing processes. The integration should be viewed as an enhancement, providing a more robust and holistic approach to AI compliance. The following steps outline a systematic approach to achieving this integration, ensuring that organizations can leverage the strengths of both their existing compliance mechanisms and the ALTAI:

- ❶ Gap analysis: Begin by conducting a thorough review of the current compliance framework in place. Identify areas that are already addressed by the framework and areas where ALTAI can provide additional insights or coverage.
- ❷ Stakeholder engagement: Engage with key stakeholders, including legal, IT, data science teams, and senior management. Their input is crucial in understanding the nuances of how AI is used within the organization and where ALTAI can be most beneficial.

- **Customize ALTAI:** Tailor the ALTAI list to align with the company's specific goals, values, and operational nuances. This might involve prioritizing certain aspects of ALTAI based on the organization's unique AI applications. An example is the study by Borg et al that sought to customize ALTAI for the sector of self-driving motor vehicles.[10]
- **Integration plan:** Develop a detailed plan outlining how ALTAI will be integrated with the existing compliance mechanisms. This should include timelines, responsibilities, and key milestones.
- **Training and capacity building:** Organize training sessions for employees to familiarize them with the ALTAI assessment. Ensure they have the knowledge and skills to effectively use and interpret it in the context of the organization's AI applications.
- **Continuous monitoring:** Once ALTAI is integrated, set up mechanisms to continuously monitor its effectiveness. This could involve periodic reviews, feedback sessions, and audits.
- **Feedback loop:** Establish a feedback loop where insights and challenges faced during the ALTAI application are regularly discussed and addressed. This ensures that the integration remains dynamic and evolves based on real-world experiences. A key issue to avoid is that the ALTAI assessment becomes a paper exercise, a hoop that must be jumped through without attention for the real-life consequences.
- **Review and update:** As AI technologies and applications evolve, and as new regulations or guidelines emerge, periodically revisit the integrated framework. Ensure that it remains relevant and continues to provide comprehensive coverage for AI compliance.

While the ALTAI assessment serves as a foundational tool for AI compliance, it's just one piece of a broader compliance puzzle. As organizations delve deeper into the AI realm, they'll encounter scenarios that demand a more granular examination of potential impacts. This is where the importance of impact assessments comes into play. These assessments go beyond the general framework of ALTAI, diving into the specifics of individual AI projects, policies, or systems. They provide a detailed analysis of potential consequences, ensuring that every AI initiative is launched with a clear understanding of its implications on data subjects, societal values, and legal boundaries.

Performing impact assessments

Impact assessments are systematic evaluations designed to understand the potential consequences of a project, policy, or system. Risk impact assessment models are increasingly used as a tool to consider and preserve data subjects' fundamental rights, as well as ethical and social standing.[11] In the context of AI, these assessments are crucial to ensure that the deployment and use of AI technologies are in line with societal values, ethical standards, and legal requirements. There are various types of assessment that can play a role.

Data Protection Impact Assessment (DPIA)

The General Data Protection Regulation (GDPR) introduced the concept of a Data Protection Impact Assessment (DPIA). A DPIA is a process to help organizations identify and minimize the data protection risks of a project. It is mandatory for projects that are likely to result in a high risk to the rights and freedoms of individuals, which according to the GDPR is particularly likely when dealing with "new technologies" such as AI systems.

Like the AI Act, the GDPR takes a risk-based approach. DPIAs are mandatory for "high risk" processing of personal data. Yet, the GDPR does not clarify when a risk is 'high', thus making it uncertain when a DPIA is required.[12] However, the AI Act requires deployers of AI systems to perform GDPR data protection impact assessments (DPIA) if any personal data is used in the AI system.

AI Impact Assessment (AIIA)

The AI Impact Assessment (AIIA) is a structured framework designed to evaluate the potential risks and implications of deploying AI systems. It evaluates the ethical, social, economic, and technical implications of deploying an AI system and seeks to provide organizations with a clear roadmap for understanding the potential consequences of their AI systems.

The concept of an AIIA was first promoted by the UK's Ada Lovelace Institute in an evaluation of AI usage in the National Health Service, and quickly attracted interest from European countries and EU institutions.[13] One model for an AIIA is published by the Dutch ECP Institute.[14] It provides seven steps:
1. Determine the need to perform an AIIA
2. Describe the AI application
3. Are the goal and the way the goal is reached ethical and legally justifiable?
4. Is the application reliable, safe and transparent?
5. Considerations and assessment
6. Documentation and accountability
7. Review periodically

Algorithmic Impact Assessment (AIA)

The Algorithmic Impact Assessment (AIA) is a framework designed to evaluate and mitigate the risks associated with deploying algorithmic systems, especially in public sectors. The concept of the AIA was first promoted by the AI Now Institute at New York University, with the aim of ensuring that algorithmic decisions are transparent, accountable, and free from discriminatory outcomes. Key points of attention in an AIA are:

- Transparency: Ensuring that the workings of the algorithm, its data sources, and its decision-making processes are transparent and understandable.
- Bias detection: Actively seeking and rectifying biases in both the data used to train the algorithm and in the algorithm's outcomes.
- Public engagement: Involving the public and stakeholders in discussions about the deployment and implications of the algorithm.
- Accountability: Establishing clear lines of responsibility for the algorithm's decisions and setting up mechanisms for redress in case of adverse outcomes.
- Continuous monitoring: Regularly reviewing and updating the algorithm to ensure it remains fair, accurate, and aligned with its intended purpose.

Ethical Impact Assessment (EIA)

UNESCO's Ethical Impact Assessment (EIA) is a framework designed to evaluate the ethical implications of new technologies, particularly in the field of artificial intelligence (AI).[15] The EIA aims to ensure that the development and deployment of AI technologies align with human rights, democratic values, and ethical principles. By conducting an EIA, stakeholders can identify potential ethical risks and challenges posed by AI systems, allowing them to make informed decisions and implement appropriate measures to mitigate these risks. Key points of attention in an EIA include:

- Alignment with human rights and ethical principles: The primary focus of an EIA is to ensure that the technology, especially AI, aligns with established human rights standards and ethical principles. This includes considerations of privacy, dignity, freedom, and non-discrimination.
- Identification of ethical risks: An EIA requires a thorough examination of potential ethical risks and challenges posed by the technology. This involves identifying areas where there might be unintended consequences or where the technology might be misused.
- Stakeholder engagement: Engaging with a diverse group of stakeholders, including the public, experts, and affected communities, is crucial. Their insights and perspectives can provide a holistic understanding of the ethical implications and potential real-world impacts of the technology.
- Transparency and accountability: Ensuring that the development and deployment processes of the technology are transparent is vital. This promotes trust and allows for accountability, especially if something goes wrong or if there are unintended consequences.
- Mitigation strategies: Once potential ethical risks are identified, the EIA should outline clear strategies and measures to mitigate these risks. This could include technical solutions, policy changes, or even refraining from deploying the technology in certain contexts.

Fundamental rights impact assessment (FRIA)

The Fundamental Rights Impact Assessment (FRIA) is a comprehensive evaluation framework aimed at identifying, assessing, and mitigating the potential impacts of a particular initiative, policy, or technology on fundamental rights or human rights. The European Union has been at the forefront of promoting the concept of FRIA, emphasizing its importance in the context of the digital age where technologies like AI can have profound implications on rights such as privacy, non-discrimination, and freedom of expression.

A practical framework for developing and carrying out FRIAs is proposed by Janssen et al.[16] At the highest level the framework consists of four phases:

1. Describe the purpose of the AI system, and define tasks and responsibilities of the parties involved in the design, development, use, and evaluation of the system.
2. Identify and assess the risks to rights that might occur at different stages of the AI system's development.
3. Justify whether and why the risks of possible infringements on fundamental rights identified in Phase 2 are proportionate.
4. Consider and adopt organizational and technical measures to reduce the remaining risks identified in Phases 1, 2 and/or 3. After adoption, repeat the FRIA process from Phase 1 onwards until risks have been removed or properly justified and mitigated.

The AI Act requires deployers of AI systems to perform a FRIA prior to putting high-risk AI systems into use. Such a FRIA must at least include references to the intended purpose and scope of the system and persons affected, as well as a clear analysis of risks to fundamental rights and how these will be mitigated. Applying the ALTAI assessment or any of the other assessment types in this section is a clear way to satisfy this legal requirement.

Practical tips

When performing impact assessments, it's essential to approach the task with a genuine intent to understand and mitigate potential risks, rather than merely ticking off compliance boxes. A common pitfall is treating the assessment as a mere paper exercise, which can lead to superficial evaluations and missed opportunities to address real concerns. Collaboration is key; ensuring that the assessment is not siloed within the compliance or legal departments but involves a cross-functional team can provide a holistic view of the potential impacts.

Firstly, stakeholder engagement is paramount. Engaging with a diverse set of stakeholders, including technical experts, ethicists, end-users, and potentially affected communities, can provide invaluable insights. Their diverse perspectives can highlight unforeseen risks and offer innovative mitigation strategies. Secondly, continuous iteration is crucial. The technology and societal context can evolve, so assessments should be revisited and updated regularly. Thirdly, transparency in the assessment process fosters trust among stakeholders and the public. Sharing the methodologies, findings, and mitigation strategies can demonstrate a genuine commitment to ethical AI deployment. Fourthly, training and capacity building ensure that team members understand the importance of the assessment and are equipped with the skills to carry it out effectively. Lastly, documentation is essential. Keeping a detailed record of the assessment process, findings, and decisions made can be invaluable for future reference, audits, or in case of disputes.

By approaching impact assessments with a genuine intent to understand and address potential risks, organizations can ensure that their AI deployments are not only compliant but also ethically sound and socially beneficial.

Key takeaways

This final chapter has delved deep into the multifaceted world of compliance, governance, and risk management, understanding the pivotal role of the AI Compliance Officer and the power of tools like the ALTAI Assessment whose content we have studied in the earlier chapters. This robust framework stands as more than just a set of questions; it's a beacon guiding professionals through the complex regulatory maze of AI, ensuring that systems are trustworthy and resonate with societal values.

The significance of impact assessments has also been underscored, emphasizing their role in aligning AI technologies with ethical standards, legal requirements, and the preservation of data subjects' rights. As AI continues its transformative journey across industries and societies, the importance of diligent governance and compliance will undoubtedly amplify. But with the knowledge and tools you've acquired, you're well-prepared to navigate this evolving terrain. The realm of AI compliance assessments beckons, offering opportunities to apply your expertise and make a meaningful impact.

As this book draws to a close, take a moment to reflect on the knowledge you've amassed and the potential it holds. You're not just equipped to understand the rules of AI but to actively shape its future. Embrace the challenges that lie ahead, stay curious, and champion the cause of ethical and responsible AI deployment. The world of AI is vast, and your role in it is pivotal. Share your insights, engage in meaningful discussions, and be at the forefront of this transformative era.

Appendix

Appendix

Below is a summary of the ALTAI questions cited throughout this book, followed by the page on which the question's subject matter is discussed. Chapter 10 goes into more detail on how to apply the ALTAI questions to assess an AI system's trustworthiness.

CHAPTER 3 Reinforcing Human Agency and Oversight in AI

A1. Is the AI system designed to interact, guide or take decisions by human end-users that affect humans or society? – 60
    a. Could the AI system generate confusion for some or all end-users or subjects on whether a decision, content, advice or outcome is the result of an algorithmic decision? – 61
    b. Are end-users or other subjects adequately made aware that a decision, content, advice or outcome is the result of an algorithmic decision? – 62

A2. Could the AI system generate confusion for some or all end-users or subjects on whether they are interacting with a human or AI system? – 62
    a. Are end-users or subjects informed that they are interacting with an AI system? – 62

A3. Could the AI system affect human autonomy by generating over-reliance by end-users? – 63
    a. Did you put in place procedures to avoid that end-users over-rely on the AI system? – 65

A4. Could the AI system affect human autonomy by interfering with the end-user's decision-making process in any other unintended and undesirable way? – 66
    a. Did you put in place any procedure to avoid that the AI system inadvertently affects human autonomy? – 66

A5. Does the AI system simulate social interaction with or between end-users or subjects? – 68

A6. Does the AI system risk creating human attachment, stimulating addictive behaviour, or manipulating user behaviour? Depending on which risks are possible or likely, please answer the questions below: – 70
    a. Did you take measures to deal with possible negative consequences for end-users or subjects in case they develop a disproportionate attachment to the AI System? – 71
    b. Did you take measures to minimise the risk of addiction? – 71
    c. Did you take measures to mitigate the risk of manipulation? – 71

A7. Please determine whether the AI system (choose as many as appropriate): – 72
   a. Is a self-learning or autonomous system;
   b. Is overseen by a *Human*-in-the-Loop;
   c. Is overseen by a *Human*-on-the-Loop;
   d. Is overseen by a *Human*-in-Command.
A8. Have the humans (human-in-the-loop, human-on-the-loop, human-in-command) been given specific training on how to exercise oversight? – 72
A9. Did you establish any detection and response mechanisms for undesirable adverse effects of the AI system for the end-user or subject? – 74
A10. Did you ensure a 'stop button' or procedure to safely abort an operation when needed? – 76
A11. Did you take any specific oversight and control measures to reflect the self-learning or autonomous nature of the AI system? – 77

CHAPTER 4 Robustness reliability and safeguards

B1. Could the AI system have adversarial, critical or damaging effects in case of risks or threats such as design or technical faults, defects, outages, attacks, misuse, inappropriate or malicious use? – 82
B2. Is the AI system certified for cybersecurity (e.g. the certification scheme created by the Cybersecurity Act in Europe) or compliant with specific security standards? – 82
B3. How exposed is the AI system to cyber-attacks? – 82
   a. Did you assess potential forms of attacks to which the AI system could be vulnerable? – 82
   b. Did you consider different types of vulnerabilities and potential entry points for attacks such as: – 82
      i. Data poisoning
      ii. Model evasion
      iii. Model inversion
B4. Did you put measures in place to ensure the integrity, robustness and overall security of the AI system against potential attacks over its lifecycle? – 84
B5. Did you red-team/pentest the system? – 84
B6. Did you inform end-users of the duration of security coverage and updates? – 84
   a. What length is the expected timeframe within which you provide security updates for the AI system? – 84
B7. Did you define risks, risk metrics and risk levels of the AI system in each specific use case? – 86
   a. Did you put in place a process to continuously measure and assess risks? – 86
   b. Did you inform end-users and subjects of existing or potential risks? – 86
B8. Did you identify the possible threats to the AI system (design faults, technical faults, environmental threats) and the possible consequences? – 86

B9. Did you assess the risk of possible malicious use, misuse or inappropriate use of the AI system? – 86
B10. Did you define safety criticality levels (e.g. related to human integrity) of the possible consequences of faults or misuse of the AI system?
    a. Did you assess the dependency of a critical AI system's decisions on its stable and reliable behaviour? – 89
    b. Did you align the reliability/testing requirements to the appropriate levels of stability and reliability?
B11. Did you plan fault tolerance via, e.g. a duplicated system or another parallel system (AI-based or 'conventional')? – 90
B12. Did you develop a mechanism to evaluate when the AI system has been changed to merit a new review of its technical robustness and safety? – 90
B13. Could a low level of accuracy of the AI system result in critical, adversarial or damaging consequences? – 93
B14. Did you put in place measures to ensure that the data (including training data) used to develop the AI system is up-to-date, of high quality, complete and representative of the environment the system will be deployed in? – 95
B15. Did you put in place a series of steps to monitor, and document the AI system's accuracy? – 95
B16. Did you consider whether the AI system's operation can invalidate the data or assumptions it was trained on, and how this might lead to adversarial effects? – 95
B17. Did you put processes in place to ensure that the level of accuracy of the AI system to be expected by end-users and/or subjects is properly communicated? – 96
B18. Could the AI system cause critical, adversarial, or damaging consequences (e.g. pertaining to human safety) in case of low reliability and/or reproducibility? – 97
    a. Did you put in place a well-defined process to monitor if the AI system is meeting the intended goals? – 97
    b. Did you test whether specific contexts or conditions need to be taken into account to ensure reproducibility? – 97
B19. Did you put in place verification and validation methods and documentation (e.g. logging) to evaluate and ensure different aspects of the AI system's reliability and reproducibility? – 97
    a. Did you clearly document and operationalise processes for the testing and verification of the reliability and reproducibility of the AI system?
B20. Did you define tested failsafe fallback plans to address AI system errors of whatever origin and put governance procedures in place to trigger them? – 98
B21. Did you put in place a proper procedure for handling the cases where the AI system yields results with a low confidence score? – 99
B22. Is your AI system using (online) continual learning? – 100
B23. Did you consider potential negative consequences from the AI system learning novel or unusual methods to score well on its objective function? – 100

CHAPTER 5 Data governance and Privacy in AI Systems

C1. Did you consider the impact of the AI system on the right to privacy, the right to physical, mental and/or moral integrity and the right to data protection? – 107

C2. Depending on the use case, did you establish mechanisms that allow flagging issues related to privacy concerning the AI system? – 110

C3. Is your AI system being trained, or was it developed, by using or processing personal data (including special categories of personal data)? – 111

C4. Did you put in place any of the following measures some of which are mandatory under the General Data Protection Regulation (GDPR), or a non-European equivalent? – 112

    a. Data Protection Impact Assessment (DPIA); – 112

    b. Designate a Data Protection Officer (DPO) and include them at an early state in the development, procurement or use phase of the AI system; – 113

    c. Oversight mechanisms for data processing (including limiting access to qualified personnel, mechanisms for logging data access and making modifications); – 113

    d. Measures to achieve privacy-by-design and default (e.g. encryption, pseudonymisation, aggregation, anonymisation); – 113

    e. Data minimisation, in particular personal data (including special categories of data); – 114

    f. Did you implement the right to withdraw consent, the right to object and the right to be forgotten into the development of the AI system? – 114

    g. Did you consider the privacy and data protection implications of data collected, generated or processed over the course of the AI system's life cycle? – 114

C5. Did you consider the privacy and data protection implications of the AI system's non-personal training-data or other processed non-personal data? – 115

C6. Did you align the AI system with relevant standards (e.g. ISO25, IEEE26) or widely adopted protocols for (daily) data management and governance? – 127

CHAPTER 6 Emphasizing Transparency in AI Operations

D1. Did you put in place measures that address the traceability of the AI system during its entire lifecycle? – 133

    a. Did you put in place measures to continuously assess the quality of the input data to the AI system? – 134

    b. Can you trace back which data was used by the AI system to make a certain decision(s) or recommendation(s)? – 135

    c. Can you trace back which AI model or rules led to the decision(s) or recommendation(s) of the AI system? – 136

  d. Did you put in place measures to continuously assess the quality of the output(s) of the AI system? – 137

  e. Did you put adequate logging practices in place to record the decision(s) or recommendation(s) of the AI system?

D2. Did you explain the decision(s) of the AI system to the users? – 138

D3. Do you continuously survey the users if they understand the decision(s) of the AI system? – 143

D4. In cases of interactive AI systems (e.g., chatbots, robo-lawyers), do you communicate to users that they are interacting with an AI system instead of a human? – 147

D5. Did you establish mechanisms to inform users about the purpose, criteria and limitations of the decision(s) generated by the AI system? – 147

  a. Did you communicate the benefits of the AI system to users? – 148

  b. Did you communicate the technical limitations and potential risks of the AI system to users, such as its level of accuracy and/ or error rates? – 148

  c. Did you provide appropriate training material and disclaimers to users on how to adequately use the AI system? – 149

CHAPTER 7 Fostering Fairness, Diversity, and Non-discrimination

E1. Did you establish a strategy or a set of procedures to avoid creating or reinforcing unfair bias in the AI system, both regarding the use of input data as well as for the algorithm design? – 156

E2. Did you consider diversity and representativeness of end-users and/or subjects in the data? – 161

  a. Did you test for specific target groups or problematic use cases? – 161

  b. Did you research and use publicly available technical tools, that are state-ofthe-art, to improve your understanding of the data, model and performance? – 161

  c. Did you assess and put in place processes to test and monitor for potential biases during the entire lifecycle of the AI system (e.g. biases due to possible limitations stemming from the composition of the used data sets (lack of diversity, non-representativeness)? – 161

  d. Where relevant, did you consider diversity and representativeness of end-users and or subjects in the data? – 161

E3. Did you put in place educational and awareness initiatives to help AI designers and AI developers be more aware of the possible bias they can inject in designing and developing the AI system? – 162

E4. Did you ensure a mechanism that allows for the flagging of issues related to bias, discrimination or poor performance of the AI system? – 163
    a. Did you establish clear steps and ways of communicating on how and to whom such issues can be raised? – 163
    b. oDid you identify the subjects that could potentially be (in)directly affected by the AI system, in addition to the (end-)users and/or subjects? – 163

E5. Is your definition of fairness commonly used and implemented in any phase of the process of setting up the AI system? – 164
    a. Did you consider other definitions of fairness before choosing this one? – 164
    b. Did you consult with the impacted communities about the correct definition of fairness, i.e. representatives of elderly persons or persons with disabilities? – 164
    c. Did you ensure a quantitative analysis or metrics to measure and test the applied definition of fairness? – 164
    d. Did you establish mechanisms to ensure fairness in your AI system? – 164

E6. Did you ensure that the AI system corresponds to the variety of preferences and abilities in society? – 166

E7. Did you assess whether the AI system's user interface is usable by those with special needs or disabilities or those at risk of exclusion? – 167
    a. Did you ensure that information about, and the AI system's user interface of, the AI system is accessible and usable also to users of assistive technologies (such as screen readers)? – 167
    b. Did you involve or consult with end-users or subjects in need for assistive technology during the planning and development phase of the AI system? – 167

E8. Did you ensure that Universal Design principles are taken into account during every step of the planning and development process, if applicable? – 168

E9. Did you take the impact of the AI system on the potential end-users and/or subjects into account? – 169
    a. Did you assess whether the team involved in building the AI system engaged with the possible target end-users and/or subjects? – 169
    b. Did you assess whether there could be groups who might be disproportionately affected by the outcomes of the AI system? – 169
    c. Did you assess the risk of the possible unfairness of the system onto the end-user's or subject's communities? – 169

E10. Did you consider a mechanism to include the participation of the widest range of possible stakeholders in the AI system's design and development? – 170

Appendix

CHAPTER 8 Societal and Environmental Implications of AI Systems

F1. Are there potential negative impacts of the AI system on the environment? – 170
   a. Which potential impact(s) do you identify? – 170
F2. Where possible, did you establish mechanisms to evaluate the environmental impact of the AI system's development, deployment and/or use (for example, the amount of energy used and carbon emissions)? – 180
   a. Did you define measures to reduce the environmental impact of the AI system throughout its lifecycle? – 180
F3. Does the AI system impact human work and work arrangements? – 181
F4. Did you pave the way for the introduction of the AI system in your organisation by informing and consulting with impacted workers and their representatives (trade unions, (European) work councils) in advance? – 183
F5. Did you adopt measures to ensure that the impacts of the AI system on human work are well understood? – 183
   a. Did you ensure that workers understand how the AI system operates, which capabilities it has and which it does not have? – 183
F6. Could the AI system create the risk of de-skilling of the workforce? – 183
   a. Did you take measures to counteract de-skilling risks? – 183
F7. Does the system promote or require new (digital) skills? – 183
   a. Did you provide training opportunities and materials for re- and up-skilling? – 183
F8. Could the AI system have a negative impact on society at large or democracy? – 191
   a. Did you assess the societal impact of the AI system's use beyond the (end-)user and subject, such as potentially indirectly affected stakeholders or society at large? – 191
   b. Did you take action to minimize potential societal harm of the AI system? – 191
   c. Did you take measures that ensure that the AI system does not negatively impact democracy? – 191

CHAPTER 9 Accountability and redress

G1. Did you establish mechanisms that facilitate the AI system's auditability (e.g. traceability of the development process, the sourcing of training data and the logging of the AI system's processes, outcomes, positive and negative impact)? – 203
G2. Did you ensure that the AI system can be audited by independent third parties? – 203
G3. Did you foresee any kind of external guidance or third-party auditing processes to oversee ethical concerns and accountability measures? – 204
   a. Does the involvement of these third parties go beyond the development phase? – 204
G4. Did you organise risk training and, if so, does this also inform about the potential legal framework applicable to the AI system? – 205

G5. Did you consider establishing an AI ethics review board or a similar mechanism to discuss the overall accountability and ethics practices, including potential unclear grey areas? – 205

G6. Did you establish a process to discuss and continuously monitor and assess the AI system's adherence to this Assessment List for Trustworthy AI (ALTAI)? – 205
   a. Does this process include identification and documentation of conflicts between the 6 aforementioned requirements or between different ethical principles and explanation of the 'trade-off' decisions made? – 205
   b. Did you provide appropriate training to those involved in such a process and does this also cover the legal framework applicable to the AI system? – 205

G7. Did you establish a process for third parties (e.g. suppliers, end-users, subjects, distributors/vendors or workers) to report potential vulnerabilities, risks or biases in the AI system? – 206
   a. Does this process foster revision of the risk management process? – 206

G8. For applications that can adversely affect individuals, have redress by design mechanisms been put in place? – 207

Appendix

References

CHAPTER I

[1] **Noguchi, T., Hashizume, Y., Moriyama, H., Gauthier, L., Ishikawa, Y., Matsuno, T., & Suganuma, A.** (2018, May). A practical use of expert system" AI-Q" focused on creating training data. In 2018 5th International Conference on Business and Industrial Research (ICBIR) (pp. 73-76). IEEE. [2] **Gailhofer, P., Herold, A., Schemmel, J. P., Scherf, C. S., de Stebelski, C. U., Köhler, A. R., & Braungardt, S.** (2021). *The role of artificial intelligence in the European Green Deal*. Luxembourg, Belgium: European Parliament. [3] **D.M. Nabirahni, B.R. Evans & A. Persaud,** 'Al-Khwarizmi (algorithm) and the development of algebra', *Mathematics Teaching Research Journal* 2019, 11, p. 13-17. [4] **Wagner, B.** et al. 'Algorithms and human rights. Study on the human rights dimensions of automated data processing techniques and possible regulatory implications, DGI(2017)12, prepared by the Committee of Experts on internet intermediaries (MSI-NET) for the Council of Europe' (2018) https://rm.coe.int/algorithms-and-human-rights-en-rev/16807956b5 [5] **Bordot, F.** (2022). Artificial Intelligence, Robots and Unemployment: Evidence from OECD Countries. *Journal of Innovation Economics & Management*, 37, 117-138. https://doi.org/10.3917/jie.037.0117 [6] https://rm.coe.int/algorithms-and-human-rights-en-rev/16807956b5 [7] **Dubber, M. D., Pasquale, F., & Das, S. (Eds.).** (2020). *The Oxford handbook of ethics of AI*. Oxford Handbooks. [8] **Steinhoff, J.** (2023). AI ethics as subordinated innovation network. *AI & SOCIETY*, 1-13. [9] **Green, B.** (2021). The contestation of tech ethics: A sociotechnical approach to technology ethics in practice. *Journal of Social Computing*, 2(3), 209-225. [10] **Floridi, L., Cowls, J., Beltrametti, M., Chatila, R., Chazerand, P., Dignum, V., ... & Vayena, E.** (2018). AI4People – an ethical framework for a good AI society: opportunities, risks, principles, and recommendations. *Minds and machines*, 28, 689-707. [11] **M. Haenlein & A.Kaplan,** 'A brief history of artificial intelligence: On the past, present, and future of artificial intelligence', *California management review* 2019, 61.4, p. 5-14. [12] **Floridi,** L. What the Near Future of Artificial Intelligence Co uld Be. *Philos. Technol.* 32, 1–15 (2019). https://doi.org/10.1007/s13347-019-00345-y [13] **R.S. Boyer e.a.,** 'In memoriam: Edsger W. Dijkstra 1930—2002', *Communications of the ACM* 2002, 45, 10, p. 21-22. [14] **Campbell, M., Hoane Jr, A. J., & Hsu, F. H. (2002).** Deep blue. *Artificial intelligence*, 134(1-2), 57-83. [15] **Fradkov, A. L.** (2020). Early history of machine learning. *IFAC-PapersOnLine*, 53(2), 1385-1390. [16] **Wang, F. Y., Zhang, J. J., Zheng, X., Wang, X., Yuan, Y., Dai, X., ... & Yang, L.** (2016). Where does AlphaGo go: From church-turing thesis to AlphaGo thesis and beyond. *IEEE/CAA Journal of Automatica Sinica*, 3(2), 113-120. [17] **Russell, S. J. & Norvig, P. (2010).** *Artificial intelligence a modern approach*. Pearson Education, Inc.. [18] **Turing, A.M.** (1950). Computing Machinery and Intelligence, 59 MIND 433, 442. [19] **R.S. Boyer e.a.,** 'In memoriam: Edsger W. Dijkstra 1930—2002', *Communications of the ACM* 2002, 45, 10, p. 21-22. [20] https://legalinstruments.oecd.org/en/instruments/OECD-LEGAL-0449 [21] **Hachey, K. K., Libel, T., & Partington, Z.** (2020). The impact of artificial intelligence on the military profession.

Rethinking Military Professionalism for the Changing Armed Forces, 201-211. [22] **Beard, J. M.** (2013). Autonomous weapons and human responsibilities. *Geo. J. Int'l L.*, *45*, 617 [23] **Davison, N.** (2018). A legal perspective: Autonomous weapon systems under international humanitarian law. *Convention on Certain Conventional Weapons Meeting of Experts on Lethal Autonomous Weapons Systems (LAWS)*, 11 April 2016. [24] **Campbell, J. F., & Green, K. M.** (2021). Robots as Caretakers. *Intersectional Automations: Robotics, AI, Algorithms, and Equity*, 169. [25] **Lancaster, K.** (2019). The Robotic Touch: Why there is no good reason to prefer human nurses to carebots. *Philosophy in the Contemporary World*, *25*(2), 88-109. [26] **Oriakhogba, D. O.** (2021). DABUS gains territory in South Africa and Australia: Revisiting the AI-inventorship question. *South African Intellectual Property Law Journal*, *9*(1), 87-108. [27] **Rosati, E.** (2017). The Monkey Selfie case and the concept of authorship: an EU perspective. *Journal of Intellectual Property Law & Practice*, *12*(12), 973-977. [28] **Frosio, G.** (2023). The Artificial Creatives: The Rise of Combinatorial Creativity from Dall-E to GPT-3. *Handbook of Artificial Intelligence at Work: Interconnections and Policy Implications (Edward Elgar, Forthcoming)*. [29] **Hugenholtz, P. B., & Quintais, J. P.** (2021). Copyright and artificial creation: does EU copyright law protect AI-assisted output?. *IIC-International Review of Intellectual Property and Competition Law*, *52*(9), 1190-1216. [30] **Butler, T. L.** (1981). Can a computer be an author-copyright aspects of artificial intelligence. *Comm/Ent LS*, *4*, 707.

CHAPTER 2

[1] **Sharma, R., Lopes de Sousa Jabbour, A. B., Jain, V., & Shishodia, A.** (2022). The role of digital technologies to unleash a green recovery: Pathways and pitfalls to achieve the European Green Deal. *Journal of Enterprise Information Management, 35*(1), 266-294. [2] https://eur-lex.europa.eu/legal-content/EN/TXT/?uri=COM%3A2018%3A237%3AFIN [3] **COM** (2018) 237, and in December a Coordinated Action Plan, COM (2018) 795. https://eur-lex.europa.eu/legal-content/EN/TXT/?uri=CELEX%3A52018DC0795 [4] https://eur-lex.europa.eu/legal-content/EN/TXT/?uri=COM:2018:795:FIN [5] **Floridi, L.** (2021). Establishing the rules for building trustworthy AI. *Ethics, Governance, and Policies in Artificial Intelligence*, 41-45. [6] **Justo-Hanani, R.** (2022). The politics of Artificial Intelligence regulation and governance reform in the European Union. *Policy Sciences, 55*(1), 137-159. [7] **Ulnicane, I., Knight, W., Leach, T., Stahl, B. C., & Wanjiku, W. G.** (2021). Framing governance for a contested emerging technology: Insights from AI policy. Policy and Society, 40(2), 158–177. https://doi.org/10.1080/14494 035.2020.1855800 [8] **Bradford, A.** (2020). *The Brussels effect: How the European Union rules the world.* Oxford University Press, USA. [9] **Tartaro, A.** (2023). Regulating by standards: current progress and main challenges in the standardisation of Artificial Intelligence in support of the AI Act.| Regolare con gli standard: gli attuali progressi e le sfide principali nella standardizzazione dell'intelligenza artificiale a sostegno dell'AI Act. *European Journal of Privacy Law & Technologies*, (1). [10] **Mökander, J., Axente, M., Casolari, F., & Floridi, L.** (2022). Conformity assessments and post-market monitoring: a guide to the role of auditing in the proposed European AI regulation. *Minds and Machines, 32*(2), 241-268. [11] **Floridi, L., Holweg, M., Taddeo, M., Amaya Silva, J., Mökander, J., & Wen, Y.** (2022). CapAI-A procedure for conducting conformity assessment of AI systems in line with the EU artificial intelligence act. *Available at SSRN 4064091.* [12] **De Vries, S. A.** (2013). Balancing fundamental rights with economic freedoms according to the European Court of Justice. *Utrecht L. Rev., 9*, 169. [13] **Ranchordas, S.** (2021). Experimental regulations for AI: sandboxes for morals and mores. *University of Groningen Faculty of Law Research Paper,* (7). [14] **Hacker, P.** (2023). The European AI liability directives – Critique of a half-hearted approach and lessons for the future. *Computer Law & Security Review, 51,* 105871. [15] **Matthieu Burnay & Alexandru Circiumaru, 2023.** "The AI global order: what place for the European Union?," Chapters, in: Michelle Egan & Kolja Raube & Jan Wouters & Julien Chaisse (ed.), Contestation and Polarization in Global Governance, chapter 15, pages 264-281, Edward Elgar Publishing. [16] **van Kolfschooten, H., & Shachar, C.** (2023). The Council of Europe's AI Convention (2023-2024): Promises and Pitfalls for Health Protection. *Health Policy,* 104935. [17] **Elder, E.** (2022). Wrongful Improvers as a Guiding Principle for Application of the FTC's IP Deletion Requirement. *Wash. L. Rev., 97,* 1009. [18] **Mökander, J., Juneja, P., Watson, D.S.** *et al.* The US Algorithmic Accountability Act of 2022 vs. The EU Artificial Intelligence Act: what can they learn

from each other?. *Minds & Machines 32*, 751–758 (2022). https://doi.org/10.1007/s11023-022-09612-y
[19] **Roberts, H., Cowls, J., Morley, J., Taddeo, M., Wang, V., & Floridi, L.** (2021). The Chinese approach to artificial intelligence: an analysis of policy, ethics, and regulation. *Ethics, Governance, and Policies in Artificial Intelligence*, 47-79. [20] **Filgueiras, F., & Junquilho, T. A.** (2023). The Brazilian (Non) perspective on national strategy for artificial intelligence. *Discover Artificial Intelligence, 3*(1), 7.
[21] **Belli, L., Curzi, Y., & Gaspar, W. B.** (2023). AI regulation in Brazil: Advancements, flows, and need to learn from the data protection experience. *Computer Law & Security Review, 48*, 105767.
[22] **Fatima, S., Desouza, K. C., & Dawson, G. S.** (2020). National strategic artificial intelligence plans: A multi-dimensional analysis. *Economic Analysis and Policy, 67*, 178-194. [23] **Habuka, H.** (2023). Japan's approach to AI Regulation and its impact on the 2023 G7 Presidency. *Center for Strategic&International Studies, 14*. [24] **Smuha, N. A.** (2021). From a 'race to AI' to a 'race to AI regulation': regulatory competition for artificial intelligence. *Law, Innovation and Technology, 13*(1), 57-84. [25] **Radclyffe, C., Ribeiro, M., & Wortham, R. H.** (2023). The assessment list for trustworthy artificial intelligence: A review and recommendations. *Frontiers in Artificial Intelligence, 6*, 1020592.

CHAPTER 3

[1] **Takayama, L.** (2015). Telepresence and apparent agency in human–robot interaction. In S. S. Sundar (Ed.), *The handbook of the psychology of communication technology* (pp. 160–175). Malden, MA: Wiley Blackwell. [2] **J. Greenwood, A. Seshadri & M. Yorukoglu**, 'Engines of liberation', *The Review of Economic Studies* 2005, 72/1, p. 109-133. [3] **Sarter, N. B., Woods, D. D., and Billings, C. E.** (1997). "Automation surprises," in *Handbook of human factors and ergonomics*, 2nd Edn, ed. G. Salvendy (New York, NY: Wiley), 1926–1943. [4] **Dekker, S. W. A., and Woods, D. D.** (2002). MABA-MABA or abracadabra? Progress on human-automation co-ordination. *Cogn. Technol. Work* 4, 240–244. [5] **Endsley, M. R.** (1999). Level of automation effects on performance, situation awareness and workload in a dynamic control task. Ergonomics 42, 462–492. [6] **Pagliari, M., Chambon, V., & Berberian, B.** (2022). What is new with Artificial Intelligence? Human–agent interactions through the lens of social agency. Frontiers in Psychology, 13, 954444. [7] **Barlas, Z., Hockley, W. E., & Obhi, S. S.** (2017). The effects of freedom of choice in action selection on perceived mental effort and the sense of agency. *Acta psychologica*, 180, 122-129. [8] **Cheung, A. S., & Chen, Y.** (2022). From datafication to data state: Making sense of China's social credit system and its implications. *Law & Social Inquiry*, 47(4), 1137-1171. [9] **Vokey, J. R., & Read, J. D.** (1985). Subliminal messages: Between the devil and the media. *American psychologist*, 40(11), 1231. [10] **Neuwirth, R. J.** (2022). *The EU artificial intelligence act: regulating subliminal AI systems.* Taylor & Francis. [11] **Silver, C. A., Tatler, B. W., Chakravarthi, R., and Timmermans, B.** (2020). Social agency as a continuum. *Psycho. Bull. Rev.* 28, 434–453. doi: 10.3758/s13423-020-01845-1 [12] **Vasconcelos, H., Jörke, M., Grunde-McLaughlin, M., Gerstenberg, T., Bernstein, M. S., & Krishna, R.** (2023). Explanations can reduce overreliance on ai systems during decision-making. *Proceedings of the ACM on Human-Computer Interaction*, 7(CSCW1), 1-38. [13] **Bansal, G., Wu, T., Zhou, J., Fok, R., Nushi, B., Kamar, E., ... & Weld, D.** (2021, May). Does the whole exceed its parts? the effect of AI explanations on complementary team performance. In Proceedings of the 2021 CHI Conference on Human Factors in Computing Systems (pp. 1-16). [14] **Vasconcelos, H., Jörke, M., Grunde-McLaughlin, M., Gerstenberg, T., Bernstein, M. S., & Krishna, R.** (2023). Explanations can reduce over-reliance on ai systems during decision-making. Proceedings of the ACM on Human-Computer Interaction, 7(CSCW1), 1-38. [15] **Buçinca, Z., Malaya, M. B., & Gajos, K. Z.** (2021). To trust or to think: cognitive forcing functions can reduce over-reliance on AI in AI-assisted decision-making. *Proceedings of the ACM on Human-Computer Interaction*, 5(CSCW1), 1-21. [16] **Donahoe, E., & Metzger, M. M.** (2019). Artificial intelligence and human rights. *J. Democracy*, 30, 115. [17] **Abedin, B., Meske, C., Junglas, I., Rabhi, F., & Motahari-Nezhad, H. R.** (2022). Designing and managing human-AI interactions. *Information Systems Frontiers*, 24(3), 691-697. [18] **Schuetz, S., & Venkatesh, V.** (2020). The rise of human machines: How cognitive computing systems challenge

assumptions of user-system interaction. Journal of the Association for Information Systems, 21(2), 460-482. **[19] Kędzierski, J., Kaczmarek, P., Dziergwa, M., & Tchoń, K.** (2015). Design for a robotic companion. International journal of humanoid robotics, 12(01), 1550007. **[20] Dillon, S.** (2020). The Eliza effect and its dangers: From demystification to gender critique. Journal for Cultural Research, 24(1), 1-15. **[21] Belk, R.** (2022). Artificial emotions and love and sex doll service workers. Journal of Service Research, 25(4), 521-536. **[22] Richardson, K.** (2016). Sex robot matters: slavery, the prostituted, and the rights of machines. *IEEE Technology and Society Magazine*, 35(2), 46-53. **[23] Xie, T., & Pentina, I.** (2022). Attachment theory as a framework to understand relationships with social chatbots: a case study of Replika. **[24] Cofer, D.** (2021, October). Unintended behavior in learning-enabled systems: detecting the unknown unknowns. In 2021 *IEEE/AIAA 40th Digital Avionics Systems Conference (DASC)* (pp. 1-7). IEEE. **[25] Arnold, T., & Scheutz, M.** (2018). The "big red button" is too late: an alternative model for the ethical evaluation of AI systems. *Ethics and Information Technology*, 20, 59-69.

CHAPTER 4

[1] **Papakonstantinou, V.** (2022). Cybersecurity as praxis and as a state: The EU law path towards acknowledgement of a new right to cybersecurity?. *Computer Law & Security Review, 44*, 105653. [2] **Chiara, P. G.** (2022). The IoT and the new EU cybersecurity regulatory landscape. *International Review of Law, Computers & Technology, 36*(2), 118-137. [3] **Clim, A., Toma, A., Zota, R. D., & Constantinescu, R.** (2022). The Need for Cybersecurity in Industrial Revolution and Smart Cities. *Sensors, 23*(1), 120. [4] **Bae, H., Jang, J., Jung, D., Jang, H., Ha, H., Lee, H., & Yoon, S.** (2018). Security and privacy issues in deep learning. *arXiv preprint arXiv:1807.11655.* [5] **Eykholt, K., Evtimov, I., Fernandes, E., Li, B., Rahmati, A., Xiao, C., ... & Song, D.** (2018). Robust physical-world attacks on deep learning visual classification. *In Proceedings of the IEEE conference on computer vision and pattern recognition* (pp. 1625-1634). [6] **Ozlati, S., & Yampolskiy, R.** (2017, March). The formalization of AI risk management and safety standards. *In Workshops at the Thirty-First AAAI Conference on Artificial Intelligence.* [7] **Taherdoost, H.** (2022). Understanding cybersecurity frameworks and information security standards – a review and comprehensive overview. *Electronics, 11*(14), 2181. [8] **De Haes, S., Van Grembergen, W., & Debreceny, R. S.** (2013). COBIT 5 and enterprise governance of information technology: Building blocks and research opportunities. *Journal of Information Systems, 27*(1), 307-324. [9] **Dabade, T. D.** (2012). Information technology infrastructure library (ITIL). *In Proceedings of the 4th National Conference* (pp. 25-26). [10] **Dunn Cavelty, M., & Smeets, M.** (2023). Regulatory cybersecurity governance in the making: The formation of ENISA and its struggle for epistemic authority. *Journal of European Public Policy, 30*(7), 1330-1352. [11] **Siau, K., & Wang, W.** (2018). Building trust in artificial intelligence, machine learning, and robotics. *Cutter business technology journal, 31*(2), 47-53. [12] **Hubbard, D. W.** (2009). *The Failure of Risk Management*: Why It's Broken and How to Fix It. John Wiley & Sons. [13] **Arora, A. S., Changotra, R., & Rajput, H.** (2021). to Quantitative Risk Assessment Methodologies. *Bow Ties in Process Safety and Environmental Management: Current Trends and Future Perspectives*, 211. [14] **Lior, A.** (2022). Insuring AI: The role of insurance in artificial intelligence regulation. *Harvard Journal of Law and Technology*, 1. [15] **Leffingwell, D., Meissner, M., & Langenfeld, C.** (2011). Agile software development with verification and validation in high assurance and regulated environments. *Rally Software Development Corp.* [16] **Wang, L., Zhang, X., Su, H., & Zhu, J.** (2023). A comprehensive survey of continual learning: Theory, method and application. *arXiv preprint arXiv:2302.00487.* [17] **Aljundi, R., Kelchtermans, K., & Tuytelaars, T.** (2019). Task-free continual learning. *In Proceedings of the IEEE/CVF Conference on Computer Vision and Pattern Recognition* (pp. 11254-11263).

CHAPTER 5

[1] **Westin, A. F.** (1967). *Privacy and freedom.* Atheneum. [2] **Riccardi, J. L.** (1983). The German federal data protection act of 1977: Protecting the right to privacy. Boston College International and Comparative Law Review, 6, 243. [3] **Bennett, C. J.** (2018). The European General Data Protection Regulation: An instrument for the globalization of privacy standards? Information Polity, 23(2), 239-246. [4] **Schwartz, P. M., & Solove, D. J.** (2011). The PII problem: Privacy and a new concept of personally identifiable information. *NYU Law Review,* 86, 1814. [5] **Barrett, C.** (2019). Are the EU GDPR and the California CCPA becoming the de facto global standards for data privacy and protection?. *Scitech Lawyer,* 15(3), 24-29. [6] **Haenlein, M., & Kaplan, A.** (2019). A brief history of artificial intelligence: On the past, present, and future of artificial intelligence. *California management review,* 61(4), 5-14. [7] **Zuboff, S.** (2015). Big other: surveillance capitalism and the prospects of an information civilization. *Journal of information technology,* 30(1), 75-89. [8] **Kalluri, P. R., Agnew, W., Cheng, M., Owens, K., Soldaini, L., & Birhane, A.** (2023). The Surveillance AI Pipeline. *arXiv preprint arXiv:2309.15084.* [9] **CNIL** (2023). AI how-to sheets. Retrieved from: https://www.cnil.fr/en/ai-how-sheets [10] **Cavoukian, A.** (2009). Privacy by design: The 7 foundational principles. *Information and privacy commissioner of Ontario, Canada,* 5, 12. [11] **Labadie, C., & Legner, C.** (2020). Personal Data Protection Inside and Out: Integrating Data Protection Requirements in the Data Lifecycle. *Enterprise Modelling and Information Systems Architectures (EMISAJ),* 15, 9-1. [12] **Bommasani, R., Hudson, D. A., Adeli, E., Altman, R., Arora, S., von Arx, S., ... & Liang, P.** (2021). On the opportunities and risks of foundation models. *arXiv preprint arXiv:2108.07258.* [13] **Carugati, C.** (2023). *Competition in generative artificial intelligence foundation models* (No. 14/2023). Bruegel Working Paper. [14] **Filippov, S.** (2014). *Mapping text and data mining in academic and research communities in Europe.* Lisbon Council. [15] **Rosati, E.** (2019). Copyright as an obstacle or an enabler? A European perspective on text and data mining and its role in the development of AI creativity. *Asia Pacific Law Review,* 27(2), 198-217. [16] **Ippolito, D., & Yu, Y. W. DONOTTRAIN**: A Metadata Standard for Indicating Consent for Machine Learning. Proceedings of the 40th International Conference on Machine Learning, Honolulu, Hawaii, USA. PMLR 202, 2023. [17] **Lucchi, N.** (2023). ChatGPT: A Case Study on Copyright Challenges for Generative Artificial Intelligence Systems. *European Journal of Risk Regulation,* 1-23. [18] **Frosio, G.** (2023). Should We Ban Generative AI, Incentivise it or Make it a Medium for Inclusive Creativity?. *A Research Agenda for EU Copyright Law (Edward Elgar, Forthcoming).* [19] **Omelina, L., Goga, J., Pavlovicova, J., Oravec, M., & Jansen, B.** (2021). A survey of iris datasets. *Image and Vision Computing,* 108, 104109. [20] **Ahler, D. J., Roush, C. E., & Sood, G.** (2019). The micro-task market for lemons: Data quality on Amazon's Mechanical Turk. *Political Science Research and Methods,* 1-20. [21] **Nguyen, T., Ilharco, G., Wortsman, M., Oh, S., & Schmidt, L.** (2022). Quality not quantity: On the interaction

between dataset design and robustness of clip. *Advances in Neural Information Processing Systems*, 35, 21455-21469. See also Birhane, A., Prabhu, V., Han, S., & Boddeti, V. N. (2023). On Hate Scaling Laws For Data-Swamps. arXiv preprint arXiv:2306.13141. **22 Yang, K., Qinami, K., Fei-Fei, L., Deng, J., & Russakovsky, O.** (2020, January). Towards fairer datasets: Filtering and balancing the distribution of the people subtree in the imagenet hierarchy. *In Proceedings of the 2020 conference on fairness, accountability, and transparency* (pp. 547-558). **23 M. Ebers e.a.,** 'The European Commission's Proposal for an Artificial Intelligence Act - A Critical Assessment by Members of the Robotics and AI Law Society (RAILS)', J 2021, 4, p. 589- 603 **24 Budach, L., Feuerpfeil, M., Ihde, N., Nathansen, A., Noack, N., Patzlaff, H., ... & Harmouch, H.** (2022). The effects of data quality on machine learning performance. *arXiv preprint* arXiv:2207.14529. **25 Liang, W., Tadesse, G. A., Ho, D., Fei-Fei, L., Zaharia, M., Zhang, C., & Zou, J.** (2022). Advances, challenges and opportunities in creating data for trustworthy AI. Nature Machine Intelligence, 4(8), 669-677. **26 Munappy, A., Bosch, J., Olsson, H. H., Arpteg, A., & Brinne, B.** (2019, August). Data management challenges for deep learning. In 2019 45th Euromicro Conference on Software Engineering and Advanced Applications (SEAA) (pp. 140-147). IEEE.

CHAPTER 6

[1] **Larsson, S., & Heintz, F.** (2020). Transparency in artificial intelligence. *Internet Policy Review, 9*(2). [2] **Jobin, A., Ienca, M., & Vayena, E.** (2019). The global landscape of AI ethics guidelines. *Nature Machine Intelligence, 1*(9), 389–399. [3] **Pasquale, F.** (2015). *The black box society: The secret algorithms that control money and information.* Harvard University Press. [4] **Dubber, M. D., Pasquale, F., & Das, S.** (Eds.). (2020). *The Oxford handbook of ethics of AI.* Oxford Handbooks. [5] **Lu, J., Liu, A., Dong, F., Gu, F., Gama, J., & Zhang, G.** (2018). Learning under concept drift: A review. *IEEE transactions on knowledge and data engineering, 31*(12), 2346-2363. [6] **Kreuzberger, D., Kühl, N., & Hirschl, S.** (2023). Machine learning operations (mlops): Overview, definition, and architecture. *IEEE Access.* [7] **Mora-Cantallops, M., Sánchez-Alonso, S., García-Barriocanal, E., & Sicilia, M. A.** (2021). Traceability for trustworthy ai: A review of models and tools. *Big Data and Cognitive Computing, 5*(2), 20. [8] **Plesser, H. E.** (2018). Reproducibility vs. replicability: a brief history of a confused terminology. *Frontiers in neuroinformatics, 11,* 76. [9] **Kaplan, A.** (2020). Artificial intelligence, social media, and fake news: Is this the end of democracy. *IN MEDIA & SOCIETY, 149.* [10] **Lancaster, T.** (2023). Artificial intelligence, text generation tools and ChatGPT–does digital watermarking offer a solution?. *International Journal for Educational Integrity, 19*(1), 10. [11] **Zhu, J., He, P., Fu, Q., Zhang, H., Lyu, M. R., & Zhang, D.** (2015, May). Learning to log: Helping developers make informed logging decisions. In *2015 IEEE/ACM 37th IEEE International Conference on Software Engineering* (Vol. 1, pp. 415-425). IEEE. [12] **Bosch, N., & Bosch, J.** (2020). Software logging for machine learning. *arXiv preprint arXiv:2001.10794.* [13] **Confalonieri, R., Coba, L., Wagner, B., & Besold, T. R.** (2021). A historical perspective of explainable Artificial Intelligence. *Wiley Interdisciplinary Reviews: Data Mining and Knowledge Discovery, 11*(1), e1391. [14] **Xu, F., Uszkoreit, H., Du, Y., Fan, W., Zhao, D., & Zhu, J.** (2019). Explainable AI: A brief survey on history, research areas, approaches and challenges. In *Natural Language Processing and Chinese Computing: 8th CCF International Conference, NLPCC 2019, Dunhuang, China, October 9–14, 2019, Proceedings, Part II 8* (pp. 563-574). Springer International Publishing. [15] **Bücker, M., Szepannek, G., Gosiewska, A., & Biecek, P.** (2022). Transparency, auditability, and explainability of machine learning models in credit scoring. *Journal of the Operational Research Society, 73*(1), 70-90. [16] **McCoy, L. G., Brenna, C. T., Chen, S. S., Vold, K., & Das, S.** (2022). Believing in black boxes: machine learning for healthcare does not need explainability to be evidence-based. *Journal of clinical epidemiology, 142,* 252-257. [17] **Miller, T.** (2019). Explanation in artificial intelligence: Insights from the social sciences. *Artificial intelligence, 267,* 1-38. [18] **Chromik, M., & Schuessler, M.** (2020). A Taxonomy for Human Subject Evaluation of Black-Box Explanations in XAI. *Exss-atec@ iui, 1.* [19] **Zonneveldt, S., Korb, K., & Nicholson, A.** (2010). Bayesian network classifiers for the German credit data. *Bayesian-intelligence. com/publications.* [20] **Arrieta, A. B., Díaz-**

Rodríguez, N., Del Ser, J., Bennetot, A., Tabik, S., Barbado, A., ... & Herrera, F. (2020). Explainable Artificial Intelligence (XAI): Concepts, taxonomies, opportunities and challenges toward responsible AI. *Information fusion, 58,* 82-115. [21] **Ribeiro, M. T., Singh, S., & Guestrin, C.** (2016, August). "Why should i trust you?" Explaining the predictions of any classifier. In *Proceedings of the 22nd ACM SIGKDD international conference on knowledge discovery and data mining* (pp. 1135-1144). [22] **Bordt, S., Finck, M., Raidl, E., & von Luxburg, U.** (2022, June). Post-hoc explanations fail to achieve their purpose in adversarial contexts. In *Proceedings of the 2022 ACM Conference on Fairness, Accountability, and Transparency* (pp. 891-905). [23] **Wachter, S., Mittelstadt, B., & Russell, C.** (2017). Counterfactual explanations without opening the black box: Automated decisions and the GDPR. *Harv. JL & Tech., 31,* 841. [24] **Spreitzer, N., Haned, H., & van der Linden, I.** (2022, November). Evaluating the Practicality of Counterfactual Explanations. In *Workshop on Trustworthy and Socially Responsible Machine Learning, NeurIPS 2022.* [25] **Waldman, A. E.** (2019). Power, process, and automated decision-making. *Fordham L. Rev., 88,* 613. [26] **Binns, R., & Veale, M.** (2021). Is that your final decision? Multi-stage profiling, selective effects, and Article 22 of the GDPR. *International Data Privacy Law, 11*(4), 319-332. [27] **Aloisi, A., & Potocka-Sionek, N.** (2022). De-gigging the labour market? An analysis of the 'algorithmic management' provisions in the proposed Platform Work Directive. *An Analysis of the 'Algorithmic Management' Provisions in the Proposed Platform Work Directive (July 21, 2022).* [28] **De Stefano, V.** (2022). The EU Commission's proposal for a Directive on Platform Work: an overview. *Osgoode Legal Studies Research Paper Forthcoming, Italian Labour Law e,* (1). [29] **Binns, R., & Veale, M.** (2021). Is that your final decision? Multi-stage profiling, selective effects, and Article 22 of the GDPR. *International Data Privacy Law, 11*(4), 319-332. [30] **Veale, M., & Zuiderveen Borgesius, F.** (2021). Demystifying the Draft EU Artificial Intelligence Act—Analysing the good, the bad, and the unclear elements of the proposed approach. *Computer Law Review International,* 22(4), 97-112.

CHAPTER 7

[1] **Carey, A. N., & Wu, X.** (2023). The statistical fairness field guide: perspectives from social and formal sciences. *AI and Ethics*, *3*(1), 1-23. [2] **Hellström, T., Dignum, V., & Bensch, S.** (2020). Bias in Machine Learning – What is it Good for?. *arXiv preprint arXiv:2004.00686*. [3] **Miller, K.** (2020). A matter of perspective: Discrimination, bias, and inequality in ai. In *Legal regulations, implications, and issues surrounding digital data* (pp. 182-202). IGI Global. [4] **Osoba, O. A., Welser IV, W., & Welser, W.** (2017). *An intelligence in our image: The risks of bias and errors in artificial intelligence*. Rand Corporation. [5] **Caliskan, A., Bryson, J. J., & Narayanan, A.** (2017). Semantics derived automatically from language corpora contain human-like biases. *Science*, *356*(6334), 183-186. [6] **Papakyriakopoulos, O., & Mboya, A. M.** (2023). Beyond algorithmic bias: a socio-computational interrogation of the google search by image algorithm. *Social Science Computer Review*, *41*(4), 1100-1125. [7] **Datta, A., Tschantz, M. C., & Datta, A.** (2014). Automated experiments on ad privacy settings: A tale of opacity, choice, and discrimination. *arXiv preprint arXiv:1408.6491*. [8] **Thomas, C., & Ponton-Nunez, A.** (2022). Automating judicial discretion: How algorithmic risk assessments in pretrial adjudications violate equal protection rights on the basis of race. *Law & Ineq.*, *40*, 371. [9] **Kuśmierczyk, M.** (2022). Algorithmic Bias in the Light of the GDPR and the Proposed AI Act. *In) equality. Faces of modern Europe", Wydawnictwo Centrum Studiów Niemieckich i Europejskich im. Willy'ego Brandta, Wrocław*. [10] **Chi, N., Lurie, E., & Mulligan, D. K.** (2021, July). Reconfiguring diversity and inclusion for AI ethics. In *Proceedings of the 2021 AAAI/ACM Conference on AI, Ethics, and Society* (pp. 447-457). [11] **Wirth, R., & Hipp, J.** (2000, April). CRISP-DM: Towards a standard process model for data mining. In *Proceedings of the 4th international conference on the practical applications of knowledge discovery and data mining* (Vol. 1, pp. 29-39). [12] **Martínez-Plumed, F., Contreras-Ochando, L., Ferri, C., Hernández-Orallo, J., Kull, M., Lachiche, N., ... & Flach, P.** (2019). CRISP-DM twenty years later: From data mining processes to data science trajectories. *IEEE Transactions on Knowledge and Data Engineering*, *33*(8), 3048-3061. [13] **Jo, E. S., & Gebru, T.** (2020, January). Lessons from archives: Strategies for collecting sociocultural data in machine learning. In *Proceedings of the 2020 conference on fairness, accountability, and transparency* (pp. 306-316). [14] **Holstein, K., Wortman Vaughan, J., Daumé III, H., Dudik, M., & Wallach, H.** (2019, May). Improving fairness in machine learning systems: What do industry practitioners need?. In *Proceedings of the 2019 CHI conference on human factors in computing systems* (pp. 1-16). [15] **Kaplan, J.** (2016). Artificial intelligence: Think again. *Communications of the ACM*, *60*(1), 36-38. [16] **Bittenbinder, S., Müller, C., & Tuncer, Z.** (2023). European Accessibility Act-Practice-based approaches to meeting accessibility requirements. *Mensch und Computer 2023 - Workshopband*. [17] **Martínez-Normand, L., & Pluke, M.** (2014). A decision-tree approach for the applicability of the accessibility standard EN 301 549. In *Computers Helping People*

with Special Needs: 14th International Conference, ICCHP 2014, Paris, France, July 9-11, 2014, Proceedings, Part II 14 (pp. 295-302). Springer International Publishing. **[18] Stephanidis, C., Salvendy, G., Antona, M., Chen, J. Y., Dong, J., Duffy, V. G., ... & Zhou, J.** (2019). Seven HCI grand challenges. *International Journal of Human–Computer Interaction*, 35(14), 1229-1269. **[19] Stephanidis, C.** (2021). Design for all in digital technologies. *Handbook of human factors and ergonomics*, 1187-1215. **[20] Baarslag, A.** (2022). Hurdles on the European Road to Accessibility. *The Open Issue*, 8, 11. **[21] Reich, K., & Petter, C.** (2009). eInclusion, eAccessibility and design for all issues in the context of European computer-based assessment. *The transition to computer-based assessment. New approaches to skills assessment and implications for large-scale testing*, 68-73. **[22] Lee, M. K., Kusbit, D., Kahng, A., Kim, J. T., Yuan, X., Chan, A., ... & Procaccia, A. D.** (2019). WeBuildAI: Participatory framework for algorithmic governance. *Proceedings of the ACM on Human-Computer Interaction*, 3(CSCW), 1-35. **[23] Delgado, F., Yang, S., Madaio, M., & Yang, Q.** (2021). Stakeholder Participation in AI: Beyond" Add Diverse Stakeholders and Stir". *arXiv preprint arXiv:2111.01122*. **[24] Wong, R. Y., Madaio, M. A., & Merrill, N.** (2023). Seeing like a toolkit: How toolkits envision the work of AI ethics. *Proceedings of the ACM on Human-Computer Interaction*, 7(CSCW1), 1-27. **[25] Bell, A., Nov, O., & Stoyanovich, J.** (2023). Think about the stakeholders first! Toward an algorithmic transparency playbook for regulatory compliance. *Data & Policy*, 5, e12.

CHAPTER 8

[1] **Zhong, J., Zhong, Y., Han, M., Yang, T., & Zhang, Q.** (2023). The impact of AI on carbon emissions: evidence from 66 countries. *Applied Economics*, 1-15. [2] **Li, P., Yang, J., Islam, M. A., & Ren, S.** (2023). Making AI Less" Thirsty": Uncovering and Addressing the Secret Water Footprint of AI Models. *arXiv preprint arXiv:2304.03271.* [3] **Russo, G. L.** (2023). Integrated Management of Electronic and Electric Waste (EEW) with the Application of Artificial Intelligence (AI): Future and Challenges. In *Advanced Technologies for Solid, Liquid, and Gas Waste Treatment* (pp. 23-40). CRC Press. [4] **Cowls, J., Tsamados, A., Taddeo, M., & Floridi, L.** (2021). A definition, benchmark and database of AI for social good initiatives. *Nature Machine Intelligence, 3*(2), 111-115. [5] **Rafat K, Islam S, Mahfug AA, Hossain MI, Rahman F, Momen S, et al.** (2023) Mitigating carbon footprint for knowledge distillation based deep learning model compression. PLoS ONE 18(5): e0285668. [6] **Sætra, H. S.** (2023). The AI ESG protocol: Evaluating and disclosing the environment, social, and governance implications of artificial intelligence capabilities, assets, and activities. *Sustainable Development, 31*(2), 1027-1037. [7] **SANTOS-D'AMORIM, K., & de Oliveira Miranda, M. K. F.** (2021). Misinformation, disinformation, and malinformation: clarifying the definitions and examples in disinfodemic times. *Encontros Bibli: revista eletrônica de biblioteconomia e ciência da informação, 26.* [8] **Rakha, N. A.** (2023). The Ethics of Data Mining: Lessons from the Cambridge Analytica Scandal. *International Journal of Cyber Law, 1*(1).

CHAPTER 9

[1] **Yeung, K.** (2020). Recommendation of the council on artificial intelligence (OECD). *International legal materials*, 59(1), 27-34. [2] **Busuioc, M.** (2021). Accountable artificial intelligence: Holding algorithms to account. *Public Administration Review*, 81(5), 825-836. [3] **Novelli, C., Taddeo, M. & Floridi, L.** Accountability in artificial intelligence: what it is and how it works. *AI & Soc* (2023). https://doi.org/10.1007/s00146-023-01635-y [4] **Raji, I. D., Smart, A., White, R. N., Mitchell, M., Gebru, T., Hutchinson, B., ... & Barnes, P.** (2020, January). Closing the AI accountability gap: Defining an end-to-end framework for internal algorithmic auditing. In *Proceedings of the 2020 conference on fairness, accountability, and transparency* (pp. 33-44). [5] **Bovens, M.** (2007). Analysing and assessing accountability: A conceptual framework 1. *European law journal*, 13(4), 447-468. [6] **Mitchell, M., Wu, S., Zaldivar, A., Barnes, P., Vasserman, L., Hutchinson, B., ... & Gebru, T.** (2019, January). Model cards for model reporting. In *Proceedings of the conference on fairness, accountability, and transparency* (pp. 220-229). [7] **Clark, A.** (2018). The machine learning audit – crisp-dm framework. *Isaca Journal*, 1, 42-47. [8] **Laux, J., Wachter, S., & Mittelstadt, B.** (2023). Trustworthy artificial intelligence and the European Union AI act: On the conflation of trustworthiness and acceptability of risk. *Regulation & Governance*. [9] **Srinivasan, R., & González, B. S. M.** (2022). The role of empathy for artificial intelligence accountability. *Journal of Responsible Technology*, 9, 100021. [10] **Potjewijd, G., Yakovleva, S., de Carvalho, F. A., Derrig, C., Fulton, J., Gallage-Alwis, S., ... & Wettner, V.** (2021). Mass Damage Claims for GDPR Infringements: A Multi-Jurisdictional Perspective. *Mass Claims, 5.*

CHAPTER 10

[1] **Racz, N., Weippl, E., & Seufert, A.** (2010). A frame of reference for research of integrated governance, risk and compliance (GRC). In *Communications and Multimedia Security: 11th IFIP TC 6/TC 11 International Conference, CMS 2010, Linz, Austria, May 31–June 2, 2010. Proceedings 11* (pp. 106-117). Springer Berlin Heidelberg. [2] **Ala-Pietilä, P., Bonnet, Y., Bergmann, U., Bielikova, M., Bonefeld-Dahl, C., Bauer, W., ... & Van Wynsberghe, A.** (2020). *The assessment list for trustworthy artificial intelligence (ALTAI)*. European Commission. [3] **Ali, S. M., Gupta, N., Nayak, G. K., & Lenka, R. K.** (2016, December). Big data visualization: Tools and challenges. In *2016 2nd International conference on contemporary computing and informatics (IC3I)* (pp. 656-660). IEEE. [4] **Yanfei, Y.** (2018, August). Comparison of radar chart creation methods for risk evaluation data. In *Proceedings of the 2018 International Conference on Big Data Engineering and Technology* (pp. 51-55). [5] **Rajamäki, J., Gioulekas, F., Rocha, P. A. L., Garcia, X. D. T., Ofem, P., & Tyni, J.** (2023, May). ALTAI Tool for Assessing AI-Based Technologies: Lessons Learned and Recommendations from SHAPES Pilots. In *Healthcare* (Vol. 11, No. 10, p. 1454). MDPI. [6] **Borg, M., Bronson, J., Christensson, L., Olsson, F., Lennartsson, O., Sonnsjö, E., ... & Karsberg, M.** (2021, June). Exploring the assessment list for trustworthy ai in the context of advanced driver-assistance systems. In *2021 IEEE/ACM 2nd International Workshop on Ethics in Software Engineering Research and Practice (SEthics)* (pp. 5-12). IEEE. [7] **Radclyffe, C., Ribeiro, M., & Wortham, R. H.** (2023). The assessment list for trustworthy artificial intelligence: A review and recommendations. *Frontiers in Artificial Intelligence, 6*, 1020592. [8] **Stahl, B. C., & Leach, T.** (2023). Assessing the ethical and social concerns of artificial intelligence in neuroinformatics research: An empirical test of the European Union Assessment List for Trustworthy AI (ALTAI). *AI and Ethics, 3*(3), 745-767. [9] **Golpayegani, D., Pandit, H. J., & Lewis, D.** (2022, December). Comparison and Analysis of 3 Key AI Documents: EU's Proposed AI Act, Assessment List for Trustworthy AI (ALTAI), and ISO/IEC 42001 AI Management System. In *Irish Conference on Artificial Intelligence and Cognitive Science* (pp. 189-200). Cham: Springer Nature Switzerland. [10] **Borg, M., Bronson, J., Christensson, L., Olsson, F., Lennartsson, O., Sonnsjö, E., ... & Karsberg, M.** (2021, June). Exploring the assessment list for trustworthy ai in the context of advanced driver-assistance systems. In *2021 IEEE/ACM 2nd International Workshop on Ethics in Software Engineering Research and Practice (SEthics)* (pp. 5-12). IEEE. [11] **Mantelero, A.**: AI and big data: a blueprint for a human rights, social and ethical impact assessment. Comput. Law Secur. Rev. 34(4), 754–772 (2018) [12] **Demetzou, K.** (2019). Data Protection Impact Assessment: A tool for accountability and the unclarified concept of 'high risk' in the General Data Protection Regulation. *Computer Law & Security Review, 35*(6), 105342. [13] **Stahl, B. C., Antoniou, J., Bhalla, N., Brooks, L., Jansen, P., Lindqvist, B., ... & Wright, D.** (2023). A systematic review of artificial intelligence impact assessments. *Artificial*

Intelligence Review, 1-33. **ECP Platform for the Information Provision** (2019) Artificial intelligence impact assessment. https://ecp.nl/wp-content/uploads/2019/01/Artificial-Intelligence-Impact-Assessment-English.pdf **Garcia, E.** (2021). UNESCO's Recommendation on the Ethics of AI: why it matters and what to expect from it. *The Good AI*. **Janssen, H., Seng Ah Lee, M., & Singh, J.** (2022). Practical fundamental rights impact assessments. *International Journal of Law and Information Technology, 30*(2), 200-232.

Index

A

access control – 129
accessibility – 166
accountability – 197
accuracy – 91
adversarial attacks – 83
affected person – 38
agency, human – 60
ai act – 35, **36**
ai bill of rights – 50
ai compliance officer – 205, 221
ai convention (council of europe) – 50
ai impact assessment – 230
ai liability – 47
ai system – 37
algorithmic impact assessment – 230
algorithms – 15
algoritmic accountability act (aaa) – 51
altai assessment – 34, **223**
area under curve (AUC) – 93
attachment – 70
audit of ai system – 203
automated decision making – 144
autonomous weapon systems – 27

B

bias – 125, **154**, 155
biometric surveillance – 108
black box ai – 140
brazil, regulation of ai in – 53
bug bounty – 164

C

ccambridge analytica – 17, 193
canada, regulation of ai in – 52
carbon footprint of ai – 177
carebot – 185
chief information security officer (ciso) – 219
chief risk officer – 219
china, regulation of ai in – 52
compliance – 217
conformité européene (ce) – 150
conformity assessment – **39**, 40
consumer protection law – 48
content credentials – 137
continual learning – 100
copyright infringement – 118
corporate social responsibility (csr) – 189
correlation and causation – 140
council of europe – 50
cybersecurity – 49, 85

D

damages under ai liability – 213
data management – 127
data poisoning – 82
data processing pipeline – 122
data protection impact assessment (dpia) – 112, **230**
data protection officer (dpo) – 113, 218
data quality and integrity – 120
dataset – 121, 123
deep learning – 23
definition of ai – 26
democracy and ai – 191
deployer of ai system – 37
detection and response – 74
digital decade – 33
disclaimers – 149
distributor of ai system – 38
diversity – 153
dpia – see data protecton impact assessment

E

education and awareness – 162
empathy in ai – 210
environmental impact – 177
environmental, social and governance (esg) – 187
ethical impact assessment (eia) – 231
ethics of ai – 8
expert systems – 19
explainability – 132, **138**
external accountability – 200

F

F1 score – 92
fairness – 153, 164
fallback plans – 98
false negative – 91
false positive – 91
flagging issues – 110
foundation models – 115
fundamental rights – 107
fundamental rights impact assessment – 232

G

general data protection regulation (gdpr) – 47, **111**
generative ai – 17
governance – 218
guidelines for trustworthy ai – 34, **55**

H

healthcare and ai – 185
high-level expert group (hleg) – 34
high-risk ai – 44
human-computer interaction – 170
human-in-command – 73
human-in-the-loop – 72
human-on-the-loop – 73
human-out-of-the-loop – 74

I

impact assessment – 229
importer of ai system – 38
inclusivity – 156
india, regulation of ai in – 53
insurance – 88
intellectual property – 28, **118**
internal accountability – 200
ip governance – 120

J

japan, regulation of ai in – 54

L

liability of ai – **47**
lime (local interpretable model-agnostic explanations) – 141
logging – 97, 137, 203

M

machine learning – 20
membership inference attacks – 83
model cards – 201
model evasion – 82
model inversion – 82

O

output quality – 136
overfitting – 123
over-reliance on ai – 64

P

personal data – 106, 111
personally identifiable information – 106
platform work and ai – 146, 182
precision (statistics) – 92
privacy by design and default – 113
product liability – 47
prohibited practice – 43
provider of ai system – 37

R

recall (statistics) – 92
receiver operating characteristic (ROC) – 92
redress for harm – 207
regulatory sandbox – 46
reinforcement learning – 23
reliability – 96
reporting mechanisms – 206
representative – 38
reproducibility – 96
risk management – 84, 86, 219
risks and harms – 42, 109
robustness – 81

S

sanctions under ai act – 212
science fiction – 13
self-learning ai – 77
semi-supervised learning – 23
singapore, regulation of ai in – 54
singularity – 20
smart technology – 14
social ai – 67, 69
social credit scoring – 61
social impact assessment (sia) – 179
south korea, regulation of ai in – 54
special personal data – 111
spider chart (altai) – 224
stakeholder participation – 170
stop button – 76
summer of ai – 14
supervised learning – 22
sustainable development goals (sdg) – 178

T

taxonomy of ai – 21
techlash – 17
terminator – 13
testing data – 122
traceability – 132
training data – 121
transfer learning – 23
transparency in ai – 131
true negative – 91
true positive – 91
trust in ai – 209
turing test – 24

U

uuncanny valley – 68
underfitting – 123
unintended interference – 66
united states of america, regulation of ai in – 50
universal design – 168
unsupervised learning – 22
user interface – 167

V

validation data – 121

W

water footprint of ai – 178
work environment – 181

X

xia (explainable ai) – 140